Alberta's Revolutionary Leaders

T.C. Byrne

Detselig Enterprises
Calgary, Alberta

Canadian Cataloguing in Publication Data

Byrne, T.C. (Timothy Clarke), 1907-
Alberta's revolutionary leaders

Includes biographical references.
ISBN 1-55059-024-3

1. Politicians — Alberta — Biography — . 2. Alberta
— Politics and government — 1921-1935.* 3. Alberta
— Politics and government — 1936-1971.* I. Title.
FC3674.B97 1991   971.23'02'0922   C91-091303-X
F1078.B97 1991

Detselig Enterprises Limited
P.O. Box G 399
Calgary, Alberta T3A 2G3

Cover credits (L-R): William Aberhart, Provincial Archives of Alberta,
A-2048; J.E. Brownlee, Provincial Archives of Alberta, A-433; E.C. Man-
ning, Provincial Archives of Alberta, J-107; Henry Wise Wood, Alberta
Wheat Pool.
Painting, entitled "Prairie Power," by Phyllis Palmer, an Alberta artist.

Printed in Canada
SAN 115-0324   ISBN 1-55059-024-3

I would like to dedicate this book to the memory of my grandaughter, Keltie Byrne, 1970-1991.

Table of Contents

Detselig Enterprises Ltd. appreciates the financial assistance for its 1991 publishing program from Alberta Foundation for the Literary Arts and Canada Council.

Introduction
Alberta's Revolutionary Leaders:
How They Shaped Alberta

It was August 11, 1921, Edmonton's Hotel Macdonald sparkled in the brilliant morning sunshine. Delivery wagons making their early rounds clattered in the street outside the hotel. Looking west one might see a lonely street car moving gingerly across the High Level Bridge, seemingly uncertain of its footing on this huge iron structure. The city was awakening to a tranquil summer day.

Within the hotel's foyer one could sense a quite different mood. Some 40 men were greeting each other cheerfully, even boisterously, their laughter ringing throughout the high-ceilinged room. Their camaraderie was obvious; they seemed completely at ease with each other. Their faces were deeply tanned, not fashionably so but with a texture that reflected the effects of outdoor labor. Though conventionally dressed, they lacked the sophistication of city dwellers.

No one would have mistaken the members of this early morning group to be commercial travellers, those regular habitués of pretentious railway hotels. Nor would they have mistaken them for local businessmen. To suggest that they were, in fact, political revolutionaries would have been dismissed as frivolous. They actually looked like what they were, prosperous farmers dressed in their Sunday clothes.

These men were, nonetheless, agents of a political revolution, newly elected members of Alberta's provincial legislature. They had been elected on a platform of political reform which, if instituted, would have altered drastically the character of Alberta's parliamentary government. As it turned out, that platform shaped the nature of Alberta's political life for much of this century.

These men were nominated by local organizations of the United Farmers of Alberta. In the election of July 18, 1921, 38 of the nominees won seats in the provincial legislature which, at that time, had a mem-

1

bership of 61. This political upset confounded not only Albertans but Canadians generally. Perhaps the most surprised of all were the successful candidates themselves.

In retrospect, the UFA victory seemed almost inevitable. Alberta's population in 1921 was 588,454, somewhat smaller than that of contemporary Edmonton, the province's capital. Of this population, approximately three quarters lived on farms or within a rural environment. The vast majority of Albertans were familiar with the UFA and its publications. The UFA was then at the height of its influence, with a membership exceeding 35,000 men. This did not include their wives who joined the United Farm Women's Association, an equally vigorous rural organization.

Unlike the elected members of conventional parties, these new MLAs were unprepared to form a government. They, in fact, had no designated leader, no one to undertake the initial steps necessary to exercise political power. One of the first tasks facing this group of neophyte legislators was that of appointing a leader either from within or without their own ranks. Not surprisingly, in their search they turned to members of the UFA's provincial executive.

As the men assembled in a room on the mezzanine floor of the Macdonald, one might have expected the popular president of the UFA, Henry Wise Wood, to take charge of this two-day meeting. Instead, the vice-president, Herbert Greenfield, brought the meeting to order. Wood had chosen to remain president of the UFA, a position that he continued to hold for the next 10 years. He saw government, albeit important, as only one of the several activities falling within the scope of this powerful organization's influence and control.

From the records of this historic meeting, it is difficult to determine whether Wood was actually present. He may not have been there, but his ideas were expressed by several of these recently elected members of the Legislative Assembly. All revolutions have their philosophical gurus, those who provide the ideas generating the passion that stimulates action. Henry Wise Wood's views account for much that occurred in Alberta's political history during the early 20th century.

Greenfield's selection as party leader had been approved at the first meeting of these new MLAs. All eyes were fixed on him as he spoke, each member anticipating his momentous announcement.

"I want first to impress on you the importance of absolute secrecy as to what occurs at this meeting."

Greenfield paused, savoring the drama contained in his next statement.

"Stewart has agreed to resign."

The applause, though not sustained was vigorous and genuine. The invincible Charles Stewart, that adroit and popular leader of the Liberal party had finally admitted his defeat. This was the reward that followed from an exhausting, but successful campaign.

Greenfield continued.

"Following his resignation, the lieutenant governor will instruct me to form a cabinet. It is imperative that we do not release any information about the cabinet before recommending its membership to the lieutenant governor.

"The choice of a cabinet is difficult. Very few of our members have had experience in government. We must choose the very best men irrespective of national origin or religious faith. This is the task that lies before us."

The meeting then turned to the issue of what groups might be represented in the province's executive council or cabinet. The secretary of the meeting, Mr. S. Higginbotham, a permanent employee of the UFA, reported that many special interest groups had made application for representation. For instance, the French-Canadians of the province had requested that someone should be appointed to represent their interests.

Despite the widely accepted concept of group government — a cabinet made up of representatives from various social and economic groups — the MLAs were not prepared to deal with these requests immediately. The government should have time to examine possibilities for regrouping and consolidating departments. The meeting decided to wait until the following processes were complete:

1. A careful study of the various departments.
2. A study of the financial statements for the province.
3. A study of the drought problem in southern Alberta.
4. A study of unemployment in the cities.

Lorne Proudfoot, a well-known activist in the UFA and a MLA for the constituency of Drumheller, raised two questions, at least one of which must have caused unease among not only the theorists but also the realists in the meeting.

"Mr. Chairman should we not give consideration to a representative from labor?"

The reaction of the meeting toward this proposal was positive. Farmers of that era were kindly disposed toward labor. Organized labor was to them a rather nebulous group existing largely in cities in pursuit of objectives that seemed quite remote from the economic interests of farmers. No one had as yet attempted to organize their hired men.

When Proudfoot followed up with his second proposal he was not quite so convincing.

"I need not remind you, Mr. Chairman, that the Liberals will have 14 members in this legislature. While it is true that they are constituted and recognized as the opposition, I am completely against the presence of any opposition. If we accord the Liberals this status we will have reverted to what has been anathema to those of us in the UFA — the concept of the old-line parties."

At this point, Mrs. Irene Parlby, the only woman to be elected as a UFA member, rose to express her views. Mrs. Parlby, from the Alix constituency east of Lacombe, had been active in the United Farm Women's Association, gaining thereby a prominence which had contributed to her success at the polls. She was part of a community of immigrants from England who had settled around Alix during the early part of this century. These several families had brought some wealth with them making it possible to create a lifestyle vaguely comparable to that of the British landed gentry. Her cultured upper-class accent contrasted pleasantly with the flat Canadian tones that dominated the meeting.

"Mr. Chairman, I appreciate the zeal with which Mr. Proudfoot is pursuing the interests of the Liberal party. However, I cannot accept the Liberals as an economic group. The Farmers' party now holds the confidence of the people, and I feel for that reason it should form the government."

The proposal to offer a cabinet post to the Liberals was defeated 18 to 16 with apparently four members abstaining. One wonders what would have been the response had such an invitation gone to the Liberal caucus. Greenfield submitted the following list to the meeting for its approval.

V.W. Smith	Railways and Telephones
Geo. Hoadley	Agriculture
Alex Ross	Public Works
R.G. Reid	Municipal Affairs and Public Health
J.E. Brownlee	Attorney General
H. Greenfield	Provincial Treasurer
Irene Parlby	Without Portfolio

In commenting on members contained in the list, Greenfield dwelt on the selection of Mr. Brownlee as attorney general. That he should do so reflects on the status this lawyer had achieved within a group, the members of which were not particularly enamored of practitioners in his profession.

"I have a very high opinion, formed from a close working relationship with Mr. Brownlee, and I could not see my way clear to make any other selection. I have interviewed many men seeking this position. However I would have in Mr. Brownlee a man I know personally, and a man whose judgment the executive officers of the UFA, and those of the United Grain Growers, both here and in Winnipeg, have leaned upon during these last several years."

This constitutes all that was revealed in the meeting's records about the party that was to manage Alberta's affairs for the next 14 years. We should now turn to the setting within which this government was to operate.

Notes

[1] Looking through some materials in the Provincial Archives, I chanced upon some badly typed records that caught my attention. I discovered these were the actual minutes of a meeting held some 70 years ago. This meeting was obviously the second held by these newly elected members to the Alberta provincial legislature during the 1921 election. They had been elected as representatives of the United Farmers of Alberta, the UFA. Leaving my father's farm to enter an Edmonton high school, I remember very well the caustic comments of city dwellers about welcoming the legislators by spreading straw on the steps of the legislature. I have embellished these records somewhat while maintaining the actual words of those who spoke in the meeting as recorded in the minutes.

Chapter One
The Settling of Alberta[1]

1

One of the astounding achievements in Canada's history was the building of the Canadian Pacific Railway completed in 1885. For some time prior to the driving of its final spike, the trains ambled slowly across the Northwest Territories, through the prairies that 20 years later were to become part of Saskatchewan and Alberta.

The Canadian government in 1876 purchased from the Cree Indians land that would ultimately become known as central Alberta. One year later, the Northwest Mounted Police, with its headquarters located in Fort Macleod, bought from the Sarcee and the Blackfoot tribes that portion of the Northwest Territories now encompassing southern Alberta. Although this total area had been surveyed into 65-hectare plots, until the turn of the century it remained empty of settlers, inhabited mainly by Natives who hunted the buffalo that fed on its succulent grasses.

Those empty spaces could be filled only by immigrants from outside the West. Without an active immigration policy by the Canadian government, the land would remain much as it had been for centuries — empty and unchanging except for the occasional movement of nomadic Indian tribes.

At the time of these purchases, a crucial question in nation building had yet to be answered. Which province — Quebec or Ontario — would take the lead in opening the West? The French fur traders and the early French missionaries had placed their stamp on this last frontier. Would the Quebecois capitalize on this historical advantage and claim the Last Best West, as the Canadian government later called it in advertising for settlers, for their people?

This was not to happen. The French-Canadians preferred to move south into New England, a much more accessible destination. Members of the Catholic clergy persuaded many of their parishioners to open a new frontier in northern Quebec.

A small Francophone settlement was established in the St. Paul-Bonnyville area, in north central Alberta.[2] These immigrants, however, were repatriated French Canadians, who had arrived in the West by way of the United States. Others came directly from France. This small outpost was not large enough to retain the French character of the Northwest Territories dating back to the 18th century voyageurs.

Canada had established the government of the Northwest Territories in 1875.[3] It consisted of the Northwest Council and an assembly located in Regina. Following its creation, the council introduced legislation that proposed a board of education, with a membership drawn equally from Catholic and Protestant groups, to administer two distinct denominational systems. This proposal would have introduced the Quebec system of school organization.

The assembly entered on a six-year period of bitter dispute between the proponents of the Quebec system of school organization and those preferring that of Ontario. The preponderance of Anglophone-Protestant settlement that had occurred during the 1880s left little doubt as to the outcome. The School Ordinance of 1892 established an educational design similar to that of Ontario — a common system with provision for separate schools locally, serving either a Protestant or Catholic minority.[4]

This ordinance, ultimately, provided the province of Alberta with its current system of school organization, a system that was imposed on Albertans by the federal government in 1905.

The enactments of this school ordinance by the Northwest Territories reflected the nature of the society that was evolving within its vaguely defined boundaries. The language of that society was English; its dominant religion was Protestant. In effect, its society had become a replica of that existing in Ontario.

2

Although Ontario through its early emigrants had conquered the West, it was unable to populate its new-found colony. If the West was to provide a market for Ontario's industries, it needed people. Despite this obvious lack, Canada's Conservative government had done little to encourage immigration.

Those who had developed the thriving ranching industry in southern Alberta were opposed to settlement. The ranchers, obviously, foresaw the impact of homesteaders occupying holdings from Calgary to the

United States border on land that was now available for grazing. The only way to populate the West, however, was to advertise widely the availability of free land on this western frontier.

The victory of the Liberals, led by Sir Wilfrid Laurier in 1896, brought a new approach to western settlement. The Laurier government was not disposed to listen to Alberta's ranchers. It was convinced that an active immigration policy should be initiated. Clifford Sifton, a Manitoba lawyer, was given the immigration portfolio with directions to introduce a more vigorous settlement program.

Whom to seek out as possible settlers became a significant issue in the recruitment campaign. Obviously, people similar to those living in Ontario would be most acceptable. Since the Canadian government hoped to locate these immigrants on the homesteads of western Canada, it seemed desirable to advertise for those with farming experience.

People who met these criteria could most likely be found either in the British Isles or in the United States. The response of British farmers, however, was less than rewarding. The government soon realized that it must explore new sources of immigrant supply.

Predominating views of the period on the desirable immigrant were tinged with racism. The white race was considered to be superior in intellect and general development. The conventional wisdom held that the white race had progressed to higher levels in the evolutionary process than those of other races. These conclusions were derived from applying Darwinism — the selection of superior species — to the ascent of man.

The white man was seen as occupying the highest status in the evolutionary hierarchy. According to this thinking, the next in line were those belonging to the yellow race. At the bottom of this racial hierarchy came the unfortunate blacks. This archaic theory influenced Canadian immigration policy until it was abandoned in 1967.

Apparently not all members of the white race had reached the same developmental stage. The northern Europeans, such as the Scandinavians, the Dutch, the Belgians, and the French, were considered superior to those living in either eastern or southern Europe.

Clifford Sifton, however, appeared not to hold such ethnic prejudices. He considered the eastern Europeans drawn from the peasant classes as most suitable to face the rigors of homesteading on the Canadian plains. His enthusiasm for this type of immigrant accounts for the origins of many Alberta settlers.

3

The years from 1896 to 1914, the commencement of the 20th century's first World War, were the boom years for western Canadian immigration. The election of the Laurier government, bringing a new approach to western settlement, initiated the boom.

Other factors also contributed to its acceleration. The rise in prices of farm products, particularly wheat, induced many to join this vast movement of people to the Canadian prairies. The revolution in farm machinery during the late 19th century stimulated an increasing interest in farming. Furthermore, the lowering of transportation costs for both people and farm products played a role in creating the boom.

The final years of the last century, those following the 1896 election, were devoted to advertising the attractions of prairie settlement. In 1901, that portion of the Territories that was to become Alberta had a population of 73,000 people. Considering that immigrants had been arriving from eastern Canada, Britain, and the United States for more than 15 years, that was not a particularly large figure.

Ten years later, by 1911, Alberta's population had grown to 375,000, multiplying that earlier figure by five. Each of Alberta's four major centres had expanded dramatically. Edmonton's population had escalated from 2,600 to 30,500, 12 times greater than at the century's commencement. Similarly Calgary, with a population of 4,850, had been

Arrival of settlers in Wetaskiwin.
Photo courtesy of the Provincial Archives of Alberta, A-5253.

transformed into a city of 43,700, a nine-fold increase within a brief 10-year period. The growth in the smaller centres, though not overwhelming, was still impressive. Lethbridge's population had climbed from 2,325 to 8,050. Medicine Hat, starting from a base of 1,975, tripled its numbers to 5,600.

The growth during the early years of the next decade was equally formidable. The flow of immigrants continued unabated until 1914. During the First World War, Canada was much too occupied to welcome immigrants of any kind. In fact, some of its most important sources in eastern Europe were now in enemy territory. That Alberta by 1921 had reached a population of 554,458 underscores the volume of the incoming population flow between 1910 to 1914.

The early settlement of Alberta was entirely dependent on rail transportation. Sometimes the opening of a particular area preceded the provision of rail service. Nonetheless, the distance travelled by newcomers using horse-drawn vehicles to reach the homesteads they had selected at either the Calgary or Edmonton Land Titles Office, was less than 161 kilometres.[5]

The railway lines that had crossed the province served as the basis for the settlements that had been forming throughout the central and southern areas of, first, the Northwest Territories, and after 1905, the province of Alberta.

During the boom period, two new railway lines traversed the breadth of the province. The Canadian Northern Railway, completed in 1915, entered Alberta at Lloydminster, pursuing a route through the Yellowhead Pass, to end its course in Vancouver. The Grand Trunk Pacific, the third transcontinental line binding Canada from ocean to ocean, crossed the Alberta boundary at Wainwright to reach its ultimate destination at Prince Rupert. Both these later lines, originally privately owned and controlled, met with financial reverses. The federal government was forced in 1919 to assume responsibility for both lines under the now familiar name of the Canadian National Railways.

These immigrants to the last frontier in North America were a diverse assortment of people coming from a variety of countries. But, they all had one objective. The vast majority were intent on securing a homestead on which to support themselves and, if married, their spouses and families. To do this, they had to appear at a Canadian land office and make application for a patent on a specific 65-hectare parcel of land.

The patent gave them the right to "prove up" on a particular homestead. This phrase, a very meaningful one during the province's homesteading era, implied certain obligations which the homesteader must fulfill if he or she wanted a title of ownership. He or she had to establish a residence, to be occupied for a period of three to five years. The homesteader was also required to transform a certain amount of the land from its virgin state to that of a cultivated field. Having completed these rather simple demands and convinced a land office agent of those achievements, the homesteader was granted a title. The homestead was now his or hers to continue cultivating or to sell if he or she chose to do so.

4

As we saw earlier, Canada had no active immigration policy prior to 1896. A sufficient number of settlers, nonetheless, had moved from Ontario to the Calgary region, ensuring that Alberta would become an English-speaking province. Actually Ontario-born Canadians continued to take up homesteads in Alberta throughout the first decade of the 20th century.

Some came directly to the Last Best West, others by way of the United States. They settled in and around Calgary, east of Strathmore, and south to High River and Vulcan. They could be found, as well, in most of the major towns emerging along one or the other of the three major railroads. Many of the Ontario-born became part of the business and professional classes in Alberta's pioneer society.

One group among these early settlers came from Iceland by way of North Dakota. These settlers commenced their rail journey at Winnipeg during the summer of 1888. Purchasing horses and wagons in Calgary, they struck out directly north into the prairie wilderness. One of the major hazards they encountered during their northward journey was that of fording the Red Deer River. They continued on to reach a spot on the banks of a small stream known as Medicine River. Here they settled to pursue a lifetime of farming, emphasizing the production of dairy products. Ten years after their arrival, the Dominion government granted them a post office called Markerville after C.P. Marker, dairy commissioner for the Northwest Territories government.

Another historic settlement during the opening years of the 20th century was the Barr Colony. Several thousand British immigrants in 1903 attempted homesteading near Lloydminster. Unlike the Icelandic community at Markerville, very few traces remain of this colonial venture. These early settlers moved into the towns and cities of this young province to become shopkeepers, policemen, government employees, skilled workmen and the like. With no language barrier, these British immigrants merged readily into Alberta's society, contributing their values, talents and skills. The essentially Protestant character of that society, shaped by the predominance of the Anglican, Methodist, and Presbyterian churches, may be ascribed to immigrants from Ontario, Britain, and northern Europe.

Canadian immigration officials made no distinction within the categorization of the British, which included the Scots, English and Welsh. Of the three, the Scots were the most numerous. In the 1921 census recording Alberta's population of some 600,000, 16 percent were of Scottish origin. They were widely dispersed throughout the province. One colony from the Hebrides, recruited by Father W. Macdonald, was established at Clandonald north of Vermillion. This colony did not survive. These Scottish settlers went to the cities of Edmonton, Calgary, Lethbridge, and Medicine Hat, finding employment in the building trades, small businesses, banks and in a variety of other areas.

Calgary particularly became known as a British city. It was for many years regarded as the Scottish centre of Alberta. The Scots have contributed much to the quality of life in this province. The game of curling, a small town pastime, and golf have long since captured the interest of not only Albertans, but of Canadians generally. There are few Canadians who have not heard of the Calgary Highlanders, a regiment wearing uniforms of Scottish kilts. In parade, this regiment marches vigorously to the skirl of the bag pipes. Living in Calgary during the early years of this century, one inevitably learned about the Scottish custom of "first footing" on New Year's Eve. This involved being the first to cross the threshold of a Scottish home on that significant evening.

The news of the Last Best West circulated throughout the United States around the turn of the century. Sifton saw the Americans as highly desirable settlers with similar cultural backgrounds and a common language. Attracted by the promise of free land no longer available in the United States, many Americans responded. Between 1898 and 1914, some 600,000 flooded into western Canada. By the beginning of the First World War, 22 percent of Alberta's population had been born in the States. During the mid-1920s, at least one out of every four farms was operated by immigrants from the south. Not surprisingly, the largest concentration of these farms lay between Calgary and the American border.

A large American settlement developed around Cardston, south of Lethbridge. Members of the Church of Jesus Christ of the Latter-day Saints denomination, popularly known as Mormons, moved there from Utah during the last decade of the 19th century. At first, Canadians were strongly opposed to their admission into the Northwest Territories. They objected to the practise of polygamy which had been sanctioned by the Church of the Latter-day Saints. When the Church in 1898 reversed its stand on the practise of having more than one wife at a time, the Mormons were welcomed into the continent's last frontier. By 1911, southern Alberta contained 98 Mormon communities, with a total population of 10,000.

An interesting phenomenon of this peaceful American invasion, was the diversity of backgrounds among its members. Many traced their origins back to Europe, having lived in the States for no more than one or two generations. They came from such countries as Norway, Denmark, Holland, Belgium and the Austro-Hungarian Empire. They were in search of land for their children, the price of which had become prohibitive in the United States.

American immigrants were desirable settlers for a variety of reasons. They customarily brought with them enough funds to purchase the machinery necessary to operate farms effectively. Furthermore, many had experience in both dry-land and irrigated farming. They met the requisites of the ideal model for western settlement. They worked well with eastern Canadians, supporting the major Protestant denominations such as the Methodists, Presbyterians, and Baptists. The Americans also brought with them representatives of certain evangelical sects, which may account for the many Bible colleges that have become part of Alberta's culture.

One group of immigrants not welcome in Canada was the black Americans. When the Canadian government advertised for settlers in the western and southern United States, black Americans, seeking to avoid the pressures of racial prejudice, responded. Canadian agents did their best to discourage these unwelcome settlers by describing the inclement weather and the unproductive soil in the Last Best West.

The Canadian government did not at any time legislate against the entry of black people. It preferred to keep them out by other means.

Despite the invisible barriers created by misinformation, a hardy few persisted. The occasional appearance of black men and women on the streets of Alberta's cities led to provincial protests in 1910 and 1911. The Edmonton, Calgary, Strathcona, and Fort Saskatchewan boards of Trade sent petitions to the prime minister expressing alarm over the appearance of blacks in their communities. Apparently the Canadian government hired a black American doctor to speak to black audiences in the United States. He told them the oft-repeated story of western Canada's limitations.

Despite the government's dishonest behavior, a few black settlements were established. These people sought to avoid expressions of prejudice by settling in remote areas where they met only Indians who regarded them as black white men.

One such settlement that lasted for many years was established at Amber Valley, north of the town of Athabasca. Parson Sneed led a group of 93 adults and 56 children from Oklahoma in 1910 to commence life on Alberta homesteads. Of the original group, 75 secured titles to their land. As with other rural communities, very few of their descendants remain as evidence of that early venture into the wilderness of northern Alberta.

The Scandinavians who came to the province during the immigration boom, either directly or by way of the United States, settled in the Alberta parkland. The Swedes located in Scandia, and the Norwegians in Claresholm. The names of villages and towns reflect their predominance in certain communities. These are such as Bardo, Edberg, New Norway and Malmo. Camrose Lutheran College attests to their early presence in the districts surrounding that city.

The Scandinavians met the expectations of Sifton and his cohorts directing the settlement of the West. They were from northern Europe and they were Protestant. They were, in fact, accepted readily by the West's English-speaking majority. Their assimilation was achieved within a single generation.

The immigration of German-speaking people accelerated rapidly after 1896. The Germans were predominantly Protestant, though German Catholics also settled in the Territories and subsequently, Alberta. They formed part of older settlements in Stony Plain, Edmonton, Wetaskiwin, Bashaw, and Medicine Hat. They were widely dispersed with no solid block that could be labelled as exclusively German. Many villages and hamlets acquired German names which were altered during the First World War.

German-speaking members of Mennonite sects, which followed a common Anabaptist tradition, settled between Lethbridge and Medicine Hat. They were pacifists who at that time adhered to certain rural values such as dedication to hard work and to simple and unpretentious modes of living. Eschewing the values of a mainstream society, they took pride in their own modest ways. They did not, however, live in colonies, and in this respect they differed markedly from their closest religious neighbors, the Hutterites.

As with many modern religious sects, the Hutterites are products of the Protestant Reformation. In common with the Mennonites, the Hutterian Brethern emphasize the values of an agricultural society. They also ascribe to modesty and simplicity in their style of living. Unlike the Mennonites, however, they are dedicated to communal living. Each member is expected to contribute his or her time, labor, and talents to the welfare of the community. Those who refuse are excluded. The Hutterites swear allegiance to none other than God. They are pacifists, refusing to bear arms or fight for their country.

The Hutterites moved from the United States to Canada during 1918 to 1920. They did so because of the treatment they had received from Americans after the United States entered the First World War. Nine colonies settled in southern Alberta, between Magrath and Cardston. The Canadian government actually restricted their entry in 1919, but lifted the ban in 1922. Alberta with over 116 colonies, now has more of these than any other province. The Hutterites account for a large share of the province's dairy and meat production.

Canadian officials welcomed immigrants from Holland since they conformed to the ideal model of settlers. Entering during the boom years (1896-1914), the Dutch settled in such places as Granum, Nobleford and Monarch. A large group of Dutch Catholics located at Strathmore, east of Calgary. A much smaller group found homes between Burdett and Foremost.

A Dutch community was established during 1912 in the boreal forest region some 129 kilometres northwest of Edmonton. The members of this community belonged to the Christian Reformed church which exemplifies the traditions of Dutch Calvinism. The church condemns all worldly amusements such as dancing and cardplaying. Neerlandia, this community's name, provided the isolation that kept these Dutch Calvinists from coming in contact with certain aspects of Canadian life they found unacceptable. Alberta teachers employed to teach in the Neerlandia school found living in this community a dreary experience.

The Ukrainians represented a departure from the model of desirable immigrants.[6] They came from eastern rather than northern Europe. They originated in either one or the other of two Austrian provinces, Galicia, once part of Poland, and Bukovina, formerly Romanian territory. Sifton considered immigrants drawn from the peasant classes of that region to be excellent settlers for western Canada. Agents of the Canadian government and of Canadian railways had advertised western Canada's attractions throughout these two provinces of the Austo-Hungarian Empire.

New Canadians in native Ukrainian costume.
Photo courtesy of the Provincial Archives of Alberta, B-7235.

The Ukrainians departed from the model in other respects as well. Unlike the northern Europeans, they had not come under the historic influence of Martin Luther. They were not Protestants in the Lutheran tradition. They were actually steeped in the practises of eastern Christianity. Those who came from Galicia belonged to the Ukrainian Caltholic Church — Catholics under the Roman Pope, but practising their faith by employing Greek rites. Immigrants from Bukovina were Greek

Orthodox, a church not unlike the Anglican that looked to the head of a state, the Tsar of Russia, for its leadership.

The first settlement of Ukrainians in the Northwest Territories was located at Starr near Lamont in about 1897. With this settlement as a nucleus, subsequent migration during the first decade of the 20th century extended north to the Saskatchewan River and east to Chipman, Mundare, and Vegreville. The final outlines of the block occupied by the Ukrainians commenced at Bruderheim, 65 kilometres east of Edmonton, and continued to Derwent, 48 kilometres from the Saskatchewan border, a distance of a 161 kilometres. With its southern limits at Vegreville, the Ukrainian community extended 112 kilometres northward to cross the North Saskatchewan River. The entire block covered an area of 1,610 square kilometres.

The Ukrainian settlement lies entirely within Alberta's parkland. The Ukrainians chose homesteads within this block because of its trees. Wood was a precious commodity in the regions of Europe from which they came. The land within this block in north central Alberta is generally fertile and productive, though there are some unproductive sandy stretches. The presence of trees does not always guarantee fertile soil.

The Romanians, also eastern Europeans, came from the province of Bukovina. Although they shared common geographic backgrounds with the Ukrainians, the Romanians were not Slavic in origin. They appear to have descended from the Romans. Their language is a distant relative of such romance languages as French, Spanish, and Italian. Their living standards, their customs, and their culture, however, were very much like those of the Ukrainians. In fact, they understood and spoke Ukrainian.

The Romanians located in a district near the North Saskatchewan River which they called Boian after the place they had left in Bukovina. They settled near their old neighbors with whom they had lived in Bukovina. Since they were Greek Orthodox, they shared a church with the Ukrainians at Hairy Hill. So far as the Anglophones of Alberta were concerned, they considered the Romanians to be Ukrainians. Without a knowledge of their language, there was no way for them to distinguish between these two groups of immigrants.

The Poles similarly shared an historic relationship with the Ukrainians, one deriving from centuries of close association. A major distinction between these two groups of immigrants was religion. History had placed the Poles under the influence of western rather than eastern Christianity. Consequently, Poland had become a Roman Catholic country long before the Reformation.

Well-educated Poles passed readily into Canadian society through the avenue of the Catholic church. Polish immigrants drawn from the peasant classes, however, sought out and located in the settlements of their former European neighbors. Although the Poles in Alberta frequently attended the services of the Ukrainian Catholic Church, wherever possible, they established their own church, one employing the Latin rite. Religion meant a great deal to these Polish immigrants. The major problem in practising their faith was that of securing priests who could serve them in their own language.

The initial wave of Polish immigrants, largely from the peasant classes with little formal education, came to Alberta prior to the First World War. By 1921, 20 Polish settlements had been established in the province. The first of these was located in the Wostok area north east of Edmonton. The Poles built a church there in 1905 known as Mission of St. Michael. Another settlement near Nisku south of Edmonton survived for many years before losing its Polish identity through intermarriage with people of other ethnic backgrounds, but adherents of the Catholic faith.

Polish immigrants settling around Skaro close to the North Saskatchewan River, erected a religious grotto there in 1919, reflecting the intense devotion of the Polish peasant to Catholic symbolism. The Polish mission of Krakow, east of Lamont, was the creation of a Polish priest named Father Francis Olszewski. A Polish colony at Kopernik in the Holden district on the Wainwright line, was settled by immigrants from two adjoining villages in Galicia. In Chipman, a town on the historic Canadian Northern Railway, the Poles shared a church with German Catholics. Many Poles settled throughout the Peace River block, with several families concentrating in the Clairmont district.

Since mining had been a long established industry in Poland, Polish miners were attracted to the mines of the Crowsnest Pass. Another group sought employment in mines located in the foothills close to Banff. The largest contingent of these Polish newcomers with a penchant for mining settled in the shadow of the Rockies at Colemen. Here they organized the Polish Society of Brotherly Aid. A major contribution of this society during the First World War was to convince Canadian authorities that the Polish were neither Austrian nor German. It also assisted the Poles to retain memories of their Polish culture. It provided them with a centre outside the Catholic church, since the miners, though Catholic, were not as ardent in their faith as the peasants. They were somewhat inclined toward anticlericalism.

These are but a few of the Polish settlements established during Alberta's population boom. Unlike the Ukrainians, the Poles did not locate in a block; their settlements were dispersed throughout the province. Perhaps this was because they did not arrive in the numbers typical of their erstwhile east European neighbors.

5

The year 1921 is highly significant in Alberta's history. It marks the commencement of the province's political revolution, one that was to extend over the next half century. Alberta society of the period had been shaped by the immigration taking place prior to the First World War. It was essentially an immigrant society. Albertans generally had come from somewhere else; few were born in the province, or the territories that preceded it. As a consequence, that society was characterized by its diversity. Furthermore, the Canadian government through its immigration policies, perhaps unwittingly, certainly not by design, had created a number of ethnic ghettos which would prevent rapid assimilation. This suggests that Alberta was not the melting pot the Canadian people may have expected.

Nonetheless, the members of that society, despite the diversity of their origins, shared certain common attributes. They were, with few exceptions, white and predominantly Protestant. If they were not all Anglo-Saxons, that particular genus was prevalent enough to assure the province of an equanimous future. The succeeding chapters examines that future and its occasional lapses from the state of equanimity.

Notes

[1] I am particularly indebted to a study edited by Howard and Tamara Palmer, entitled *Peoples of Alberta* with a sub-title "Portraits of Cultural Diversity," published by Western Producer Prairie Books of Saskatoon, Saskatchewan. It proved an excellent source in rounding out information on the diversity of Alberta's population in 1921.

[2] During its early years, the town of St. Paul was known as St. Paul de Métis, indicating the nature of the early settlement. The title was dropped with the building of the railway from Edmonton to St. Paul, completed in 1919.

[3] Statutes of Canada, 38 Victoria, c48 sec.3.

4 Ordinances of the Northwest Territories, No 22 of 1892 sec 5. Information on the above statutes was contained in Cecil Lingard, *Territorial Government in Canada* (Toronto: University of Toronto Press, 1946). These were cited in a doctoral thesis by T.C. Byrne "Historical Development of Provincial Leadership in High School Education" (University of Colorado, 1956).

5 Such a trip was made by the author with his parents in 1909 by stage coach along the Victoria Trail. This road followed the northern bank of the Saskatchewan River to a point called Pine Creek, located on the most northerly bend of that river, a distance of some 97 kilometres from Fort Saskatchewan. With the coming of the railway in 1918, the Pine Creek post office became known as Waskatenau.

6 T.C. Byrne, "The Ukranian Community on North Central Alberta," Masters Thesis (Edmonton: University of Alberta,1937).

Chapter Two
Henry Wise Wood and the UFA

1

If one were to select the factor of prime importance to the opening of western Canada, it would undoubtedly be an achievement in biological science. This was the development of hard spring wheat that ripened 10 to 12 days earlier than any other variety. With "Red Fife," as it was called, farmers could harvest their crops earlier, thereby avoiding early autumn frosts. This wheat, originating first in Ontario, was taken by Canadian immigrants to Minnesota, eventually to reach Manitoba toward the end of the 1860s.

This contribution to agricultural science was further enhanced in 1904 by the achievements of William and Charles Saunders, a father and son team. They developed marquis wheat which advanced the ripening process yet another eight days. This high-quality spring wheat became western Canada's staple commodity in the production of agricultural wealth.

The expansion in wheat farming provided Alberta with its dominant economic reality throughout the first half of this century. To illustrate, in 1916, land devoted to wheat in Alberta had reached 607,000 hectares. By 1921, that figure had increased to 1,862,000 hectares, a tripling of the land devoted to wheat production within a five-year period. Albertans, particularly those living in the southern part of the province, were fast becoming dependent on the income derived from a single crop. For the next three decades, the economy of the province rose and fell concurrent with the price of wheat. Like cotton in the southern United Sates, wheat had become master of the Alberta farmer's destiny.

These early settlers were not without their farm organizations. At the turn of the century, two groups competed for support within what was to become Alberta's farm population. One, called the Canadian Society for Equity, was an import from the United States. The American Equity Society exemplified the agrarian movement for reform in the American

Northwest, which was designed to assist farmers through the establishment of cooperative enterprises. Similarly the Canadian Society for Equity had entered into various cooperative endeavors which had not been particularly successful financially.

The other farm organization, the Alberta Farmers' Association, was local in origin. It had gained recognition by holding agricultural fairs that demonstrated the capabilities of western agriculture for variety in the production of field crops.

One may find parallels of these two associations among Canada's labor organizations. The Equity Society exemplified the international labor unions that spoke for workers, irrespective of national origin, calling for "Workers of the world to unite, you have nothing to lose but your chains." The Alberta Farmers' Association appealed to farmers on the basis of national identity.

This intense competition for membership was obviously counterproductive. Members of both organizations soon found that limited room existed when two associations sought support from the same group of

Grain elevators at Edmonton.
Photo courtesy of the Provincial Archives of Alberta, Brown Collection, B-1215.

patrons. Eventually, both groups of members reached similar conclusions — that amalgamation was imperative. This mutual conclusion led in 1909 to the formation of the United Farmers of Alberta.

Considering the diverse backgrounds of these early settlers, one might expect them to be a variegated lot. Nonetheless, by the time of the UFA's formation, the typical Alberta farmer had begun to emerge. True, he had much in common with the industrial worker in that the performance of his work involved considerable strength and a diversity of physical skills. In most respects, however, he differed markedly from his industrial compatriot. Typically, the farmer operated his farm through total family effort. His wife and children were an integral part of his labor force. Only occasionally did he resort to employing casual labor, quite often provided through harvest excursions from eastern Canada.

The farmer was obviously much more than a laborer. He was primarily a land owner, with his 120-hectare estate valued from $50 to $125 per hectare. He was, in fact, an entrepreneur with an investment in farm machinery, frequently equal to that in his land. He dealt with and was dependent on two important industries, those of banking and insurance.

The farmer's relationship with the government was intimate and continuous. Government decisions based on policies generated to meet needs created in other parts of Canada might affect adversely the income he received from his grain.

In fact, the Alberta farmer's economic welfare was often influenced by events occurring or decisions made in remote parts of the world. The supply of, and the demand for wheat in such distant nations as Russia or China sometimes determined the price a farmer received for it in Canada.

The farmer saw himself as the province's sole economic generator. Wheat and, to a lesser extent, meat were the major exports entering either interprovincial or international trade from this completely agricultural province. Production from the mines and the forests had long since ceased to be of major significance. Those who lived in the cities generally rendered services for each other and for the farmer who brought in the wealth that, in the long run, paid for such services.

In the predominantly rural province of that period, employees of government, the railroads, and the wholesale distributors were dependent on the farmer for their ultimate source of income. Despite the arrogance of many urban dwellers, the farmer was convinced that he alone carried the economic burden of maintaining Alberta's urban population.

2

Those who in 1909 designed the UFA's constitution also included its major objectives. The overriding purpose of this new organization was to assist Alberta's farmers in their farming practises. Not surprisingly, these objectives reflected the range of interests generated by such practises. The objectives were actually dictated by the many complex issues that affected the farmer's welfare throughout the early part of the 20th century.

The constitution opened with a statement on a role the United Farmers of Alberta refused to accept. It was not a political party! This new organization did not propose adopting the policy of any political party, nor the candidature of any politician. Politicians generally, and party politicians in particular, were apparently anathema to those who prepared this founding statement.

The major and overriding objective of the new organization was to forward the interests of producers of grain and livestock. This meant securing profitable prices for all products that were the fruits of their labor. To achieve this would require increased emphasis on the marketing of grain. Granaries, elevators and warehouses would have to be built for storing the farmers' produce during the course of its orderly sale. The founders of the UFA abhorred combines among traders which were designed to dispose of grain in the interests of speculators rather than producers.

Designers of the UFA's constitution obviously recognized that governments do not always act in the best interests of producers. Farmers needed legislation that assured them equable rates for the transportation of their products. They had to request the Canadian government to open new markets and to enlarge those already in existence.

It was advantageous for young men taking over farms from their parents to learn about the impact of legislation. They had to watch out for, and evaluate, proposed legislation as to its probable effects on farm operation and be prepared, from time to time, to recommend legislative enactments designed to meet changing conditions.

Farmers, of necessity, were dependent on certain service industries. Banks, for instance, provided services to farmers in the form of loans.

Consequently, interest rates were of continuing concern to them. Foreclosures on mortgage debt were a constant threat to those who may have had difficulty in meeting payments because of poor crop conditions.

Farmers also depended on securing adequate crop insurance at reasonable rates. The rates of insurance premiums, in areas with a high incidence of hail storms, often became onerous.

To promote social intercourse, UFA locals attempted to organize leisure activities for its members such as picnics, box socials, or dances, depending on local interests. One suspects that this objective might have been achieved more successfully through the United Farm Women of Alberta (UFWA), a counterpart of the UFA, designed to meet the needs of the women living in rural Alberta.

3

Henry Wise Wood's career and that of the UFA were inextricably interwoven. Following his arrival in Alberta to settle in Carstairs, Wood joined the Canadian Equity Society. After the amalgamation, he became an active member of the UFA, not only in the Carstairs local, but also at the organization's annual convention. During the convention of 1915, Henry Wise Wood was elected vice-president of the provincial association.

Following the death of President James Speakman in 1916, Wood defeated Rice Sheppard, an Edmonton farmer, in a contest to decide Speakman's successor. He held the position of president until 1931, a period during which the UFA reached the zenith and commenced the decline of its influence in provincial affairs.

Henry Wise Wood was born in Ralls County, Missouri, in 1861. He grew up there during the American Civil War and the years following that internal struggle between the northern industrial states and those of the agricultural south.

His father, a slave owner, had fought on the side of the South in the Confederate Army. Despite the loss of his slaves following the war, John Wood gave Henry educational opportunities that were exceptional for a farmer's son in those days. He sent Henry to a rural school for a few years, later placing him in a private school, followed by two years in what might now be termed a liberal arts college.

Although Henry Wood terminated his formal schooling at the age of 22, he had developed an interest in both literature and philosophy that

Henry Wise Wood.
Photo courtesy of the Alberta Wheat Pool.

he retained throughout his life. Through his study of those disciplines, he became capable of organizing and expressing ideas in clear, though sometimes ornate, prose.

His intellectual interests were those one might expect from an intelligent university undergraduate. He had read, for instance, Adam Smith's *Wealth of the Nations*, and had explored the writings of John Stuart Mills, books more likely to have been read by undergraduates in the 19th, than in the 20th century.

Why did this man with a family of four sons decide in his middle years to emigrate to Canada? Perhaps the answer to this question existed in his family. Although he managed his father's farm, he did not own it. Nor could he see any hope to buy a farm, either for himself or for any of his sons, land values being what they were in Missouri.

The news of this new Canadian frontier with its available free land had reached that state. Intrigued, Wood visited the Territories in 1904 and satisfied with what he saw, he returned the next year to settle on a farm he had purchased in the district of Carstairs. He brought with him, not only his wife and family and his intellectual interests, but also a deep dedication to an agrarian lifestyle and farming as a vocation.

Henry Wise Wood was 55 when he assumed the presidency of the UFA in 1916. During the intervening years since leaving Missouri, he had become a Canadian citizen and had learned something about the country he had adopted in mid-life.

He found in Canada much that was familiar. He was surrounded by farmers in a province that was strictly agricultural. Rather than looking southward, he now looked east to his adopted country's industrial core, and to the sources of the political power that governed its decision making.

The UFA was an unusual organization, highly decentralized in some respects, though centralized in others. Ten farmers could organize a local anywhere within the province, and its members were then free to participate in the affairs of the association. They could prepare resolutions and forward these to head office for the consideration of the annual convention. If accepted by the convention, the intent of the resolution would apply to all other locals within the province. Every local was bound by decisions taken at the annual convention.

This made the annual convention an extremely significant meeting in the life of the organization. Each local could send delegates varying in number according to its size. As the number of locals increased, so did the size of the convention, reaching at times an assembly of 500 delegates. Although the directors met periodically throughout the year, the major decisions of the organization were reached on the floor of the convention. Granted that a skillful official, such as the president, could influence delegates to support or oppose certain resolutions, the delegates were, nonetheless, free to follow their own judgments in the shaping of policy.

An earlier comment pointed to the UFA as the province's most powerful organization throughout the '20s. The only means of communication for much of the decade was either the daily or weekly newspaper. The radio became available toward the end of the '20s, but it was not completely entrenched in every Alberta home until the early '30s. Until that time, the convention was the most effective means of disseminating information throughout Alberta's rural population. Political leaders of the UFA during that period used the convention as their power base. Anyone who could influence the assembled delegates, and hence the UFA locals, was able to gain and retain political power.

Henry Wise Wood was a master of convention politics. He knew his audience well, its predispositions and its biases. He rarely chaired general assemblies during the debates on resolutions, preferring rather to leave such tasks to other members of the executive. He did not enter debates except at strategic points when he sensed the convention might be heading toward a decision that UFA members would later regret. During his interventions, he dealt with the topic under discussion precisely and with telling effect.

Wood was a tall man, somewhat gaunt in appearance, completely bald, with deep-set brown eyes. Unassuming in manner, he possessed a personal magnetism that attracted not only his farming colleagues, but others who met him away from his customary settings. The personal quality most often attributed to him was that of integrity. Whether he spoke to individuals, small groups or mass meetings, his words carried deep conviction of the ideas he was expressing. To those who listened, they were words of wisdom. At times, though not often, those words revealed the passion he often felt beneath his invariably calm exterior.

The period of the First World War and its aftermath, created special problems for western farmers. Members of the UFA, through their locals, brought these problems to the floor of the convention in the form of resolutions. Though many of these were ill-conceived, they nonetheless grew from the reality of the times.

In his presidential addresses Wood reacted to these problems, problems that he shared with members of his audience. This series of addresses, added to each year throughout his term of office, was published in *The Grain Growers' Guide*, a magazine for farmers. The series encompassed Wood's philosophy of government and his views on cooperative marketing.

4

Not surprisingly, Henry Wise Wood was concerned with the impact of industrialism on the farming class. The United States had passed through the first phase of the Industrial Revolution during Wood's upbringing in the late 19th century. Canada was taking its first tentative steps along the same path during the early years of the 20th century.

Wood was convinced that the industrial society was both individualistic and competitive. To exist in such a society, organization was imperative. Any class or group of people had to organize if it wished to identify and further its interests in this highly competitive world. The classes that organized during the early years of the industrial era, such as those of commerce and banking, proceeded to exploit the unorganized.

Farmers as a class continued to be individualistic and competitive. As the last of all affected groups to organize they, in Wood's view, had been the most victimized of all.

In supporting the concepts of class identification and interest, Wood could have been accused of following Karl Marx's teachings. Marx's ringing appeal, calling on workers to unite against the evils of capitalism, resounded throughout the industrial world during the 19th century. He foresaw an extended period of class warfare before those workers would gain their just benefits within an industrialized society.

Wood departed from the Marxian view, however, in that he identified cooperation rather competition as the basic law of a democratic social order. The first step toward the fulfillment of this law lay in the organization of individual classes, each to explore and define its own set of economic and social needs. As each class began comprehending problems from its own particular perspective, it would inevitably develop its understanding in a broader, more democratic way. The eventual reconciliation of conflict would occur through class organization and interclass cooperation toward the full achievement of a cooperative society.

Wood reacted negatively to the argument that to gain its ends the UFA should become actively engaged in politics. He was completely opposed, to the establishment of a new political party. His view was that a party, since it purported to represent many groups, did an inadequate job of speaking for any one of them.

However, he did agree to the UFA entering politics as an organization. In this case, it would speak for and interpret the interests of a single group or class. The entrance of other groups representing the interests of other classes would end the exploitation of class by class to bring about what Wood considered the major concept in governing — the cooperative commonwealth.

The principles underlying group government are inconsistent with those providing the foundations of cabinet government. A cabinet or executive council exercises and holds power if it retains the support of the majority of members in the legislature. Quite obviously, a government by the representatives of one or more groups need only maintain the support of the class or classes for which it speaks.

Group government spokesmen, nonetheless, introduced the principle of proportional representation to make sure that minorities had someone to speak for them in the legislature.

The nomination of candidates and the costs of their election became the responsibility of the combined locals within a constituency. The elected member, in effect, was a delegate from this coterie of locals and could be recalled if unsatisfactory. This perception of the legislator's role was in direct contradiction to the bipartisan system then existing in Canada as well as the United States.

Henry Wise Wood saw political parties as being employed by organized interests. The rewards for their employment were favorable tariff rates, resource grants, and public franchises. To establish a cooperative commonwealth, the old party system had to be destroyed. Henry Wise Wood and the UFA took giant strides toward terminating professional politics in Alberta for much of this century.

5

The UFA's decision to enter politics was neither hasty nor impetuous. It grew from events that occurred throughout the first 12 years of its existence. Each event inexorably pushed UFA members to conclude that political action had become imperative.

Extreme fluctuations in the price of wheat acted as a persistent and overriding pressure for direct action. Local elevator agents paid farmers a price based on daily quotations from Liverpool, less shipping costs. These costs, including rail and ocean transport, storage and insurance, seemingly moved in only one direction — upwards. The farmer frequently found that higher prices did not guarantee increased income.

The *Wartime Elections Act* created wide dissension among many Canadians. The Union government under Sir Robert Borden, reacting to pressures from zealous anglophone patriots, enacted legislation arousing bitter hostility within several groups. The act disenfranchised all immigrants from countries within the Central Powers (i.e., the Germanic and Austro-Hungarian Empires) who had not been naturalized before 1902.

For farmers generally, the most annoying of government actions was the cancellation of exemptions from military service for their sons. Depriving the family farm of its most important labor source did little to endear Borden's bipartisan government to members of the UFA.

The Canadian Council of Agriculture, a national organization formed from representatives of farmers' associations across Canada, provided leadership for the various agrarian movements that had emerged in almost every province. Henry Wise Wood had been an active member of the council as UFA representative from the time of his election as president in 1916.

The council in that year had published a farmer's platform which was widely accepted among provincial associations. In 1918, the council revised the original version and submitted the revision to its corporate members for their approval. This platform announced what farmers expected from any political party seeking their support.

The council advocated an immediate reduction in tariffs insisting, as well, that the Canadian government should accept the reciprocity treaty currently being offered by the United States. It advised that the government consider personal income tax, and inheritance, and corporation taxes as sources of income, rather than depending on tariff duties. It also felt that the government should levy a tax on unimproved land, presumably to encourage landowners, to use such land more productively.

The platform advocated, as well, public ownership of all forms of transportation and communication. Ostensibly, this meant railways and telephones, since radio and television were still far in the future. Other items included proportional representation, the initial and direct legislation reflecting the influence of Henry Wise Wood. Another plank apparently expressed the agrarian view on international relations. It insisted that Canada should join the League of Nations.

The free-trade issue dated back to the election of 1910. Sir Wilfrid Laurier, leader of the Liberal government, had made free trade with the United States the major plank in his campaign, adopting the slogan "Reciprocity, rest in prosperity." He was opposed by Sir Robert Borden, leader of the Conservative party, who had adopted a national policy, one that promoted the protection of Canada's infant industries. His slogan might well have been that of a former Conservative prime minister, "No truck nor trade with the Yankees."

The UFA, as well as the farm organizations in Saskatchewan and Manitoba, supported Sir Wilfrid Laurier. The wheat farmers of the West, forced to sell their staple product in a world market, had little use for a national policy that protected the economically inefficient farm machine factories of eastern Canada.

In effect, the Canadian council's platform of 1918 became the national policy of western farmers. Sir Robert Borden, leader of the then Union government, would under no circumstance accept a platform that included a free-trade proviso. He had very little sympathy for the views of western Canadian farmers. Sir Wilfrid Laurier, leader of the Liberal rump that remained loyal to him after the defection of those who had joined the Union government, was no longer a force in Canadian politics.

The pressure mounted throughout the locals for direct political action. The issue was not whether the UFA should undertake political action. This had been accepted by all factions within the association. The issue was how that action might be undertaken. Should the UFA enter politics directly or through the formation of another political party?

Feelings ran high during the 1919 convention, with the tide of opinion flowing in the direction of a separate political organization. The convention unanimously approved a resolution recommending the formation of an agrarian political party. This was to be achieved through the establishment of a political action committee. Following this convention, the then Liberal government of the province announced a bi-election in the Cochrane constituency. The UFA political action candidate was victorious.

Wood was undoubtedly chagrined by the outcome of the 1919 convention. Nor was he particularly jubilant over the Cochrane victory. He had attempted to work with the political action committee, the members of which had brusquely informed him that they were acting independently of the executive.

This was what Wood had feared might happen. Irrespective of a title which implied the UFA in politics, the political action committee seemingly regarded itself as an agrarian political party ready to seek support in the same manner as either the Liberals or Conservatives.

The issue was settled during the 1920 convention when Wood's leadership was threatened by the followers of the political action committee. They were, in effect, challenging Wood's ideas on group government. A resolution by Perrin Baker sought to combine all activities of the UFA — social, educational, economic, and political — under the direction of the central executive. The Baker resolution was passed almost unanimously.

At the same time, Wood defeated his opponent for the presidency, establishing that the ideas he had been developing through his annual addresses were supported by the UFA. He had created the class organization that was to dominate provincial affairs for the next 14 years.

6

Alberta's political history during the first 16 years of its legal existence followed a pattern set by the older members of the Canadian Federation. Albertans accepted the two-party system of the Northwest Territories as foreordained, the major change being that the elected members of the Legislative Assembly would travel to Edmonton rather than Regina.

Albertans supported the Liberal party during the province's first four elections. The predisposition of Albertans to vote Liberal emerged at the first election in 1905. In the first legislature of 25 members, the Conservative opposition contained only three MLAs. As the province's population increased, the provincial legislature grew accordingly. With each successive election the ratio of government to opposition altered somewhat, yet the Liberals continued to retain a decided majority. In the wartime election of 1917, for instance, the Liberals captured 34 seats, the Conservatives two, with two constituencies returning independents, and one declaring for Labor.

The election of 1921 was, however, startlingly different. A newcomer to Alberta's political scene, not even a political party but a farmers' organization, had been swept into power by capturing 38 seats, reducing the Liberals to 15, and obliterating the Conservatives completely. Furthermore, the Legislative Assembly would include four independents and four representatives of Labor, a decided increase in the members who were not clearly aligned with any party. Albertans had rejected bipartisan politics decisively.

This political upset created excitement and trepidation throughout the province. It undoubtedly caught the attention of Canadians generally, particularly those involved in the political process.

Albertans had unquestionably opted in favor of group government. The province's rural voters had asserted their political power. Alberta's farmers had, in fact, assumed control of the legislature. The division between rural and urban support had become astoundingly clear. No UFA candidates had been elected in either of the province's two major cities. Actually, the only government supporter to win a seat in those two cities throughout the UFA regime was J.F. Lymburn, an Edmonton lawyer who succeeded in doing so during the sixth and seventh legislatures from 1926 to 1935.

This political reversal aroused consternation, skepticism and even humor among the business groups of the province. Small town businessmen feared competition from cooperative stores established by UFA locals. Urban dwellers, particularly those living in Edmonton, suggested scattering straw on the steps of the Legislative Assembly to welcome the rural legislators. This was the era when farmers were viewed as lacking in sophistication, implied by such descriptive epithets as "rube," "hick," and "hayseed."

The election results were actually a protest against bipartisan politics. Alberta's rural voters had become convinced that very little difference existed between the two old-line parties at either provincial or federal levels. In a sense, the results constituted a revolution, a peaceful one undoubtedly, but nonetheless one that registered strong distaste for the status quo.

Strangely enough, the movement emerged from the rank and file of Alberta's rural population. Dissatisfied farmers used the organization they had created to seize control of the province's governing structures. In so doing, they set a pattern for change that was ultimately adopted by other Canadian provinces. The farmers' movement emerged in the provinces of Saskatchewan, Manitoba, and Ontario. The movement actually ended the predominance of the two-party system in Canada at both levels of government, provincial and federal.

The 1921 victory marked the high point in UFA support among Alberta farmers. The number of paid up members during that year reached 35,000. Several forces throughout the 20th century contributed to the decline of the UFA. The most influential of those ultimately was that which depleted the farming population, transforming Canada into a nation of urban dwellers. This was the evolution of a farming technology that made large farms not only possible, but economically desirable.

The UFA commenced its decline in membership immediately following its first election victory. That decline arose not from its inadequacies, but from its achievements. One of the greatest contributions of UFA leadership to the welfare of Alberta farmers existed in its organization of the Alberta Wheat Pool.

7

Western Canadian farmers, even those diversified in their production of food commodities, depend on one crop as their staple source of income — wheat. The history of western agriculture centres on the development of wheat strains appropriate to prairie climate, on the storage and movement of this product, and on opening and maintaining world markets for its disposal.

The search for effective marketing methods occupied the attention of western farmers following the First World War. One proposal, widely supported, was that the government establish a wheat marketing board comparable to that which had existed during the First World War. This, however, was not met with great favor by the federal government. The greatest difficulty seemed to be that of securing competent officials to serve on the proposed board.

Henry Wise Wood was opposed to such a board. He strongly believed that marketing should depend on the initiative of producers, rather than on the efforts of government. He argued that farmers, through their organization, should explore the possibilities of cooperative marketing.

Farmers were very much opposed to the currently existing marketing methods, with privately owned grain companies purchasing their grain at prices determined by the Winnipeg Grain Exchange.

Pressure for action mounted during the years following the election of the farmers' government. Finally, the UFA executive responding to this pressure decided to explore the feasibility of cooperative marketing. During July of 1923, the executive instructed President Wood to invite the outstanding expert in North America on cooperative marketing to visit Alberta.

Aaron Sapiro had worked with fruit growers to establish the California Fruit Growers' Association. The association then contracted with its members to dispose of their fruit over a five-year period. Giving the growers a small initial payment, the association sold the fruit, returning the profits of the sale to the producer. The California experiment in cooperative marketing had become a model attracting worldwide attention.

Sapiro proved to be an effective salesman for cooperative marketing. He insisted that the model he had devised for the fruit growers could be readily adopted by Canada's wheat growers. He caught the attention not only of the audience he addressed, but of western Canadians generally.

UFA members responded enthusiastically, convinced that the pool should be launched to market the current year's crop. Wood agreed, somewhat reluctantly, to become president of the proposed Alberta Wheat Pool.

In assuming this responsibility, he sought the assistance of his close friend, the Hon. J.E. Brownlee, who had become attorney general in the UFA government. Together they designed the operation of this venture into cooperative marketing. They planned the nature of the contract to be signed by each wheat pool member. They approached the Canadian banks to arrange the necessary financing which was to be backed by the Alberta government. The banks actually advanced $15 million for the initial payments. The Alberta Wheat Pool commenced operation on October 29, 1923.

On July 5, 1924, The Canadian Cooperative Wheat Producers Ltd. reported the results of its first year's operation. This organization was owned by the three pools of the prairie provinces, with each pool investing in its establishment. Its responsibility was to sell Canadian wheat to the various world markets. During that first year of operation, it had sold 34 million bushels of wheat, over 40 percent of that produced in the three western provinces at better than average returns.

Each provincial wheat pool distributed contracts to farmers prepared to use this method of marketing their wheat. It collected the grain from the privately owned elevators committed to handling wheat pool business, delivered it to terminals, and paid farmers their initial and final payments. In time, the three pools built their own elevators throughout the provinces to serve wheat pool members.

The success of the Alberta Wheat Pool led to the establishment of cooperative organizations dedicated to the sale of other farm products. These pools dealt with such products as livestock, cream, eggs, and poultry. None of these pools, however, gained the stature of the wheat pool, an experiment in cooperative marketing that still exists.

Henry Wise Wood wearing the cross of Companion of St. Michael and St. George awarded for service to agriculture.
Courtesy of the Alberta Wheat Pool.

Henry Wise Wood, until his retirement in 1931, retained the presidency of both the UFA and the Alberta Wheat Pool. He continued his post with the Wheat Pool until 1937. One wonders which of these two organizations he considered the most important of his contributions to Alberta farmers. Actually, the establishment of the Wheat Pool contributed to the decline of the UFA. Farmers tended to support the pools rather than the parent organization. However, the UFA may have achieved its ultimate service to farmers by giving birth to cooperative marketing.

During Wood's tenure as president of these two organizations, wheat farming continued to be the province's dominant industry. The farmer, obviously, was the most significant worker contributing to the provincial economy. Throughout that time, the UFA controlled provincial affairs. In reality, during this period Wood played the role of Alberta's uncrowned king.

Chapter Three
John Edward Brownlee

1

Alberta's political history for the decade following the UFA's first election victory centres on the careers of two men, Henry Wise Wood and J.E. Brownlee. The two men enjoyed a close friendship which endured throughout Wood's years as a farm leader, one based on mutual liking and respect. Although quite unlike in backgrounds and social interests, they shared many common views. Together they wielded considerable power during the early years of the province's peaceful political revolution initiated by the 1921 election results.

Brownlee, born in 1883, was at least a generation younger than Wood. He was brought up in Lambton County, Ontario, the son of William Brownlee, a rural storekeeper, and Christine Shaw Brownlee, both second generation Canadians. He attended high school and model school in nearby Sarnia. This latter institution was the 19th century version of a teacher training college from which Brownlee secured a third class teaching certificate.

Most notable in his educational career was the nature of his university program. A member of the Methodist church, he attended Victoria College, an affiliate of the University of Toronto. During his undergraduate studies, he emphasized courses in history and political science, electing to follow an honors program in the latter discipline.

As a student, he was diligent, often brilliant, and invariably well organized. One of the attributes Brownlee shared with Wood was that of religious conviction. Brownlee was more than a nominal member of the Methodist church. He was, in fact, an active participant in its activities, taking charge occasionally of Sunday school classes. Methodist doctrine of the period stressed the importance of service to others, a value that influenced Brownlee throughout his public career.

As we saw earlier, Wood too was a religious man, a member of the Campbellite Sect, a sect dedicated to Bible study, particularly the New

Testament. During his early years, Wood also conducted Bible classes. He saw his role, as a follower of Christ, to be that of working in the interest of social improvement.

These two men, both members of Protestant sects emphasizing Christianity as a way of life, exemplified this in their public careers. Both men were inherently cautious, hesitant to arrive at decisions or embark on courses of action without carefully weighing the consequences.

Wood, though something of an ideological reformer, was nonetheless not given to expect simple or ready solutions to social problems. He was convinced that the pace of change must necessarily be slow. Brownlee, too, was unlikely to act hastily. Though liberal in his views, he was incapable of radical action. He was, in fact, conventional in dress and manner, as well as in his economic theories.

Neither of these two men could be regarded as likely revolutionary leaders. Brownlee's comments on the role of farm organizations reflected his abhorrence of radicalism. He insisted that a government could not operate on a higher plane than that occupied by most of its citizens. No reform could be accomplished until the feelings and perceptions of the majority of people had been crystallized and shaped into some form of opinion. The education of people in these intellectual processes is of the greatest importance. Brownlee maintained that farm organizations must dedicate their efforts toward preparing their members for change.

2

Following his graduation from the University of Toronto, Brownlee left for Calgary to article with the law firm of Lougheed, Bennet, Alison and McLaws. Later he changed to the firm of Main, Jephson and Adams. He was admitted to the bar on December 16, 1912, joining the firm with which he had been articling.

In July, he was appointed solicitor for the United Grain Growers Co., an appointment that reflected Brownlee's growing interest in farm organizations. Shortly after this appointment, he accepted the position of manager of UGG Securities. Their Calgary offices were in the same building as those of the UFA. This proximity of offices led to his close acquaintanceship with UFA officials, including Henry Wise Wood, one that accounted for Brownlee's subsequent career.

Following the 1921 election, Brownlee accepted Greenfield's invitation to join his cabinet as attorney general. He was immediately forced to secure a seat in the Legislative Assembly. The death of a member elected to represent the Ponoka constituency opened a vacancy for him. He continued to represent this constituency until his defeat and retirement from politics in 1935. During that time, he addressed audiences in school houses throughout the constituency and frequently attended UFA picnics that were the high points in the social life of rural Albertans.

Despite his experience as vice-president of the UFA, Greenfield was far from being an effective premier. He did not fall short in his ability as a public speaker, though he was frequently beset with bouts of laryngitis that rendered him temporarily speechless. He was also an excellent host to

Herbert Greenfield,
Alberta premier, 1921-1925.
Photo courtesy of the Provincial Archives of Alberta, A-6267.

prominent visitors, showing off the provincial legislature with obvious pride. However, he avoided political problems, preferring to ignore them, presumably with the hope that they would eventually disappear. His major weakness was his seeming inability to either interpret or defend government policy in the legislature. He relied on Brownlee, increasingly, to perform that role.

During his first years in the legislature, Brownlee developed a speaking style appropriate to the Legislative Assembly. Lean and quite tall in stature, he was youthful yet mature, even grave in appearance. In delivery, his manner verged on the judicial, with occasional traces of school masterly authority. Invariably well prepared, Brownlee could be devastating in debate with his opposition critics. Contrasted with the backbenchers of the UFA, he was a veritable intellectual giant. The rank and file of UFA members gloried in Brownlee's debating strength as he ruthlessly disposed of opposition arguments.

The seeds of dissent that would finally defeat the UFA government were apparent in the annual conventions of the early '20s. Farmers were enduring the impact of high interest rates, as well as threats of foreclosures from banks and mortgage companies. In constant dread of losing their livelihood, many farmers turned to their organization and to the government they had elected for protection. Radical thinkers advocated solutions that created uneasiness with certain UFA leaders.

One group of dissidents insisted that the problem existed in Canada's financial institutions. George Bevington, a convention activist, had read a treatise by Major C.H. Douglas identifying bankers as the villains in the economic tragedy. Douglas thought that consumers did not have enough money or credit to buy all the products being produced in an industrial society. He thought this chronic shortage in purchasing power must be remedied by government.

Another group would be content if the government issued bonds covering the complete debt of Alberta's farmers. The government could then exchange these directly for Dominion treasury notes. With these funds it would be able to make loans to debtors at cost. A third sought satisfaction in the establishment of a provincial bank, one that would operate for service rather than profit.

Pressures from these groups commenced during the 1922 UFA convention, reaching a high point in that of 1923. Several resolutions demanding radical action by government reached the convention floor. These dealt with such drastic issues as an extension of the *Drought Relief Act* and provincial funding of farm debt. One, less radical in impact, advocated that the Alberta government obtain a bank charter and establish a provincial bank.

Brownlee never hesitated to intervene in convention debates. On such resolutions as these, he was quick to respond. Facing an audience filled with fruitless anger against forces beyond its control, Brownlee employed rational argument, using such words as these:

"Gentlemen, the government realizes the serious situation of farmers in this province. However, I should like you to consider this fact. The government has the second highest per capita debt in Canada. We actually need $13 million to replace past borrowings."

A voice from the audience interjected. "Another effort to keep us in perpetual serfdom!"

Ignoring the comment, Brownlee continued. "The amortization plan you put forward this morning would practically double the province's debt. This would force every man, woman and child to pay more to retire the debt than in any other province. I ask you to have faith in your government. As a result of certain resolutions, we may find it difficult to carry on for another year."

Whether it was Brownlee's appeal, or Wood's steady hand that defeated the more radical of these resolutions is difficult to say. It was probably the combined efforts of both leaders. The convention was ultimately satisfied with a request that the government make application for a provincial bank charter.

Brownlee was complimented for his control over a convention on the brink of despair. His firm stand against radical proposals strengthened his hand in dealing with banks and mortgage companies. He could now request these organizations to be more moderate in their actions, not to be hasty in foreclosures. He eventually assumed the role of mediator between debtors and creditors.

The resolution on the provincial bank was revived once more during the 1924 convention. The persistent George Bevington, leading a small group intent on monetary reform, presented a resolution insisting that the government act on last year's request to apply for a bank charter. Bevington's hopes had been revived, one suspects, by his invitation to appear before the federal government's select committee on banking. He had presented a discourse to the committee on the movement of blood through the circulatory system as being analogous to the flow of credit through society.

Although Brownlee had made certain concessions in the form of provincial savings certificates, he made no effort to apply for a bank charter. He was afraid that such a venture might lead to the weakening of the province's financial position. This time Wood dealt with Bevington in the following terse statement.

"Not only is the establishment of a bank not fundamental to the solution of our financial problems, but also the financial question is not fundamental to the solution of our social problems.

"The farmers' problem is not that they cannot contract more debts. It is because the income they receive for their product is not sufficient. They must have more say about the price of their products."

Wood, by his intervention turned the convention against the monetary reformers to defeat overwhelmingly Bevington's resolution. Neither

Wood nor Bevington could foresee the day when such a resolution would be successful. Wood had not permanently eliminated the seeds of this dissent.

By 1924, the UFA members in the Legislative Assembly had become increasingly critical of Greenfield's leadership. A small group of those members, fearing defeat if Greenfield remained premier entering the next election, started agitating for a change. The replacement, obviously, would be the attorney general.

Brownlee was firm in his rejection of such a proposal. He actually indicated that if Greenfield was forced to resign, he also would resign. To demonstrate his sincerity, Brownlee tendered his resignation to become effective if and when this took place. The insurgents proposing a transfer in leadership persuaded Wood to exert pressure on Brownlee. Brownlee relented, agreeing to accept the leadership only if it met with Greenfield's approval. Greenfield resigned on November 23, 1924, recommending to Lt. Gov. Egbert that Brownlee be asked to form a government.

As premier, Brownlee faced several problems. Above all else, however, he considered that of balancing the budget to be the most imperative. This could only be achieved if he were able to sell the provincial railways. Of these, the two major lines were the Edmonton, Dunvegan and British Columbia (E.D.& B.C.), and the Alberta Great Waterways (A.G.W.). The interest on the debts these lines had accumulated, together with the shortfalls in their operational costs, imposed heavy financial burdens on the province.

3

Alberta had not yet secured control over its natural resources. At the time of the prairie provinces' establishment, the federal government had prudently retained control over their natural wealth including their land, their forests, and the minerals lying below the earth's surface. The Laurier government argued that there were too few people in these newly formed jurisdictions to assume responsibility for the their natural resources. In retrospect, one might conclude that the federal government needed to retain control of western land as part of its homestead policy.

The unresolved problem of resource ownership continued to sour relationships between all three prairie provinces and the federal govern-

J.E. Brownlee, Alberta premier, 1925-1934.
Photo courtesy of the Provincial Archives of Alberta, A-433.

ment. A favorable solution to it would undoubtedly assure success in the provincial election to take place no later than 1926. Winning that election was now Brownlee's top priority.

Since Brownlee had met with little success in his attempts to solve either of the two major problems — selling the province's two major railways, or securing its natural resources — he resorted to an attack on the party system. Campaigning vigorously throughout the province, Brownlee exhorted members of rural audiences to remain faithful to their government in such words as the following:

"I believe that the farmers of this province are going to say, as they said five years ago, that we want something better than the party system. We want those people who go up to Edmonton to be able to face the issues that affect our homes and our children; and forgetting about artificial divisions, to try to solve these problems from the viewpoint only of improving the welfare and the conditions of the people of the province."

Strangely enough, Brownlee made no references to group government. Perhaps this was unnecessary since he was speaking for a party that, with one or two exceptions, was solidly made up of those engaged in farming. Despite his obvious lack of sympathy for the more theoretical of Wood's ideas, their friendship remained strong. With Wood's interests increasingly directed toward the affairs of the Alberta Wheat Pool, and with a successful election behind him, Brownlee was becoming more and more the voice of the UFA.

4

The years of the sixth legislature, 1926-1930, were the best of the 14 during which the UFA held office. The period was one of general prosperity, with the world price for wheat remaining relatively high throughout. The West was favored with a series of good crops which, combined with these prices, rewarded farmers with a period of unprecedented financial well being. This gave Brownlee an opportunity to fulfill his most cherished ambition — to further the growth of cooperative marketing which he and Wood had initiated, and to deal with the province's budgetary problems.

By February 1929, Brownlee had reached an agreement with Canada's two major railways, the Canadian Pacific and the Canadian National, to purchase the E.D.& B.C., the A.G.W. and the Pembina Valley lines. The two companies assumed a debt of $9.5 million and agreed to pay the province $10 million in two instalments during 1929 and 1933. Furthermore, they lifted a yearly burden of one million dollars from the province's exchequer. Altogether the province wrote off some $15 million as an expenditure on northern development. Alberta did not become directly involved in further railway construction until the building of the Alberta Resources Railway, between Grande Prairie and the main line of the CNR, during 1964 to 1966 under the Manning Government.

As we have seen earlier, the federal government had retained the province's natural resources at the time of Alberta's creation. During the period of its stewardship, the federal government had used these resources for the purposes of Canada generally, with the understanding that it would compensate the province for lost revenues.

In its generous way, Canada had granted aproximately 200,000 hectares of land to eastern corporations for the construction of railways in British Columbia, Manitoba, and Ontario. The Canadian government had also rewarded other corporations with mineral leases to search for and exploit Alberta's coal and oil deposits.

During the early '20s, the most significant resource issue was that of hydroelectricity. The city of Calgary since 1909 had been supplied with electricity by the Calgary Power Company, a corporation with its head office in Montreal. Calgary Power applied for water rights in the Upper Bow watershed, including Spray Lakes, a region rich in water power potential. The government, supported by the UFA executive, maintained that the small towns and farm homes of rural Alberta should not have to depend on power supplied by a company interested in profits for non-Albertans.

Brownlee made a formal application for a priority permit entitling the province to the water power rights concerned. The federal government denied Alberta these rights. In denying this request, Canada had ignored not only the wishes of the provincial government, but those of most Albertans.

The natural resources issue continued to fester throughout the '20s. During 1925, Prime Minister King appointed a special committee, including himself and four members of his cabinet along with two representatives from Alberta, to study the question of extending control over its resources to each of the three prairie provinces. Typically, Mackenzie King was proving evasive by indicating his desire for further study.

The following year, the issue appeared on the verge of resolution. An historical problem, however, one that periodically thrusts itself into Canada's federal-provincial relations, forestalled its final settlement. Brownlee discovered that the agreement he had signed and the bill proposed by King were not identical in substance.

The complication arose with the transfer of lands, and funds deriving from them, that had been designated for the support of schools, organized under section 17 of the *Alberta Act*. This particular section ordained that since the territorial government had introduced separate schools into the territories prior to the establishment of Alberta, that province must continue to provide for them.

In the signed agreement no reference had been made to this proviso. Prime Minister King's Quebec lieutenant, the Hon. E. LaPointe, wanted this reference to section 17 in the bill to assure Quebec's premier, Henri Bourassa, that the rights of the French-Catholic minority in Alberta were being safeguarded. This was obviously a political move that had little to do with the agreement.

Brownlee objected to the reference. He argued that if section 17 was valid, then this inclusion was unnecessary. If it was invalid, it ought not to be legalized by such a statement. No one from Alberta had challenged the constitutionality of section 17, nor was the province interested in doing so by distinguishing between its separate and public school systems in the distribution of these funds. Mackenzie King held back the bill in order to test the legitimacy of section 17.

The legislative mill ground slowly under the wily leadership of Mackenzie King. By 1929, however, his officials had revised the section on school lands in the proposed bill. The federal government had agreed that subsidies to the provinces should be continued in perpetuity as compensation for the resources Canada had alienated during its period of their administration. This was to be paid to each province on the basis of population.

Brownlee immediately protested the unfairness of this proposal. Based on population, Saskatchewan would be paid $950,000, as opposed to Alberta's payment of $526,000; yet Alberta's resources far exceeded those of Saskatchewan in value. Brownlee argued that a sliding scale providing for increases in the subsidy as population grew was imperative.

On December 11, 1929, Premier J.E. Brownlee, and ministers George Hoadley and John Lymburn, met Prime Minister Mackenzie King and his supporters in King's Ottawa office suite. The recurring failures of such meetings over several years undoubtedly made the members of each group somewhat edgy. Manitoba had already settled for a perpetual subsidy and a cash settlement of $4 million. Brownlee asked for a similar payment, which meant going back to 1870, the date of Manitoba's entrance into Confederation.

King was obviously upset by this request. He rose abruptly. Attempting to control his anger, he looked directly at Brownlee, saying icily:

"Put it in writing Brownlee. We'll deal with it after Christmas."

With these words he walked out of the room.

Brownlee stood and turning to his delegation directed them to carry on with the discussion. He too then strode from the room.

The startled officials in both groups recognized they could get nowhere without their leaders. Each group agreed that it would try to persuade its leader to return to the meeting in the afternoon. They were both successful.

During the afternoon, Brownlee told King of the offer which R.B. Bennett, the leader of the Opposition, had said he would make to the prairie provinces if he won the next election. Brownlee continued to argue that Alberta should receive a larger subsidy than Manitoba. King, now recovered from his pique, invited Brownlee to stay over until the next day.

King immediately held a cabinet meeting recommending approval of Brownlee's request. Some members were reluctant to agree. King, however, insisted that the government settle with Alberta as well as Manitoba to forestall Saskatchewan from asking for better terms. Both Brownlee of Alberta and John Bracken of Manitoba were ready to sign.

King entertained the Alberta delegation for dinner at Laurier House, his official residence, that same evening. During its course, King and Brownlee arrived at an agreement on transferring control of the province's resources to the Alberta government. The amount of the additional payment was left to the decision of a commission.

Premier Brownlee and Prime Minister MacKenzie King, 1930.
(front row, third and fourth from left, respectively)
Photo courtesy of the Provincial Archives of Alberta, A-10924.

The agreement was signed on December 14, before Brownlee and Bracken returned home. It placed both these provinces on the same level as those that had entered Confederation in 1867. The terms granted Alberta were much more favorable than those offered in 1926.

Brownlee had secured for the province 35,400,000 hectares of land, the world's largest coal deposits and hydroelectric potential, and one-third of the world's supply of oil and gas. This was the greatest achievement of Brownlee's career as premier of the province.

When Brownlee returned home on December 17, he was met at the station by a large group of cheering Edmontonians. Even the Newsboys Band, one established by the owner of Mike's News Stand, was out to welcome home Alberta's conquering hero. Brownlee had become the province's man of the year.

5

Had Brownlee chosen to retire from political life following this achievement, he would have entered history as one of Alberta's great premiers. He decided to remain, however, perhaps to savor his negotiating successes through further political victories. Within a brief span of time, those successes were replaced by a series of ignominious failures. Five years later Brownlee, defeated in his own constituency, was forced to abandon his political career; the movement he headed obliterated as a political force, and his personal reputation tarnished beyond repair.

The years of the seventh legislature, 1930-1935, were sad ones for the UFA. They must, without doubt, have caused Henry Wise Wood much anguish. His good friend Brownlee was excoriated by the press. The radical element which he and Brownlee had silenced so effectively 10 years previously had gained control of the convention to demand actions that for both were anathema. Group government had ended in disastrous defeat. His beloved wheat pool had been threatened by financial crisis.

The Brownlee government, enormously popular at the termination of the sixth legislature, encountered problems during the seventh for which it had no effective solutions. The cabinet was beset by minor scandals, titillating stories of wife swapping between two cabinet ministers. There was nothing, however, that a resignation or two would not have cured had Brownlee been more alert.

Perhaps the cabinet's greatest defect was its failure to keep in touch with the convention. Separated from that body, the government was cut off from the people it had been elected to serve. The most condemnatory statement heard throughout rural Alberta was that cabinet ministers, having spent so much time in the city, had become urbanized. Many farmers were saying that they could see little difference between the UFA and the old-line parties. For a government wholly dependent on rural votes, these were fatal perceptions.

The government was attempting to cope with forces and events over which it had little control. The most devastating of these was the inexorable downward movement in the price of wheat. The first appearance of this remorseless trend came in 1929, immediately following a crash in the New York stock market. The price of wheat on the Winnipeg Grain Exchange plummeted from a high of $1.78 per bushel to $1.20, a drop of nearly 60 cents. The direction having been set, it continued its descent, to reach a low in 1932 of 40 cents, the lowest price in 400 years.

On the day of that occurrence, Brownlee had called on the Mounted Police to dispense a peaceful hunger march of 1,000 men on the Legislative Assembly.

This downward trek in wheat prices had engendered a crisis for the wheat pool. The pool had granted farmers an initial price in 1929 that was higher than the actual by the time the wheat had been marketed. This had placed the wheat pool in financial straits. Brownlee spent a great deal of time during 1930 attempting to assist the three western pools through their difficulties.

The three western premiers took their problems to R.B. Bennett who had been elected prime minister of Canada in 1930. On behalf of the premiers, Brownlee set out three courses of action for Bennett's consideration. One course proposed a fixed price of 70 cents per bushel which Bennett, an advocate of the free market, flatly rejected. A second course recommended that the federal government assume the provincial role of guaranteeing the banks against loss in carrying the pools. A third proposed that Canada establish a stabilization board with sufficient funding to purchase wheat when the market fell below minimum levels.

Mr. Bennett was not impressed with any of these proposals involving government intervention in the marketing of wheat.

The banks indicated they were ready to continue carrying the pools, provided they could get some control over their operation. They demanded that their man, I. McFarland, be appointed general manager, obviously to protect their interests. Farmers generally pressed for a return to a government appointed national wheat board to market Canadian wheat, one comparable to that set up during the First World War.

The appointment of this board ended the international aspects of the three wheat pools. Each pool became, in effect, a purchaser of wheat only, delivering it to the board for its disposal.

The second problem facing western governments was that of falling tax revenues. This, too, was the inevitable outcome of low farm income. The bond market refused to absorb the securities not only of the western, but of all Canadian provinces. During those years, the federal treasury became the bank of last resort for most provinces.

Much of the fiscal impoverishment among the western provinces, resulted from relief payments to their unemployed citizens. Here again, the premiers approached the Canadian government, insisting that it ought to bear at least 35 to 50 percent of those expenditures. Bennett's reply was that the provinces should balance their budgets!

"If they are unable to do so," said Canada's lordly prime minister, "their governments should accept a controller appointed by the federal government."

Provincial governments had little leeway in the balancing of expenditures with revenues. They could cut back on services such as schools, health institutions, mothers' allowances, old age pensions and the like. On the other hand, they might default on the payment of interest on debts, or on exchange premiums. They needed desperately advances against treasury bills to meet expenditures on unemployment relief, a stark necessity in both rural and urban areas.

Brownlee held deep seated convictions about government and its operation. He regarded government as a corporation to be run in a businesslike manner. His dedication to a balanced budget, doubtless, emanated from a firm belief in the principle that the business of government is business. With Brownlee, this was a rational view rationally derived, yet adhered to with almost religious conviction. He frequently said that he would do anything to help the people, provided it did not worsen the province's financial resources.

Brownlee's devotion to a balanced budget led him to reduce government expenditures ruthlessly. These cuts affected the simplest improvements, such as that of installing an electric lift in the legislature. In 1931, the government closed its three agricultural schools at a time when the sons and daughters of farmers needed training to maintain and improve their family farms. The civil service was reduced from 2,566 to 1,600, a drastic reduction in personnel that had its effects on service.

By 1933, Brownlee had reduced the cost of government by $8 million, a 50 percent reduction from 1929. The reduction of grants to the school boards of the province was equally drastic, with many rural boards paying salaries to their teachers well below the poverty line.

Though Brownlee's actions may have appeared extremely conservative to Albertans, he was regarded as a radical thinker in other parts of Canada. In July, 1933, the federal government set up a royal commission on banking and currency. The commission was chaired by Lord Mac-Millan, an eminent British jurist, with such other members as Sir Charles Addis, a director of the Bank of England, Sir Thomas White, former minister of finance for Canada, Beaudry Lemieu, general manager of the Banque Canadian National, and J.E. Brownlee, the only non-banker.

The purpose of the commission was to recommend measures for promoting the revival of trade and enterprise, and for improving the economic welfare of Canadians in general.

The commission's recommendations were of far-reaching impact. A leading and major proposal was that of establishing a central bank for Canada. No less important was the recommendation for an inquiry into current provisions for rural credit with a view to improving these if deemed desirable.

Brownlee's views on the structure and role of a central bank found their way into the report. He argued that the central bank should be a public institution designed not for profit, but for the achievement of a national purpose. Of necessity then, the chairman and the board of directors should be appointed by the government. As for the bank's role, it must be concerned with such matters as the supply of money within the country and interest rates. Obviously, these are both related to the state of the national economy.

That Canada's central bank was eventually established along the lines advocated by Brownlee represents a major achievement for which he has received little credit.

6

Any account of Brownlee's career would be incomplete without reference to the events leading to his resignation as premier in July of 1934. Central among these was the Brownlee case, one that reached the British Privy Council before it passed into history several years after its first appearance in Canadian courts.

During the course of the 1930 election campaign, Brownlee visited the town of Edson. He was entertained there by Mr. Allan MacMillan, a former mayor of Edson and a supporter of the Brownlee government. The MacMillan family drove Brownlee to Luscar, a mining community some 80 kilometres south of Edson, for a political meeting. Brownlee rode in the back seat of the car with the MacMillans' daughter, Vivian, a recent high school graduate. Throughout the pleasant afternoon drive, Brownlee and Vivian chatted about the sorts of topics a middle-aged man might conceive of interest to a young lady not yet 20 years of age.

Before leaving Edson, Brownlee commented to MacMillan that he might find a position for Vivian in government service if she were interested in pursuing a career away from home. He said, also, that both he and Mrs. Brownlee would be pleased to have her stay with them until she was located.

Vivian later took advantage of that invitation. Employed as a clerk in the attorney general's branch, Vivian visited the Brownlee residence frequently, making it her second home.

On August 3, 1933, Vivian MacMillan and her father, Allan Mac-Millan, commenced legal action against J.E. Brownlee, alleging seduction. The trial by judge and jury resulting from this action took place in Edmonton, during July of 1934. The evidence submitted by Vivian Macmillan, in response to the questioning of her lawyer, Mr. Neal D. Maclean, became front page news not only in Alberta, but across Canada.

Vivian maintained that Brownlee had seduced her quite early during her many visits to the Brownlee home. She described a living arrangement within the Brownlee home that, to say the least, was unusual. Mrs. Brownlee slept in one room with one of their two young boys, and Mr. Brownlee occupied another room, with the other son.

When she visited the Brownlee home, Vivian indicated that she slept in a room designated as the maid's room. The premier would arrange for her to come to his bed by flushing the toilet and walking lock step with her to conceal the noise of her passage.

Vivian testified that this liaison was carried on outside, as well. Brownlee had taken her on drives in his government car over country roads, immediately west of Edmonton, in the direction of Stony Plain.

The jury accepted Vivian's evidence as true. Perhaps members of the jury did so because they found this evidence so bizarre, they concluded that no one could have fabricated such a fantastic story! The jury members agreed, that the plaintiff had suffered damage to the extent of $2,000. Allan MacMillan was awarded a damage payment of $5,000. Mr. Justice Ives disagreed with the awards and dismissed the action.[1]

Following this pronouncement, Brownlee resigned as premier. The case wound its tortuous way upward to the Court of Appeal, the Supreme Court of Canada, finally reaching the Privy Council in England. During the course of its advance over these legal hurdles, Vivian was awarded $10,000, with no recognition for her father's claim.

The appeal judge concluded that there was no incontrovertible evidence of sexual intercourse. Whether the cautious and upright

Brownlee was guilty of seduction is still a matter of conjecture. Only Brownlee and Vivian knew the truth and the evidence each gave was mutually contradictory.

The case probably did not alter the political future of the UFA government. Its fate in the 1935 election had been determined before the Brownlee case emerged to absorb the attention of all Albertans. Quite apart from the explicit details revealed in the trial, the events of the seventh legislature lead inexorably to the demise of the government. It appeared completely immobilized from the start of the legislature, bereft of ideas on how to meet the problems it was facing, and quite incapable of the drastic actions for which Albertans were clamoring.

In the meantime, a new prophet had emerged in the south. William Aberhart, a Calgary school principal, had almost unwittingly started a movement that was spreading throughout southern Alberta with the speed of a prairie fire.

Brownlee spent the last two years of his political career trying to counter this movement with rational argument. The people, however, were calling for a revival of the political revolution with greater public anger than existed in 1921. The UFA government was headed for defeat.

Following the 1935 election, Brownlee returned to his position with the United Grain Growers, one that he had left 20 years earlier. He died in 1961. The following comment which appeared in the *Saskatoon Star Phoenix* is a most appropriate epitaph for this outstanding Albertan.

"He was not inclined to become evangelistic about farming problems as popular causes to be exploited and placed out of proportion. He preferred a businesslike, professional approach to them, and his personal policy of reasoned argument distinguished him in his public career."

Notes

[1] The events of the trial, including the recommendations of the jury and the decision taken by Mr. Justive Ives, were reported in the July 3, 1934, copy of the *Edmonton Bulletin.*

Chapter Four
The UFA and the CCF

1

When Henry Wise Wood retired as president of the UFA in 1931 he had served in that post for 15 years. That organization had been in existence since 1909 and had provided a government for Alberta since 1921. At this juncture in Alberta's history, we should examine the UFA to see what it actually was before tracing its eventual destiny.

The UFA had been part of a movement. Walter Young, in his book *The Anatomy of a Party,* discusses the nature of a movement and how it differs from a political party.[1] A movement is an action or venture undertaken by a group of people that originates from a set of ideas. These ideas involve not only intellectual concepts, but also emotional attachments to those concepts. They are felt as well as understood.

The action or venture, irrespective of where it first emerges, invariably extends beyond a local community, encompassing inevitably a series of events. A movement of consequence seeks to influence by establishing new modes of thinking, new patterns in behavior, and new arrangements in social relationships. People who originate a movement, and those who become its adherents, cling to its ideology. In essence, they accept it almost as a faith.

The ideas and the values exemplified by the UFA were shared by similar farmers' organizations across Canada. Whether the farmers' movement first originated in Ontario or Alberta, the east or the west, is difficult to say, although one suspects that the UFO preceded the UFA. The movement seems to have emerged simultaneously in most provinces, taking somewhat different organizational forms in each.

The provincial movement reflected an attachment to an agrarian lifestyle, and a certain suspicion of most urban dwellers. The vitality of the farmers' movement was generated by the centrality of its focus on the family farm, a predominant and powerful social force during the early years of this century.

A political party, though it may start as a movement, rarely retains its ideological origins. The overriding purpose of a political party is to gain and hold power, which means winning elections. Failure to get elected forces a political party to reexamine its objectives and the views it expresses. A party frequently modifies those views in the search for platforms that might appeal to the electorate.

Relationships between the UFA as a movement and its political offspring remained harmonious throughout the decade of the '20s. This friendly rapport was engendered by a period of prosperity and expansion. The UFA's child, the Alberta Wheat Pool, had seemingly solved the farmers' marketing problems, providing them with unprecedented prosperity as the decade moved to its close. The relationships were further facilitated by the close friendship between the president of the UFA and the premier of the province.

The early years of the succeeding decade saw a marked change in the rapport existing between the UFA movement and the political party it had spawned. Wood's retirement from the UFA presidency in 1931 brought new leadership to the fore. Robert Gardiner, MP, assumed the presidency of the farmers' organization. Norman Priestley remained as its secretary, providing continuity in that office.

Robert Gardiner' s background, his recent experience, and his views were quite unlike those of Henry Wise Wood. He had been elected to the federal parliament in 1921 in the political upset that had changed the character of Alberta's provincial government and had sent a group of members to Ottawa strongly opposed to Canada's bipartisan system. Some 65 members from western Canada joined in parliamentary ranks led by T.A. Crerar, a former Liberal. He had resigned from that party because of Mackenzie King's cautious avoidance of free-trade legislation.

This western group heralded their coming by announcing they were members of the Progressive party. Despite its appealing title, the party began to disintegrate almost immediately. J.S. Woodsworth, leader of a tiny contingent of Labor members, had been elected from a working-class riding in North Winnipeg. One of Canada's great parliamentarians, Woodsworth courted a small group of Progressives who had decided to speak not only for farmers, but also for the labor elements of their constituencies.

These dissidents became known as the "Ginger Group," so-called because of the vigorous spirit with which they attacked the parliamentary status quo. They protested a greater loyalty to their constituents than to the Progressive party. Robert Gardiner was a member of this group. From 1924 on, the Ginger Group worked closely with Woodsworth in attempting to build a coalition that could well have been labelled farmer-labor.

2

In retrospect, the decade of the '30s stands out in the 20th century. To borrow a descriptive phrase from a great English novelist, "They were the worst of times and the best of times."[2] Unquestionably the decade is noteworthy for the despair and disaster that beset Alberta's society in common with those of other western Canadian provinces.

As we saw earlier, the price of Alberta's major farm product — wheat — reached a low unparalleled during the last four centuries. The number of people on relief (i.e., securing municipal aid for life support) had reached phenomenal figures. Those who were unemployed represented the mainstream rather than the exception in the province's towns and cities.

The bright side of the coin reflected the best of times. The degree of altruistic feeling and behavior in this decade undoubtedly exceeded that of any other.

Two major movements, each charged with admirable motives and worthy intent, emerged in response to the human needs created by the decade's events. These two movements, both politically oriented, exerted their influence on Alberta's subsequent history. Both movements are relevant to understanding the nature of Alberta's society, though one was infinitely more influential than the other. Through what can only be described as a vagary of history, the other movement played a highly significant role in shaping the destiny of Alberta's provincial twin, Saskatchewan.

It is difficult to distinguish between the two movements in terms of time. They both caught the attention of Albertans during the early '30s. It is equally difficult to draw distinctions between them by referring to geographical origins. Both could be described as originating in the city of Calgary. That one became exclusively identified with Alberta, while the other placed its indelible stamp on the Saskatchewan story, can only be explained as historical irony.

As the title indicates, this chapter is concerned with the UFA, and the Cooperative Commonwealth Federation, the CCF. The role of the CCF, a movement-cum-political party, in shaping the events of Alberta's social history, is quite indirect, some might say non-existent. Yet certain reforms now universal across Canada, such as unemployment insurance and medicare, were first proposed by the CCF.

The series of actions leading to the establishment of the CCF are an essential part of this story. They, in fact, provide its historical setting. The first of these is a movement not widely recognized or remembered. Actually, one so obscure that it has, perhaps, escaped the eyes of all but the most vigilant of Canadian historians. This was the League for Social Reconstruction, an organization formed in 1930 that lasted until the early '40s. Despite its limited life span, the League was quite influential. It became, for a time, the brain trust of the CCF.

The League was initiated by intellectuals, professors in the universities of McGill and Toronto. They were convinced that Canada needed an organization comparable to the Fabian Society in England, one that had become widely known throughout the English-speaking world. Fabius was a Roman general, a man of wisdom, who apparently preferred to practise delay tactics, rather than precipitate military action. The modern Fabians were socialists who, unlike Karl Marx with his emphasis on class conflict, insisted that people should be persuaded to accept socialism through the peaceful processes of education and eventual enlightenment.

The Socialist League spread rapidly across Canada, appealing to people not unlike those who initiated the movement. Very soon groups dedicated to the study of socialism appeared in most of Canada's major cities. The eastern leaders, such as Eugene Forsey, Frank Scott and Frank Underhill, approached J.S. Woodsworth inviting him to become honorary president. Woodsworth was delighted to accept, seeing this organization as fulfilling a need which he had frequently voiced.

The league described itself as "an association of men and women who were working for the establishment in Canada of a social order in which the basic principles regulating production, distribution, and service will be the common good rather than private profit."[3] With this purpose, Woodsworth was in complete agreement.

Woodsworth had been a Methodist minister until 1919 when he resigned in protest against his church's support of the First World War.

He was an inspirational speaker, an evangelist dedicated to the cause of Christian socialism. Although a representative of labor, he was equally familiar with the problems of the western farmers. As a leader, he was revered by both groups.

During May of 1932, a group including four labor MPs — J.S. Woodsworth, William Irvine, A.U. Heaps and Angus MacInnis — met in Ottawa. The purpose of the meeting was to plan the establishment of a Commonwealth party. Woodsworth was chosen as president of this embryonic political group. The person allocated organizing responsibility for Alberta was none other than Robert Gardiner, president of the UFA.

The occasion for launching the new party was to follow the annual meeting of various labor groups to be held in Calgary during July of 1932. Robert Gardiner had invited these labor groups to hold their conference in this young prairie city with its magnificent view of the Rocky Mountains.

Following the labor conference, the meeting to launch Canada's newest political party took place. The chairmen of the various convention committees were such prominent people as M.J. Coldwell, a school principal and alderman from Regina, Norman Priestley, secretary of the UFA, and Dr. W.H. Alexander, a classics professor from the University of Alberta.[4]

The delegates from Alberta represented the UFA and the Canadian and Dominion labor parties. Delegates speaking for the Socialist Party of Canada came from British Columbia. Manitoba provided delegates who announced their attachment to the Independent Labor party. The United Farmers of Canada (Saskatchewan section) sent delegates accompanied by representatives of the Independent and Cooperative Labor party. A representative of the Canadian Brotherhood of Railway Employees completed the founding assembly.

Certain broad decisions were reached during this meeting. After some debate, its members concluded that the name of the new party should be the Cooperative Commonwealth Federation (CCF). The concept of a federation implied that the organization would include within its framework several groups, presumably all those who had attended this founding gathering. They were identified broadly, under the categories of farmer, labor and socialist.

The overriding purpose of this new party was to establish in Canada a cooperative commonwealth in which the basic principle regulating production, distribution and exchange would be the supplying of human needs, rather than the making of profits. Its organizational structure would consist of a council and an executive for each province to deal with provincial political issues and activities. It would have a national council and executive to direct its attention to federal matters.

The meeting outlined a program of action for this political newcomer. It should seek to establish a planned system of social economy for the production, distribution and exchange of all goods and services. This implied a centrality of control over economic affairs unprecedented in Canada, even in wartime.

The CCF was expected to transform the banking, credit, and financial system of the nation by assuming control of its institutions either through government ownership or regulation. Bankers were not loved by these western Canadians; neither were mortgage companies, nor for that matter, anyone in the business of loaning money during a period when foreclosures had become a threat to many farmers.

Furthermore, these people were convinced that the natural wealth of a province should be exploited not for the benefit of private interests, but for public well-being.

Those who had launched this new party were realistic enough to realize that a socialist heaven could not be achieved overnight. In the meantime, there must be adequate provision for insurance against crop failure, illness, accidents, old age, and unemployment during the transition from the unhappy present to the ideal future — a socialist state.

These requests may not seem particularly radical, but one must recognize that they appeared, at that time, to be startlingly so. Canada's press, irrespective of its locale, was quick to condemn the CCF as a potentially dangerous party. As usual, many suggested that its proposals were communistic. The fact that the Communist party of Canada was equally critical of the CCF was ignored by members of the press anxious to protect Canadian society from the dangers of a Marxian dictatorship.

3

The extensive program outlined during the founding meeting was provisional. The party as yet lacked organization and properly elected officials. The CCF would have to hold its first convention, establish its own direction, purposes, and programs. In the meantime, a temporary committee could commence the formidable task of getting this infant party en route to maturity.

The CCF's first convention was held as anticipated in Regina during July of 1933. The organization of provincial councils, each with its own executive, was complete. In addition, the establishment of a national council had also been accomplished. J.S. Woodworth headed the National Executive.

It is interesting to note the backgrounds of the leading figures in this new party that threatened the security of the Canadian nation. M.J. Coldwell and C.M. Fines were teachers; Iven Cook and King Gordon were clergymen; Elmer Roper, F. Pritchard and A.E. Partridge were journalists. With a former Methodist minister as leader, this does not appear to have been an exceedingly dangerous revolutionary group.

The major achievement of the first convention was the Regina Manifesto. The Provisional National Council had asked the research committee of the League for Social Reconstruction to produce a document that would form the basis of such a statement. This was to be considered by the Regina meeting. Underhill of the League produced a first draft which was reviewed by the research committee. The revised version was forwarded to the National Council. This document provided the foundation for the Regina Manifesto.

Gerald Grant and David Reisman, in a book entitled *The Perpetual Dream,* talk about two types of reform, telic and popular.[5] A telic reform of a social system seeks to alter its overriding objective and the mode of operation for its achievement, thereby introducing a very basic change. A popular reform proposes a change within the system, but does not seek to transform its essential purpose.

The Regina Manifesto announced by the CCF proposed a major telic reform in these words:

"The CCF is a federation of organizations whose purpose is the establishment in Canada of a cooperative commonwealth in which the principle regulating production, distribution and exchange will be the supplying of human needs and not the making of profits. We aim to replace the present capitalist system, with its inherent injustice and inhumanity, by a social order from which the dominating of one class by another will be eliminated, and in which economic planning will supersede unregulated private enterprise and competition, and in which genuine democratic self-government, based on economic equality, will be possible."

This statement unquestionably posed a telic reform. To eliminate the profit motive from business and industry would undoubtedly strike at the very basis of a free-enterprise system. The methods by which this was to be achieved, however, were far from revolutionary. The CCF maintained that the way to institute this reform was through education.

During its lifetime, the CCF produced a stream of publications informing Canadians about the virtues of socialism and the evils of capitalism. Considering the nature of its leadership, one is not surprised at the emphasis placed on education. Its leaders believed firmly in the rationality of mankind.

Much of the manifesto was devoted to explicating how this was to be achieved. It proposed, for instance, the establishment of a national planning commission consisting of a small body of economists, engineers, and statisticians assisted by a technical staff.

The document insisted on the socialization, which, in effect, meant government ownership of all banking, currency, and credit institutions. Furthermore, socialization should extend also, to the transportation, communication, and electrical power industries, as well as any services essential for social planning.

The CCF also proposed a series of popular reforms, those that could be initiated without altering the present economic system. In fact, by pressing for these reforms, the CCF made its greatest contribution to Canadian society during the brief 28 years of its existence. It stressed the importance of security in tenure to its farmer members, in effect, freedom from mortgage foreclosures. It advocated insurance against crop failures, the removal of tariff burdens on the operation of agriculture, improving the efficiency of export trade in farm products and the like.

The CCF was also sensitive to the needs of labor. The leaders of the movement demonstrated a keen understanding of the problems workers encountered in Canadian industry during the early part of this century. They proposed, in the Regina Manifesto, a national labor code guaranteeing Canadian workers maximum income and leisure, insurance against the menace of illness, accidents, old age, and unemployment.

They also proposed that workers enjoy freedom of association and effective participation in the management of their industries and organizations.

The manifesto focused on the maintenance of health. The document argued for publicly organized and supported hospital and medical care that would be as freely available as the currently well-established educational services. Attention would be paid not only to the cure, but also to the prevention of illness. All citizens, irrespective of income, would enjoy the benefit of these services.

The manifesto directed attention to amending the Canadian constitution, which at that time was the *British North America Act*. Framers of the document were convinced that the national government should have greater powers to deal with Canada's economic development. The need for increased central authority grew from Canada's growing industrialization with its centralization of economic and financial power. Further amendments protecting the rights of racial and religious minorities were also recommended.

Leaders of the CCF, through its manifesto, took a strong stand on senate reform. They concluded that the Canadian senate should be abolished. So many appointments had been made to that body of those who represent capitalistic interests that it had become one of the most reactionary assemblies in the civilized world.

The manifesto dealt with Canada's external affairs. Leaders of the CCF favored international cooperation, such as that achieved through the League of Nations. Since, however, most nations within the League were governed by capitalistic regimes, that organization reflected their views. Rescuing the League from the control of these powers would be extremely difficult.

Furthermore, Canada needed to establish her autonomy as an independent nation within the British Commonwealth. It had to avoid building a British economic empire to replace the former political one. To do so might lead to further world wars. Canada had to refuse to become involved in any more wars with the objective of making the world safe for capitalism.

The manifesto did not avoid the problem of taxation and public finance. Those who created the CCF saw the need for a new taxation policy, one that would address the glaring inequalities of income. They were also convinced that they had to eliminate systems of public finance that seemingly created nothing but public debt.

CCF members saw the current methods of securing revenue through custom duties, and sales taxes as placing the burden on the masses. They proposed a drastic extension of income, corporation, and inheritance taxes, graduated according to the ability to pay. This would be the major means of raising funds during the transition period to a socialist state.

The manifesto proposed the elimination as soon as possible of the parasitic interest-receiving class. One might anticipate that the election of a CCF government in Canada would result in an immediate flight of capital.

The CCF, through its manifesto, went on record for freedom of speech and of assembly for all, irrespective of nationality or religion. The document pointed out that there had been an alarming growth of fascist tendencies among all governing authorities. This had been exemplified in the behavior of police in preventing certain public meetings. It was evident in the deportation of immigrants who were attracted to Canada through propagandistic advertising. They now found themselves victims of an executive department, without any appeals to the courts. One cannot fail to admire the dedication of CCF members to the principles of democracy.

The manifesto emphasized the need for an emergency program, arising from current problems. It stated that the federal government should deal directly with the critical unemployment situation since the resulting widespread suffering could not be relieved adequately by either municipal or provincial authorities. The Dominion government was the only agency with the financial resources sufficient to ameliorate the most horrendous social disaster of this century.

What the CCF proposed in the pages of its official document was a far-reaching program of public expenditure on housing, slum clearance, hospitals, libraries, schools, community halls, parks, recreational projects, reforestation, rural electrification, and the elimination of grade crossings. This was to be financed by the issue of credit based on national wealth. Such a program would have met not only the problem of unemployment, but also that of social need. The last statement in the manifesto announced that no CCF government would rest content until it had eradicated capitalism and put into operation the full program of socialized planning which would lead to the establishment, in Canada, of the Cooperative Commonwealth.

4

The CCF's manifesto in its focus on popular reforms particularly, provides an historical mirror, reflecting a view of the 30s, perhaps the most unusual decade of the 20th century. Given an opportunity, the CCF's proposals might well have dealt with the social and economic problems of that disastrous decade. That opportunity, however, did not arise.

Before the movement had disappeared in 1961 to become the New Democratic Party, one province, at least, had turned to the CCF seeking a solution for its problems following the Second World War. This was the province of Saskatchewan, Alberta's historical twin. One cannot conclude the story of the CCF without examining its impact on the life of that province.

The man who led the CCF to an election victory in 1944 was T.C. (Tommy) Douglas. Douglas had been a CCF member in the federal parliament before resigning to win the premiership of Alberta's neighboring province. The CCF victory was overwhelming, 47 out of 52 constituencies.

Douglas had been a Baptist minister before entering politics. A rather small man, Douglas made up for his diminutive stature with his sharp intellect and his ineffable sense of humor.

At the outset of his career as Saskatchewan's premier, Douglas maintained that government should own only those industries within which monopolies might gain control. As long as competition prevailed, ownership might well remain in private hands. He pointed to certain industries or businesses, such as banking, railways, and packing plants, as those susceptible to monopolistic control leading to the exploitation of people.

During the years 1944 to 1961, the Douglas government placed changing emphases on public, private, and cooperative development in Saskatchewan. Douglas, in fact, leaned heavily on two agencies outside government for support and guidance. One of these, the Education Planning and Advisory Board (EPAB), was chaired by an economist. The role of the board was to guide the government in those decisions affecting the economic growth of the province. The second of these

T.C. Douglas at the Jubilee Auditorium, Calgary, 1968.
Photo courtesy of the Provincial Archives of Alberta,
Edmonton Journal Collection, T-221.

agencies, the Legislative Advisory Committee, assisted the government in the formulation of legislation. These agencies compensated for cabinet ministers lacking in social and economic knowledge.

One is somewhat amazed by the pragmatic policies formulated by this presumably socialistic government. The government insisted that it welcomed private enterprise in the development of Saskatchewan's resources. The major requirement was that of avoiding monopolistic ownership.

Saskatchewan recognized three types of ownership — public, private, and cooperative. Each had its place in formulating an economic strategy for the province. When Douglas retired as premier in 1961, these three types were still recognized. The role for private enterprise had been greatly increased during his premiership.

The Douglas government not only encouraged, but facilitated, the growth of cooperative enterprise. Actually, social democrats throughout the western world advocated the adoption of cooperative ownership. This type of entrepreneurship provided for greater control over the economy by local producers and consumers. The ownership of a cooperative firm ultimately resided in the hands of those using the service. Quite obviously the "co-ops," their familiar title, existed for use rather than profit.

A variety of these organizations was established during the Douglas regime. The largest marketing cooperative common throughout each of the prairie provinces was the provincial wheat pool. Another illustration emerging during the "co-op" era was the livestock cooperative, obviously another producer's organization.

Consumers' cooperatives, both wholesale and retail, provided consumers with a variety of products at lower prices. The objective was to eliminate the middle man, a symbolic figure for which the farmer had little regard.

The Saskatchewan Cooperative Credit Society played the role of a credit union. The need for money to finance these enterprises emerging in this strictly agricultural province became a basic necessity. This society pooled investment to be distributed among the province's major cooperatives. The society sometimes turned to government for both direct and indirect assistance. It developed a multi-faceted financial system to accumulate resources for a membership seeking financial aid for future developments.

The government did not depart completely from its socialistic faith. It passed the *Crown Corporations Act,* creating a government finance office. This agency was to act as a holding company, financial controller, and coordinator of Crown corporations.

To further the exploitation of Saskatchewan's natural wealth, the Douglas government invested in exploration, research and the mapping of mineral resources. It left prospecting to private enterprise. Furthermore, it was forced to encourage private investment if any resource development was to occur. To illustrate, several private firms competed in the production of potash. Without an infiltration of private enterprise into this socialistic bastion, no resource development of consequence would have taken place. Similarly, in the discovery and production of oil, private investment was essential. A share in provincial mining profits was achieved for the people of Saskatchewan through the imposition of royalties.

The government controlled the natural gas industry by owning the distribution system. In the field of transportation, communication, and power, the Douglas government fulfilled its mandate for social ownership.

One cannot do justice to Saskatchewan's CCF government without reference to its social aid programs. Relief, that ignominious term for social assistance during the '30s, came under the administration of municipal governments throughout Canada. It was financed jointly by these local bodies and the provinces' departments of municipal affairs.

Needy persons, during that decade of despair, turned to local governments for social assistance and for medical aid. One of the requirements before that aid was forthcoming stipulated that the applicant must have lived in the municipality, whether city, town, village or rural, for at least one year.

The Douglas government's first reform, instituted in 1945, provided free medical, hospital, dental, and nursing services for pensioners and for the recipients of mothers' allowances and their dependents. A further reform reflected not so much a substantive change as one of attitude. Relief inspectors were renamed social welfare officers.

The Social Assistance Act of 1959 expressed in legal terms the values governing the views and actions of the CCF government following some 15 years experience in provincial administration. The act set out two basic principles in the provision of public assistance:

1. Municipalities must accept full responsibility for administering social aid.
2. Persons in genuine need should receive adequate support.

In presenting the act to the legislature, the minister for social welfare expressed the government's views on social assistance. These views were delineated in the following points:

1. Every person has the right to social aid where the need can be demonstrated irrespective of race, creed, residence, or citizenship.
2. No individual should have to meet a test of moral worthiness in order to secure social aid.
3. Every individual receiving social aid should have the right to plan his life as he chooses. He should have the right to decide how he uses social aid except if he fails to provide the necessities of life for himself and his dependents — where he shall live and what services he wishes to accept. He should also receive the aid in cash.
4. His privacy must be respected.
5. He should have the right to appeal decisions on aid.
6. He should have the right and the obligation to take such responsibility as he can in seeking a solution to his financial problem.

5

In Canada, many third parties have emerged, thrived for a period of time and then disappeared. As we have seen, the CCF, born in 1932, held its first convention in 1933. In 1961, it met its demise, ending a short career of 28 years. It is true that its successor, the New Democratic Party, carries on with traditions inherited from its political progenitor. The NDP however has established itself as a highly important minor political party on the federal scene. It has, in fact, threatened to supplant the Liberal party as one of Canada's two major parties.

The CCF failed to achieve such a status. One might conclude that it remained, more as a movement than a political party until its disappearance in 1961. This, however, would not be entirely correct.

The CCF was undoubtedly a protest movement. As we saw earlier, movements demand support on the grounds of moral justification. On the other hand, a political party garners adherents by holding out the possibility that it will form the government at the next election. While one may be attracted by a party platform, these are in reality largely designed to achieve electoral success. Despite electioneering rhetoric, the purpose of most platforms is to command a majority at the next election, not to achieve the moral regeneration of a society.

If the CCF is to be judged by the success it achieved for its proposed telic reform, then it failed abysmally. It did not end the reign of capitalism. CCF supporters were convinced that this was a worthy purpose. It was the moral justification for the effort they expended. The party attracted dedicated amateurs, those who had discovered the truth and were intent on enlightening others. While the CCF gained many adherents, it fell far short of reshaping Canadian society into a socialist mold.

The movement nonetheless left its mark on Canadian society, including that of Alberta. That it did so resulted not only from the ideas it presented, but also from the quality of its leadership. Men such as Woodworth, Coldwell, Douglas, and David Lewis were eloquent in their presentations, reflecting a deep conviction of their concern for the needs of people.

In his efforts to counter the growing appeal of the CCF, Mackenzie King, prime minister of Canada from 1926-1930 and 1935-1948, was forced to pay heed to pressures for change. Conceivably, King may have used the threat of a CCF government as a means of achieving his own ends. In any event, King, by introducing such reforms as old age pensions and unemployment insurance, moved Canada along the route to a welfare state.

In the chapters ahead, we examine the emergence of another movement, one also originating during the decade of the '30s. That movement was generated by the same set of social and economic conditions that gave rise to the CCF. Interestingly, both movements have their roots in Alberta. Both were stimulated by events and people outside its boundaries. The Social Credit movement, however, played an infinitely more significant role in shaping Alberta's future than did the CCF.

Notes

[1] W.D. Young, *The Anatomy of a Party* (Toronto: University of Toronto Press, 1969), Chapter One.

[2] Charles Dickens, *The Tale of Two Cities*.

[3] Young, "Quotation on the League for Social Reconstruction." The quotation cited provided the major objective of the "League for Social Reconstruction." As Young points out, membership in this national organization was made up of representatives drawn from Canada's universities of that period.

[4] Dr. W.H. Alexander, a classics professor at the University of Alberta was an active member of the "League for Social Reconstruction." The author of this book still remembers his brilliant lectures on "Classics in English" during the 1930-31 university term.

[5] Gerald Grant and David Reisman, *The Perpetual Dream* (Chicago: The University of Chicago Press, 1978).

Chapter Five
William Aberhart
Teacher and Preacher

1

The decade of the '30s, the worst and the best of times, spawned more than one movement. The disastrous economic conditions of that eventful decade spawned two of these social manifestations that had as their objective the amelioration of human suffering deriving from the Depression. While both movements gave birth to governments designed to achieve their major purpose, they were otherwise quite dissimilar.

The Social Credit movement created a government quite unlike that generated by the UFA. With a mandate to introduce Social Credit, this government was the first of its kind in Canada, or for that matter anywhere else. A political party in British Columbia later borrowed the title but failed to adopt its philosophy. Albertans may well boast of having had the only genuine Social Credit government in history.

This is directly attributable to William Aberhart. Had he chosen to remain in the province of his birth, the Social Credit movement would not have gained sufficient momentum to capture the attention and win the support of most Albertans. George Bevington had introduced Social Credit theories to the UFA convention in 1923. Neither he nor any of his like-minded colleagues, however, were capable of turning its complex proposals for financial reform into a movement powerful enough to destroy the UFA as a political force and reduce the two old-line parties beyond the point of recovery for several decades. Only an Aberhart could have performed such a feat.

Although William Aberhart and Henry Wise Wood had little in common, they were both prophets of Alberta's political revolution. Wood provided the rationale for the UFA's entry into politics. His message emphasized the necessity for group government, the group being that of the farming class. He insisted that a class must define its special needs before cooperating with other classes toward the achievement of a just society.

Aberhart, almost unwittingly, entered the revolutionary movement at a time when many UFA members were losing confidence in their own government. His message had nothing to do with group government, though he had slight regard for either of the old-line parties. He brought Albertans a reason to hope when many had despaired of the future.

Like Wood, Aberhart was a religious man; both were students of the Bible. Aberhart had adopted the fundamentalist's position — that everything appearing in the Bible was literally true. For him, the Bible was the ultimate source of truth. Wood, on the other hand, was more selective in his choice of scriptures, preferring to use as his model those of St. John who, in his epistles, had stressed the importance of social reconstruction.

Although Aberhart proudly signed the baccalaureate title (B.A.) following his name, there is little to suggest that he had become seriously involved in reading the great writers of either his own or earlier centuries. Despite his more limited formal education, Wood had studied these writers. From his analysis of their works, he evolved a philosophy that inspired Alberta's political revolution.

Aberhart adapted his political message from the publications of C.H. Douglas, or from other authors' interpretations of those publications. Aberhart accepted Douglas' theories more as articles of faith than as concepts for critical analysis. Having done so, he became an ardent missionary in spreading the gospel they enunciated. Perhaps all great missionaries have been limited in their critical capabilities.

Aberhart shared one quality with both Brownlee and Wood. He was equally as cautious as they when it came to the expenditures of funds, either his own or the public's. His behavior as premier manifested a quite unexpected caution. The ardent reformer, intent on revolutionary change, became a balanced and careful, even hesitant statesman. This transformation shocked many of his followers, leading to consequences influencing the story of Aberhart's premiership.

Premier Aberhart, 1935.
Photo courtesy of Provincial Archives of Alberta, A-437.

2

William Aberhart was born on December 30, 1878, near Egmondville, a village near Seaforth, Ontario. He came from a large family, six boys and two girls, William being the fourth to join their ranks. The Aberharts were Presbyterians, not particularly devout, though they followed the practices of their church with reasonable attention to custom.

Aberhart attended a collegiate institute in Seaforth during his high school years. His post-secondary education included a year at Chatham Business College, from which he received a commercial specialist certificate. Following this year, he entered Hamilton Normal School. Aberhart completed his arts degree extramurally with Queens University.

During his studies in these various institutions, he favored mathematics, a subject in which he had achieved the greatest success. As an extramural student, he was unlikely to have pursued any discipline in depth. In fact, little evidence exists to suggest that during the course of those studies he had read, or even recognized, such great writers as Adam Smith, Jeremy Bentham, John Stewart Mills, or Karl Marx. These were the literary giants dominating an undergraduate course in arts at the turn of the century.

Although Aberhart's serious reading appears to have been restricted to the scriptures, he had a bright and active mind. He was a quick learner, grasping information readily with a marked capacity for retention and recall. He was deeply interested in foreign languages, continuing the study of both French and Spanish throughout his adult life to the point of being able to communicate in them with a fair degree of skill. This lifelong hobby was reflected in his professional zeal as a teacher of grammar.

Strangely, this dedication to the linguistic disciplines had apparently little effect on his speech. Either through early formed habit or political design, Aberhart often expressed himself in language that was far from grammatically perfect.

As with most people, Aberhart had both his strengths and his limitations. His capacity for organization verged on the order of genius. This he manifested in all that he undertook in his teaching of arithmetic, in the performance of his role as school principal and in the structuring of his religious enterprises.

Whether dealing with facts, ideas or people, Aberhart displayed an extraordinary talent for order and arrangement to achieve his purposes. On the other hand, he appeared incapable of analysis. He could comprehend ideas, arrange them in order, and translate them into graphic design. He seemed, however, unable or unwilling to test their validity, examine their implications, or determine their relationships within broader patterns of thought. He did not analyze ideas; he accepted or rejected them according to patterns of belief that had become firmly fixed in his youth.

Aberhart's religious faith evolved through contacts outside his home. He gained his first memorable experience through a series of revival meetings which he attended in his boyhood. The preacher pounded his pulpit as he exhorted his audience to forsake the ways of a sinner by adopting those of Christ. Aberhart was strongly impressed by the effect this evangelical preacher was creating on his listeners through such an athletic exhibition. This led him, actually, to emulate the evangelist, in the privacy of a woodlot, by thumping on a stump as he harangued an invisible audience among the surrounding trees.

At the age of 28 in 1906, Aberhart underwent a second experience reinforcing his early fascination with evangelism. He became a member of a men's Bible class under the charge of Dr. William Nichol of the First Presbyterian Church in Brantford. This man, a physician by vocation, was a follower of a well-known clergyman who adhered to and sermonized on premillennial doctrines, those that presaged the return of Christ to reign over the earth for 1,000 peaceful years — a millennium. Although Nichol was not a clergyman, he was widely respected as a Bible scholar and a confirmed premillennian.

Stimulated by Nichol's interpretations of Bible prophecy, Aberhart took his first steps toward cultivating the avocation of Bible teaching by organizing a class among his staff members at the school at which he was principal. The class directed its attention toward the Book of Revelations, and Aberhart prepared and delivered several papers on the contents of this perplexing volume.

After this initial foray into Bible instruction, Aberhart conducted a class at the Zion church in Brantford. His preparatory study under Nichol, and his subsequent ventures into Bible instruction prepared him for the challenges of serving the larger community.

Other facets of Aberhart's activities in Ontario reveal something of the man who was to play a leading part in Alberta's history. During his high school and college years, he was an outstanding athlete. Tall and strong, he played individualistic games such as tennis and badminton with a vigor reflecting both his physical capabilities and his desire to win. He also excelled in football, frequently leading his team to victory in intercollegiate competition. He played in the late 1890s with the Hurons, a well-known amateur team that won a Canadian championship. When playing he was cheered on by fans with shouts of "Go Whitey go!" the nickname deriving from his exceedingly blonde hair.

Aberhart had the respect of his teammates, but never their love. They recognized his desire to play the role of star, evidenced by his constant avoidance of effective team play by refusing to pass the ball when it was advantageous to do so.

In 1910, Aberhart accepted an invitation to join the Calgary Public School staff. Like Brownlee, who arrived in Calgary during the same year, Aberhart responded to the call of the West and to the appeal of this prairie city located in sight of the Rockies. Unlike Brownlee, however, he had become well-established professionally in Brantford. He had, in fact, reached the mature age of 31, married, with a family of two young girls.

The decision to "go West" must not have been easy for the Aberharts. If they could have foreseen the events of the following 30 years, one wonders if they might have refused the call.

3

Aberhart received a royal welcome from a group of Calgary teachers on his arrival following the Easter break in 1910. This was a rare courtesy extended to few recruits joining the Calgary Public staff, particularly as the system increased in size. Aberhart's rise in the system was rapid, considering that he assumed the principalship of Alexander School at the beginning of the next school year. His major and final promotion in the Calgary system came during 1915.

In response to North Hill residents' demands for a high school, the Calgary Public Board established the Crescent Heights High School in 1913. However, the board was not prepared to build the school until enrollments justified such an expenditure. For the first two years, the small group of Crescent Heights' staff and students moved from school to school, seeking accommodation wherever it became available. With the appointment of Aberhart as principal, Crescent Heights High School ended its peripatetic career. It was given a home in the Balmoral Public School, a short distance north of its final location.

During the 13 years that Crescent Heights High shared accommodation with Balmoral Public, Aberhart must have walked by the proposed sight frequently, hoping, perhaps, that a miracle might have hastened the construction of his longed-for school building. Completed in 1929, Crescent Heights was, for a time, one of the outstanding high school buildings in the province.

Despite the trend toward the non-teaching principalship then emerging in Alberta's high schools, Aberhart continued to teach a course in commercial arithmetic. He had reduced this course to a series of basic principles or assumptions which he outlined on a number of charts. He included, as well, methods for the application of these generalized statements to the solution of problems. He required students to memorize these statements, and he assigned problems providing practise in their application. His was essentially a memorization approach to the processes of teaching and learning.

Much has been said about Aberhart's capabilities as a school principal. He was undoubtedly an excellent organizer, a desirable trait in any principal. At the beginning of the school year, a principal must design a time table that allocates students to classes according to their needs, and assigns those classes to the various members of his teaching staff. Meeting this organizational challenge with a minimum of friction in a large high school, during its first week of operation, is a Herculean task.

Aberhart probably accomplished these administrative chores more effectively than most principals of his time. Moreover, he was aware of the likes and dislikes of his staff members in their professional practise. He did his best to assign teachers to the courses they enjoyed teaching, and for which they were best prepared professionally.

He was extremely loyal to his staff members, defending them against criticism from the public, though he may have remonstrated with some of them in private. As a principal, he played the role of father figure, exercising discipline within his family, but ready to shield its members from external abuse.

4

Though few of his staff members accused Aberhart of neglecting his duties as principal, his real interest lay in the pursuit of his second career. After some trial runs with other Protestant denominations, Aberhart finally settled in the Westbourne Baptist, a sect much more sympathetic to fundamentalist views.

Using this church as a base, he began building his reputation not only as a Bible teacher, but as a preacher. Although he was unable to fulfill completely the role of minister for the Westbourne congregation, he preached regularly two sermons each Sunday, and directed week night prayer meetings. Westbourne Baptist actually became Aberhart's church, much to the chagrin of some of its members.

These dissatisfied members, however, found it difficult to argue with success. Aberhart transformed a church limited in membership to one with an expanding and active congregation. One aspect of the dynamism with which he transfused this church's activities was demonstrated in

William Aberhart on the air.
Photo courtesy of the Provincial Archives of Alberta, A-2043.

1919 through the birth of the Calgary Prophetic Bible Conference. This organization was an outgrowth of Aberhart's Sunday afternoon classes on Biblical prophecy.

These conference meetings proved so popular that their locale was ultimately transferred to the Palace Theatre with seating capacity for 2,200 people. By the mid-'20s, Aberhart had a following in Calgary of several thousand.

Aberhart's organization of Bible institute classes in Westbourne Baptist was an innovation generated by conference activity. The institute was designed to train students in the practise of Bible study, offering a program not unlike that of a theological seminary. Aberhart became dean of the institute, eventually drawing his staff from those who had previously taken courses from him. Within a year or two, the institute was attracting students not only from Alberta, but also from Saskatchewan and British Columbia.

The next step in Aberhart's climb to fame occurred in 1925. He, himself, did not conceptualize this step, though it was the most important of his career. An official within the Bible conference approached the founder of CFCN Radio with the suggestion that Aberhart should go on air.

On a Sunday afternoon in November 1925, Aberhart presented his first "on air" sermon from the stage of Calgary's Palace Theatre. The experiment was instantly successful. Almost immediately, people responded enthusiastically with letters of commendation and support. Within a very short time, Aberhart had moved from novice to master of this new communication medium.

He became adept at expressing a variety of emotions such as anger, contempt, sorrow, biting humor, and particularly, evangelical inspiration. His radio audience grew rapidly, extending beyond the boundaries of Alberta into neighboring Canadian provinces and American states.

Aberhart's leadership in Westbourne Baptist generated activities that exerted pressures on the church's accommodation. This led members of the Bible conference to consider the construction of not only a new church, but also a Bible institute. The proposed building would contain an auditorium to serve both as church and lecture hall, a school assembly room, with accommodation for some 300 students, and a students' residence.

The curriculum designed for the proposed Bible institute was an intriguing feature of the plan. The subjects suggested were Bible knowledge, personal evangelism, homiletics (the art of preaching), public speaking, and Bible teaching. The curriculum would prepare not only Bible instructors and evangelists, but also premillennian preachers.

Within two years the Bible conference had completed its new institute. No longer dependent on a theatre, Aberhart now had a base of operation over which he had full control. Furthermore, the link with CFCN gave him entry into the homes of most Albertans. He now occupied a singular position for making an impact on the province should he elect to do so.

Aberhart's two careers, pursued during his first 25 years in Calgary, each contributed to his ultimate destiny. His career as a school principal provided him with security. It may not have been his major passion in life, but the income from it permitted him to feed that passion free from financial worries. He could preach the gospel with little or no concern about facing a penniless retirement.

His career as an evangelist afforded him an outlet for his boundless energy and a source of satisfaction for his equally boundless ego. William Aberhart had created the Prophetic Bible Institute, an organization that would influence life in Alberta during the '30s more than any other single institution. This marks the significance of Aberhart's second career.

Chapter Six
The Advent of Social Credit

1

The story of Aberhart's first encounter with the doctrines of Social Credit is familiar to many Albertans. An Edmonton high school teacher, Charles Scarborough met Major C.H. Douglas, the founder of Social Credit, on a trip to England in 1925. During the course of the lengthy sea voyage, Douglas introduced Scarborough to his economic theories, apparently convincing him of their validity.

As the Depression deepened during the early '30s, memories of those long discussions with this British military man and professional engineer were constantly in Scarborough's mind. Having had the good fortune to encounter Major Douglas, Scarborough became convinced that he ought to take some overt action toward making his economic theories available to western Canadians.

Scarborough was a modest man. He knew that he had neither the capacity nor the vigor to promulgate Douglas' theories widely throughout the province. He realized it would take someone with the talents of a propagandist, or even a missionary, to arouse the public's interest in Social Credit. Not surprisingly, his thoughts turned to William Aberhart, a fellow teacher, whom he had met casually over several summers, one whose avocation as a preacher he had found intriguing.

This was the era of external examinations. The provincial Department of Education imposed year-end examination papers, in the high schools of the province, on students finishing grades 11 and 12. These were then shipped to Edmonton for marking. The department appointed teachers from those various high schools to evaluate the papers under the supervision of one of its officials.

Teachers enjoyed this experience, finding it not only professionally, but also financially rewarding. They worked hard during the day, relaxing in the evenings by attending shows, playing tennis or golf, or visiting friends. A number of them stayed in St. Stephen's College, the

Major C.H. Douglas, founder of the Social Credit movement.
Photo courtesy of the Provincial Archives of Alberta, PA 1688/1.

Presyterian presence on the University of Alberta's campus, a building located not far from the Provincial Normal School, where the papers were being stored and marked. Many friendships had been formed through the close associations created by this three-week marking session.

Scarborough had spent several sessions with Aberhart during these marking enterprises. He had begun to relate the story of his encounter with Douglas and Social Credit theory soon after his return from England. Aberhart listened to these recitations, but at first was quite unresponsive to Scarborough's arguments. He agreed that something was amiss in the economic system, but he was not convinced that Douglas' economics provided a solution.

As the Depression deepened, however, Aberhart became more concerned. He was deeply shocked by the suicide of one of his students, an act that had been attributed to the financial difficulties his family had been undergoing.

By the summer of 1932, the Depression had intensified its ruthless hold on western Canada. Scarborough felt even more strongly that he must convince Aberhart to adopt the Douglas cause. Employing another approach, he suggested that Aberhart read Maurice Colborne's *Employment or War* in which the author had dealt with Douglas' theories in readable prose. Scarborough discussed the book's substance with Aberhart at some length one eventful summer evening in St. Stephen's College. He left the book with him on condition that Aberhart study it further. Aberhart did so, completing the task as the early morning sun lit up his room.

As Aberhart walked to his marking assignment next morning, he was convinced that Douglas' Social Credit theory was the answer to Alberta's economic problems. True to form, he made little attempt to analyze the ideas Colborne had explored. He accepted them because they fit within his perception of the world. During that night he had undergone a form of religious experience. The doctrines of Social Credit had now become part of his faith.

2

Having experienced a conversion, Aberhart the missionary was eager to convert others to his new-found economic religion. His first step was to secure permission from the Prophetic Bible Institute's Board of Management to introduce Social Credit doctrines into his broadcasts.

The board saw no reason to deny such a request since these doctrines appeared to fall within the scope of biblical prophecy. The board did not envisage, nor did Aberhart, that this approval would lead to the formation of a political party.

Aberhart was at first cautious in altering the character of his Sunday afternoon broadcasts. From the beginning, he viewed Social Credit doctrines as the fulfillment of Christian prophecy. As one might expect from a teacher, he raised questions, the responses to which directed attention to Social Credit principles.

The central theme in his talks underscored the significance of the shortage of purchasing power as the reason for a depressed economy. This statement constituted the core of the Social Credit faith, the doctrine that provided a rationale for both its economic theory and its proposed reforms. The statement is not as simplistic as it first appears.

Social Crediters argued that this shortage is endemic within our economic system. They illustrated this by using the **A+B** theorem. **A** represents the flow of money into the economy in the form of the wages, salaries, dividends, and profits paid out as the direct costs of such factors in production as buildings, labor, and transportation.

B, on the other hand, symbolizes payments for the indirect costs of depreciation, bank charges, raw materials, and knowledge. Though these latter components create legitimate charges against the production process, adding to its costs, frequently insufficient flows of money or credit enter the system in recognition of their economic contribution.

The total costs of production had to include all direct and indirect costs, i.e., **A+B**. Since the flow of money and/or credit into the system is insufficient to cover all the components represented by **B**, there exists a chronic shortage of purchasing power in the economic system. This condition makes it financially impossible for people in an industrial society to purchase all the products that society produces.

Those who control credit (e.g., banks and other financial institutions) keep it in short supply for their own special purposes. It becomes imperative for a society to make up this deficiency through direct payments to their citizens.

Aberhart's biblical sermons, with their admixture of economic theory, began to attract attention throughout Calgary. Those who were on relief became regular listeners to broadcasts from the Prophetic Bible Institute.

Responding to this widespread interest, Aberhart offered a series of evening lectures on Social Credit at the institute. These were delivered to the first Social Credit study group, comprising 30 students, to make its appearance in the province. That group was a harbinger of a movement yet to emerge.

With this initial venture into organized study groups, Aberhart had raised his mission to a new level of activity. He prepared charts and leaflets, covering such topics as "The Present Method of Business," "The Social Credit Concept," and "Purchasing Power in the Hands of the Consumer."

This led finally, to the publication of the so-called Yellow Pamphlet in 1933, entitled "The Douglas System of Economics." Although unsigned, quite obviously Aberhart had written it. This document formed the basis of a dispute between Douglas and Aberhart as the movement progressed.

Through this first study group, Aberhart had produced a number of graduates that had not only accepted Social Credit economic theory, but were also prepared to indoctrinate others into the faith. The pressure for study groups mounted not only in Calgary, but within other cities and towns of southern Alberta.

Responding to an appeal from Aberhart, these graduates commenced organizing groups in Calgary, meeting wherever space was available in the city's schools, halls, and homes. By 1934, Social Credit had become the major topic of conversation among Calgarians. Almost simultaneously, study group activity spread throughout southern Alberta.

The institute became the focus of this study group movement. Aberhart announced meetings of various study groups over the air each Sunday afternoon. Ernest Manning, Aberhart's star pupil and first graduate of the institute's Bible school, in his capacity as secretary of the institute, made arrangements for these meetings. Sometimes a former pupil of Crescent Heights High School living in one of the surrounding towns organized a study group, hoping to get Aberhart as speaker. The many demands on his time in Calgary, however, made this difficult. Nonetheless, Albertans beyond Calgary's boundaries were anxious to meet the prophet in person.

Not every study group in Calgary regarded Aberhart as the infallible interpreter of Douglas' theories. Charles G. Palmer, a Calgary businessman who had suffered financial reverses during the Depression, was instrumental in organizing the New Age Club. This club attracted several of the city's brightest intellects who met periodically to explore Social Credit theories. Spurning association with the Prophetic Bible Institute, the club affiliated directly with the Social Credit Secretariat in London. It pursued objectives similar to those of Aberhart, but with a much more limited audience.

Aberhart's study groups, though of special appeal to those on relief, included a broad range of Alberta's population. Many of the UFA locals forsook their traditional activities for studies of credit deficiencies. Small town dwellers, long since barred from participation in farmers' affairs, now became involved, along with their rural neighbors, in the pursuit of knowledge about Social Credit. Generally, members of the professional classes, particularly those with university backgrounds, remained aloof. Even among these Albertans, however, there were many exceptions.

3

By 1935, Aberhart had transformed the province into a vast classroom containing hundreds of study groups. In retrospect, this appears an incredible achievement, almost beyond belief. How could this man in such a short space of time have captured the attention of, and forced his will upon, so many people?

During the period between 1932 — the year of Aberhart's discovery of Social Credit — and 1935, the Depression had deepened, casting a pall over the province that enveloped many families in feelings of uncertainty verging on despair. More and more families had been forced to apply for relief, a form of government support that carried with it a distinctive social stigma. The majority of Albertans were becoming increasingly distraught, not only with anxiety over their loss of income, but with the apparent contradiction between so much poverty in the midst of such obvious abundance.

They were in search of meaning, some explanation of how this could have occurred. Furthermore, the solution Aberhart proposed — that of paying each adult Albertan a social dividend of $25 each month — would have gone far toward meeting the needs of large numbers of people.

Although the number of study group members rapidly exceeded those who were Aberhart's followers in Biblical prophecy, these originals were still a significant number. Furthermore, many of those attracted by his Social Credit teachings felt comfortable with economic solutions expressed in biblical language. Through his prophetic allusions, Aberhart cloaked Social Credit principles with an aura of respectability that enhanced their authenticity. By combining the skills of a teacher with those of a preacher, he transformed reasoned argument into doctrinal statements of faith. As a true millennarian, he painted a picture of righteousness with which the control of credit would be wrested from the few — those 50 big shots in eastern Canada — for the advantage of the many, a truly Christian and democratic achievement.

These study groups were not entirely spontaneous. Someone must have taken the initiative in their organization. Despite radio broadcasts and printed study materials, the groups required additional nurturing. They needed the occasional inspirational visit from an outside speaker, perhaps a minor leader in the movement. Many such people emerged from the original study group in the Prophetic Bible Institute; some came from other sources. Aberhart's messianic personality attracted capable people who were prepared to act as his disciples in the crusade for Social Credit. The following two leaders in the organizing and nurturing of groups stand out — one an ardent Aberhart follower, the other, one who looked to Douglas' publications as the source of his knowledge about Social Credit.

Born, educated and trained as a teacher in Nova Scotia, Edith Cox came West in 1912 to teach in the one-room schools of the prairies. Discouraged by the living conditions she encountered in rural Saskatchewan, she took a business course as an avenue to a banking career. This was an unusual decision for a female to take at that time, since banking was then viewed as a man's vocation. Nonetheless, Edith Cox persisted, eventually locating in a branch bank at Killam, Alberta. Here she met and married the principal of the local high school, Mr. W.H. Rogers. The Rogers moved to Calgary in 1929, where they both became intimately acquainted with Aberhart. They were somewhat skeptical of his premillennian prophesies, but they responded enthusiastically to his advocacy of Social Credit.

Mrs. Rogers was a member of the first study group at the institute, thereby becoming a charter member of the Social Credit movement. She was instrumental in organizing study group procedures in Calgary by moving their locale out of the institute into the homes, schools, and halls of the city. Her enthusiasm and enterprise were such that she was appointed women's organizer. In fulfilling this role, she focused her attention on working-class women through a series of mass meetings in Calgary's Labor Temple.

Perhaps her greatest contribution lay in her determination to carry the Social Credit movement beyond Calgary's boundaries. She, more than any of the early leaders in the movement, was intimately acquainted with rural and small town Alberta. In 1934, she proposed touring the province to hold meetings and organize study groups wherever possible in order to disseminate the Social Credit message.

Aberhart was at first opposed to this proposal, pointing to the costs involved in such tours. When she persisted, he gave in grudgingly indicating that she would have to finance these trips through local

Mrs. Edith Rogers.
Photo courtesy of Edmonton Public Schools Archives and Museum.

donations generated at the meetings. He maintained "living off the land" as a general policy applying to all who responded to invitations from outside Calgary.

Mrs. Rogers, accompanied by her husband and Henry Unwin, another advocate of Social Credit, initiated the tours on a trip to Granum, Alberta, in a rickety Model T ford. Throughout the summer of 1934, this troupe toured the towns and villages of southern Alberta, holding mass meetings in halls, churches, and school houses, and leaving behind a trail of study groups. The troupe encountered some opposition, often from UFA members of the provincial legislature. Generally, however, these meetings were evidence of solid support for these Social Credit missionaries. By the winter of 1935, they had moved into northern Alberta covering up to, but not including, the Peace River block.

Finally, these missionaries tackled Edmonton, the last bastion to capitulate to the persuasive eloquence of Edith Rogers. Her crowning achievement of the tour was the organization of a mass meeting in an Edmonton rink during Easter week, one at which Aberhart addressed a crowd of 9,000 people.

Throughout her travels, Edith Rogers' support for Aberhart was single-minded and unalloyed. She saw him as the real leader of the movement, proclaiming her antagonism fiercely toward any manoeuvre to displace him. During the brief period from February to May of 1935, a time within which Aberhart had resigned from the chairmanship of the Social Credit League through differences with the followers of Douglas, Edith Rogers called publicly for his return. She criticized vehemently the so-called Douglasites for their attempted takeover of the movement. She not only cajoled Aberhart into fresh offensives toward forwarding the Social Credit cause, she supported him loyally when he responded. Her dedication was surpassed only by one other leader, Ernest Manning.

Not all who pioneered the Social Credit movement, throughout the three-year period leading to the August election of 1935, were equally as loyal. Earl Ansley, a teacher in central Alberta, and a student of Douglas' theories, had never been closely associated with such Calgary dissidents as Charles McGregor who headed the Social Credit League during Aberhart's absence. Ansley, nonetheless, had exhibited signs of independence early in his speaking career as a Social Credit advocate. He had gleaned his knowledge of Social Credit by reading Douglas' books. As a teacher, he felt confident that he was equally as capable as Aberhart of interpreting Social Credit theories. Ansley had commenced organizing constituency associations during the summer of 1934, at a time when Aberhart was still protesting that his study group activity was for educational purposes only.

Although Ansley eventually won Aberhart's approval as a candidate for the Leduc Constituency, he travelled widely throughout several constituencies prior to the election. His address to the organizational meeting of the Camrose constituency was memorable, marking him as a rising star among Social Credit leaders. Unlike Mrs Rogers, however, he had not been a member of the famous class of 30. His loyalty to Aberhart was opportunistic. He recognized his public appeal, but he had little respect for Aberhart's knowledge of the theories he was expounding.

4

Despite the number of supporters Aberhart had acquired, he was not without his dissidents. As we have seen, both the New Age and Open Mind clubs, Calgary groups equally intent on studying Douglas' theories, took strong exception to his interpretations of Social Credit contained in the Yellow Pamphlet. When the members of these two Calgary clubs criticized his renditions of Social Credit theory, Aberhart replied indignantly that these had met with Douglas' blessing.

The members of these clubs then referred the document to the Social Credit secretariat in London. The outcome of this referral was a letter from Douglas to Aberhart demanding his name be removed from the pamphlet. Furthermore, Douglas insisted that he would not recognize Aberhart's movement as a genuine Social Credit endeavor.

Aberhart's response to this request was to resign from the presidency of the Social Credit League. While announcing his resignation over the air, Aberhart attacked Tony Kerslake and Lance Collins, both of whom had been responsible for referring the pamphlet to the London secretariat. Adopting the role of martyr, Aberhart confided to his radio audience that this would be his final address on the principles of Social Credit.

The next event in the series, leading to Aberhart's triumphant return to the movement's leadership, occurred in Edmonton. This took the shape of an enquiry into Social Credit conducted by the agricultural committee of Alberta's eighth legislature during its spring session of 1934.

The purpose of the enquiry was twofold: to elicit a system of Social Credit from the witnesses appearing before it, and to hear evidence on the possibility of operating the Douglas plan of Social Credit in Alberta. Those who had been invited to appear before the hearing were such luminaries as Major Douglas of London, Professor G.A. Elliot of the University of Alberta, Aberhart, and representatives from Calgary's New Age Club, Herbert Boyd and Lance Collins.

Aberhart presented the views he had expressed in the Yellow Pamphlet, maintaining that a system of Social Credit could be introduced by distributing a social dividend in the form of credit notes to all adult Canadian citizens living in Alberta.

Boyd and Collins argued that Social Credit could not be adopted by the province because of constitutional limitations. They advocated approaching the federal government to lay the foundation for a dominion-wide Social Credit movement.

Douglas was somewhat equivocal in his presentation. He agreed that Social Credit could work in Alberta, but admitted the province did not have the power to institute a national dividend. Professor Elliot, expressing the views of an orthodox economist, insisted that prices are set by the interaction of the supply of goods and services with the demand for them. In the long run, the price received by producers must cover the costs of production or they will cease producing either goods or services.

Despite these hearings, the UFA government had no intention of adopting Social Credit as a policy. The enquiry was a way of demonstrating that such a decision would not be within the constitutional powers exercised by the province. From the government's point of view, the enquiry conducted by its agricultural committee had been successful. It had brought out clearly the differences that existed within the Social Credit movement by demonstrating the rift that had developed between Douglas and Aberhart.

No doubt government members had congratulated each other for having nipped the seemingly fragile Social Credit plant in the bud. However, they were obviously unaware of the enquiry's unanticipated consequences. It had brought Aberhart, one of its major stars, into the provincial limelight, giving him a degree of publicity which he could not have matched from his Calgary base. The enquiry had actually set the stage for Mrs. Rogers successful tour throughout rural and small town Alberta. Social Credit had been transformed from a Calgary phenomenon into a province-wide movement.

Douglas' trip to Alberta had not improved relationships with his Canadian disciple. Two incidents reveal this, the first occurring on his arrival, the second following his appearance at the enquiry. Aberhart had gone to the train to greet Douglas and welcome him to Alberta. On his descent from the train, Douglas brushed Aberhart aside, going directly to Collins who was also there waiting for the appearance of the Social Credit founder.

The second incident took place in Calgary. The Open Mind Club invited Douglas to attend a public meeting in Calgary. Since Aberhart had at that time resigned as president of the Social Credit League, organizers of the meeting felt free to ignore him. When his followers in the CPR yards heard of this, they threatened not only to boycott the meeting, but also to prevent its occurrence. Bearing this threat in mind, the organizers of the meeting invited Aberhart to sit with other eminent Calgarians on the platform. Aberhart, fearing a disturbance, agreed to accept the belated invitation.

A Calgary alderman, who was also president of the local Canadian Club, presided over the meeting held in the Sarcee Army Barracks. The mayor of Calgary welcomed Douglas to the city. After a brief introduction, the chairman invited Douglas to address the vast audience congregated to hear him. Douglas responded by delivering a two-hour lecture that was highly abstract and exceedingly dull. Members of the audience listened patiently with few interruptions. When the chairman rose to thank Douglas, it became apparent that he intended not only to refrain from inviting Aberhart to speak, but also to ignore his presence completely.

At this obvious insult to Aberhart the audience erupted. With shouts of "We want Aberhart," a group rushed forward to engulf the platform. The crowd broke into an uproar. The chairman, with remarkable presence of mind, called for "God Save the King." During its noisy rendition, the platform guests quickly retreated.

Aberhart, quite unexpectedly, met Douglas later in the Officers' Mess. This encounter did neither of them credit. Aberhart accused Douglas of sabotaging his Yellow Pamphlet. Douglas responded with a demeaning remark. Within a few seconds their meeting turned into a vituperative shouting match, with each employing a vocabulary so coarse that it shocked all those present.

By the end of April, Charles McGregor had demonstrated his lack of appeal to members of the Social Credit League. Discouraged by his inability to play a leadership role, he announced his resignation. Aberhart refused to resume the presidency, however, until League members begged him to return. When this finally occurred, he stated the terms on which he would once more assume leadership of the movement. He demanded that all members of the New Age Club holding positions on the executive of the Social Credit League resign.

Having achieved the removal of his critics, Aberhart resumed the presidency of the league in May of 1934, four months after his resignation. He was now completely in charge of the Social Credit movement, the supreme interpreter of its theories. The defeated Douglasites ultimately formed the Douglas Social Credit League, turning their attention mainly to federal rather than provincial politics.

Despite the criticism of purists in Douglas' Social Credit theory, Aberhart appears to have grasped its quintessence. As with any good teacher, he simplified its basic principles, making them comprehensible to the general public, something Douglas either would or could not do.

Moreover, Aberhart was inclined to interpret economic theory in moralistic terms. The just price, for instance, was one consistent with the value of justice, which is not always true of the market price.

The orthodox economist maintains that the price of any good or service in a free market is set by the interaction of its supply with the demand it generates. That price is neither just nor unjust; it is, rather, the inevitable consequence of an economic system in action. One hastens to add that this only happens "in the long run."

Aberhart and Douglas differed in whom they identified as controlling the issuing of credit for their own selfish purposes. Douglas identified this group as Europe's international bankers, most of whom he claimed to be Jews. A strong element of anti-Semitism appears in Douglas' works. Aberhart, on the other hand, levelled his ire at the "Fifty Big Shots" in eastern Canada. While he derided these faceless individuals for their role in controlling credit, he did not single out the members of any particular religious denomination for special condemnation.

5

Aberhart held firmly, even tenaciously, to the perception of Social Credit as an educational, not a political movement. He declared frequently that he wanted some political party, ostensibly the one in power, to adopt and institute the monetary reforms proposed by Douglas. He saw his role as being that of educating the public about, and convincing the majority of its members for the need to introduce Social Credit into the province. He did not, and in this he appears to have been sincere, wish to undertake the task of bringing about the necessary changes himself.

This perception of the Social Credit movement was consistent with that of Douglas. Douglas was an engineer and amateur economist, not a political revolutionary. The Douglas approach was reflected in the responses to his theories followed by other Commonwealth countries. Many New Zealanders and Australians showed an interest in Douglas Social Credit during the '30s and '40s.

Douglas made more than one visit to these two countries in response to invitations from one or more of their political parties. New Zealand's Labor party, for instance, adopted Social Credit along with other types of reform in their election platforms during the '30s. A Social Credit party in that Commonwealth country ran candidates in 1955, winning

11 percent of the vote, but failing to win any seats. Since that time, the Social Credit party has succeeded in increasing its share of votes, but has never had more than one representative in New Zealand parliament.

Three major political parties vied for public support in Alberta during the period leading to the election of 1935. The UFA with 30 MLAs, formed the government as it had done since 1921. The Liberal party, having 11 members in the legislature, served as the opposition. George Howson, its leader, was an aggressive politician intent on restoring his party to a governing role, one which it had not occupied for several years. D.M. Duggan, head of an Edmonton investment agency, was content to lead his party of six members, recognizing that the Conservatives at that time had little chance of gaining much in rural Alberta. Of the remaining seven members, four were designated as Labor representatives, who usually voted with the government, and three chose to sit as independents.

Howson played a devious political game throughout the life of the province's seventh legislature. He sensed the weakening of support for the UFA government in the province and was anxious to do everything he could to instigate a coup at the coming election. It was alleged that he had been influential in persuading the MacMillans to undertake the lawsuit ending Brownlee's political career. He flirted with Social Credit as a means of embarrassing the government. Neither he, nor any of his followers, were likely to adopt any form of Social Credit as part of their party platform.

As a political realist, D.M. Duggan, leader of the small Conservative party in the provincial legislature, had little zest for planning to overthrow the UFA government. As a member of the Baptist church, Duggan might have been prepared to accept Aberhart, the Baptist preacher. As head of an Edmonton investment agency, however, he was unlikely to look with favor on Aberhart, the monetary reformer. He would have found it exceedingly difficult to approve a policy that proposed issuing monthly credit certificates, valued at $25, to every adult citizen of Alberta.

As for the UFA— the organization whose political party had governed Alberta since 1921 — it was comprised of at least four factions. The government itself, that is Premier E.G. Reid and the members of his cabinet, considered Social Credit proposals, either those of Douglas or Aberhart, to be complete nonsense. The government was reticent in branding it as such. It preferred, rather, to say it was unconstitutional.

A second faction, many members of which had been instrumental in establishing the Cooperative Commonwealth Federation — a party with mildly socialist objectives — was sympathetic toward monetary reform. This faction was disposed to invite Douglas back to Alberta.

A third faction of convinced socialists strongly supported the fledgling CCF party. This faction wanted nothing to do with Social Credit. Its members saw it as an attempt to avoid undertaking essential social reform, that of transferring industrial ownership in Canada from private to public hands.

The final and predominating faction numerically encompassed the thousands of UFA members on the verge of joining Social Credit ranks.

The press is a powerful voice either in opposition to, or in support of, an emerging political movement. Reporters are unimpressed by eloquence, quick to spot inconsistencies in argument, and eager to pierce the protective armor of public figures. Their most potent weapon, however, if they wish either to destroy a budding politician or prevent his rise to power, is one they find most difficult to employ — the weapon of silence.

Aberhart's appearance at the government enquiry transformed him into a public figure. Whatever members of the provincial press thought of Aberhart's message, they could no longer ignore it, nor could they relegate it to the back pages of their publications. Aberhart's pronouncements had become front page material.

The province's leading newspapers were intensely critical of Aberhart's proposals. The *Calga*ry Herald and the *Edmonton* Journal, both castigated him roundly in their editorials. They dismissed Aberhart as one who did not understand the implications of what he was proposing. The *Edmo*nton Bulletin, now extinct, was virulent in its denunciation of Social Credit, either of the Douglas or Aberhart variety. Only the *Calgary* Albertan, yet to become the *Calgary Sun*, gave him, if not enthusiastic, at least mild support. This paper was, in fact, echoing the views of a Calgary majority.

Stung by the *Calgary Herald*'s criticism, Aberhart decided to start his own paper. On July 20, 1934, the Social Credit League issued the first copy of the *Soci*al Credit Chronicle. The paper carried articles by outstanding writers in England and America who were supporters of Social Credit. These included Sir Oswald Mosely, leader of the English green-shirt movement, a pseudo-fascist organization, and Father Coughlin, a fiery right-wing priest and radio evangelist in the United States. The *Chronicle*, an avid supporter of Social Credit, found its way into many of the province's homes. It was not the sole factor leading to Aberhart's election victory, but it was undoubtedly one of them.

6

Aberhart and Manning had travelled about the province during the summers of 1933 and 1934. They were both aware of the ground swell of support rising among Alberta's farmers, whether UFA members or not. This may have been one reason why Aberhart delayed his decision on direct political involvement.

Conceivably the rank and file of UFA members, by passing a resolution at a convention, might have forced their leaders to accept Social Credit. One suspects, however, that Aberhart's hesitation was consistent with his general approach to decision making. He preferred yielding to the pressures of public opinion, rather than moving ahead of them.

Despite Ansley's constituency activities, and the crusade of the Rogers' troupe, Aberhart still clung to the position that Social Credit was an educational movement. The events of 1934, nonetheless, had been pushing him further along the road to political action. The final event leading to his full acceptance of political involvement occurred in February of 1935. This took place at the annual convention of the UFA in Calgary.

A resolution had been forwarded to the executive from several locals, all expressing the same intent. This resolution, among the most important of any to reach the floor of the convention, was couched in the following words:

"Therefore be it resolved that a system of Social Credit as outlined by William Aberhart be put as a plank in the UFA provincial platform to be brought before the electorate at the next provincial election."

Brownlee, up until his resignation as premier in July of 1934, had vigorously opposed pressures from the rank and file of members to adopt this stance. His resignation and the events leading to it had weakened his voice in the association. Nevertheless, another voice had emerged which was equally as adamant as that of Brownlee's in its opposition to such a resolution.

Norman Priestly, vice-president of the UFA, was an exceedingly brilliant public speaker. Educated as an Anglican clergyman, he had devoted many years to the cooperative movement. For some seven months, he argued against an irrational approach to economics, politics, and religion. He gave the UFA heroic leadership to the end of its period as the most powerful organization in the province, displaying brilliant qualities in a struggle within which emotion eventually triumphed over reason.

By invitation, Aberhart spoke to the delegates during the convention. His address was largely polemical, though much more restrained than those he delivered over the radio. He dwelt on his favorite topic, the flow of credit through the economic system. He argued that it could best be understood by using the analogy of the flow of blood through the human body. The heart pumps many quarts of blood through the body each day, yet the actual amount of blood contained within the circulatory system is within the neighborhood of four quarts.

Presumably, the moral of this story is that a small amount of credit issued by government to its citizens would have a major effect on the economy, provided it was immediately put into circulation.

The motion asking the convention to adopt Social Credit as part of the UFA platform was defeated by a substantial majority. This defeat might have been construed as a victory for the UFA executive which, at the time, it appeared to be. Actually, while the defeat was decisive, many delegates had abstained from voting.

The end result was a wholesale departure of members from the association. The UFA's roster in 1935 listed a membership of 9,838, down from a high in 1921 of 37,883, a loss of 27,883 members during a period when that organization appeared to be completely in control of the provincial government.

The convention's rejection of Social Credit may have finally convinced Aberhart that he could not avoid political involvement. That evening, he and his intimate friends gathered at Calgary's Mandarin Cafe — a customary meeting place — to discuss the implications of the convention's decision. The talk turned inevitably to the election that must be held sometime in 1935. Although Aberhart refrained from revealing his views, the consensus of the discussion — that political action was now inevitable — must have troubled him. So much remained to be done in an unfamiliar field of activity. He had not anticipated anything like this when he commenced weaving Social Credit theory into his Sunday afternoon sermons three years previously.

Reid's government was not unaware of the erosion that was occurring in UFA membership. Certainly his announcement on February 22 of the government's decision to bring Douglas to Alberta a second time reflected a mood of despair rather than one of positive action. It obviously appeared to contravene the convention's refusal to accept Social Credit as a plank in the UFA's election platform. If the government was convinced that the introduction of Social Credit was "ultra vires" of provincial authority, why have anything further to do with either Douglas or Aberhart?

R.G. Reid, Alberta premier, 1934-1935.
Photo courtesy of the Provincial Archives of Alberta, A-439.

The government, nonetheless, appointed Douglas as its principal adviser. He was awarded a two-year contract, within which he was to prepare a plan of action, and for which he would be paid the sum of $5,000. This decision, however, did nothing to settle the unrest within the rank and file of UFA membership. On the contrary, the uproar over the following question increased. Was the government actually sincere, or was this merely a ruse to regain political support?

The government displayed yet another symptom of futility when it invited Aberhart, as well, to come to Edmonton. It offered him an office, a staff of accountants, stenographers, and clerks if he would develop a plan for the introduction of Social Credit. The politically sensitive Calgary School Board immediately provided him with a leave of absence for the period he would be away saving the government.

As usual, Aberhart temporized waiting for his followers to advise him. Several local constituency groups recommended he not accept the government's invitation. As they said, he had already fulfilled his duty when he appeared before the agricultural committee in 1934. Aberhart finally declined, replying that he must follow the guidance of his people.

As evidence that it still clung hopefully to rationalism as a way of countering Aberhart's arguments, the government requested two reports, one from Dean Weir, head of the University of Alberta law faculty, and the other from Professor G. Elliot, chairman of the university's economics department. Both men reiterated in more scholarly fashion the views they had expressed at the enquiry before the agricultural committee. Dean Weir predicted that any attempt to distribute credit certificates of any form would be *ultra vires* of the *British North* America Act. Professor Elliot argued that the impact of distributing either money or credit would be inflationary, causing prices to rise, which would defeat the purposes of the initial distribution. Furthermore, any such experiment involving free handouts of credit certificates would undoubtedly redound on the province's credit rating.

Douglas' second coming, unlike the first, caught the attention of many Canadians outside of Alberta. As he proceeded across Canada by way of the CPR, he was interviewed by reporters in search of a front page news story. They sought to discover his attitude toward Brownlee who, though no longer the head of Alberta's government, was still good copy for any Canadian newspaper. In Winnipeg, he made two comments on Social Credit in Alberta. He saw difficulty with the payment of $25 per month to Alberta residents, and he was completely opposed to the formation of a Social Credit political party.

Although Douglas once more repudiated the contents of the Yellow Pamphlet, he refused to meet the expectations of at least some members of Alberta's government. He would not denigrate Aberhart. He, in fact, wrote to Aberhart, advising him to pay no attention to statements which he had not signed, nor those taken out of context, this, despite their previous bitter encounter at the Officer's Mess in the Sarcee barracks. Douglas saw his assignment in Alberta as being that of formulating a preliminary plan for the introduction of Social Credit.

That plan, when complete, was contained in a document entitled "First Interim Report on the Possibility of the Application of Social Credit Principles to the Province of Alberta." In this report, Douglas distinguished between the use of public credit, and strategies for acquiring the power to deal with the public credit issue. He recognized that the Canadian government had granted authority for printing money to the Bank of Canada at the time of its establishment. However, up until 1945, Canadian banks retained the power, in diminishing degrees, to issue certain bank notes as they had been doing prior to the establishment of the Bank of Canada.

Douglas outlined the preliminary steps the province might take to achieve the power of issuing a medium of exchange. The objective was to establish a circulating system of money or credit under the control of the province, almost as if it were a sovereign state.

Having secured this authority, the province would then organize credit institutions, presumably similar to banks, which were to extend credit to individuals or companies. The effect of this credit or monetary expansion would be to increase the demand for goods and services. At the same time, the province would accumulate foreign exchange. A supply of money that was acceptable outside the province would be essential for carrying on trade.

As the next step, Douglas insisted that government should reduce taxes dramatically. This would have the effect of shifting the financial burden from the people to the provincial government. That body would then generate its own support through the issuance of credit. To prevent any inflation that might occur, Douglas recommended the introduction of price controls. Since the objective of the proposed system was to monetize the natural wealth of the province, the government would have to immediately undertake a vigorous development of its internal resources.

Douglas' final recommendation was perhaps the most difficult to achieve. He insisted that in order to accomplish these reforms, a coalition government would have to be established in the province. Douglas was not enamored of party politics, the essence of which is legislation emerging through the interplay of a government in debate with an official opposition. He viewed parliamentary debate to be not only a waste of time, but also counterproductive. He saw the government's role as being that of expressing the demands of people, and then appointing experts to fulfill those demands. A coalition government would not spend time debating issues. It would, rather, expedite the process of meeting public need.

Douglas' appointment was to little avail. UFA membership had continued to decline, until it was only a fourth of what it had been at the commencement of the '20s. Social Crediters, no longer a small group confined within the boundaries of Calgary, spoke out with the fury of religious zealots. They castigated both the press and the government for trying to compromise the one man who could save Alberta.

7

The election of 1935 generated the most bitter campaign in the history of Canadian politics. This was, in part, due to the polemical nature of Aberhart's radio addresses. It might also be explained by his transformation of a political battle into a type of religious warfare. It could be attributed, as well, to the despair of a people who, longing for a savior and having found him, became hostile toward anyone or anything that might prevent his accession to power.

The province's political and social elite must also share part of the blame. The UFA had lost touch with its supporters and, lacking imaginative leadership in dealing with the worst Depression of this century, continued to proclaim the importance of balancing the budget. The rift between the haves and the have nots widened, as the unemployed were harried from one end of the nation to the other by the RCMP acting as gendarmes of the established order.

As we saw earlier, Aberhart had become a master of radio communication. The microphone for him became an instrument of power, one that gave him control over a vast, though remote audience. Most great actors, which Aberhart undoubtedly was, crave the responses of a live audience, those subliminal messages that pass between them and others enthralled by their art. Aberhart apparently succeeded in sending and receiving these messages by air.

Aberhart evolved and delivered a radio program throughout several months prior to the election called "The Man from Mars." This creature, speaking English with a strange accent presumably suggestive of an extraterrestrial traveller, asked a number of ostensibly naive but exceedingly pointed questions. Aberhart's difficulties in explaining the inconsistencies in the Canadian economic system to this interested but puzzled visitor not only entertained his listeners, but also highlighted points in his version of Social Credit. It was both an amusing and persuasive series of dialogues that few Albertans of that period missed hearing.

Aberhart was extremely sensitive to criticism, responding with ridicule to his critics, often using vituperative language. He labelled those critics as crooks, scheming politicians, insincere office seekers, and the like. He branded one person, whom he did not name, as being guilty not only of fornication, but also of grafting and hypocrisy. He described the arguments of his opponents as the ravings of henchmen serving high finance. He compared these men to those who had betrayed

Christ. He adjured his listeners to show their contempt for his most devastating critic, Norman Priestly, by turning off the radio during his broadcasts.

The organization of local associations, based on representatives of study groups drawn from the four zones or subdivisions of each constituency, was completed by April 5, 1935. The first Social Credit convention was held on that date in Calgary. Aberhart, in his address to the convention, insisted that he must have a voice in the selection of candidates. As he said to the meeting:

"If you are not prepared to let me have any say in the choice of my supporters, then you will not have me for a leader."

This threat resulted in a resolution giving Aberhart the power to select his legislative supporters from a list of three or four possible candidates. These were to be nominated by each of the local constituency associations.

Several similar meetings followed throughout the province, all of which confirmed the Calgary decision. In his addresses to those meetings, Aberhart defended his method of selecting candidates. He stressed the theme, one familiar to rural voters, that democracy had been ruined by party politics. It had become an arena for wire-pulling crookedness. Because of his selection methods, his opponents accused him of being a dictator. He responded with this statement, one that rang out at every meeting:

"The spirit of Christ has gripped me. I am only seeking to clothe, feed and shelter starving people. If that is what you call a dictator, then I am one."

Following the conventions, the Social Credit movement performed the final rituals of candidate selection. To facilitate these rituals, the province had been organized into seven divisional conferences located in these areas: the Peace River Block, areas on each side of the North Saskatchewan River, central Alberta, Calgary rural, southern Alberta, and Calgary and Edmonton as one conference. Aberhart and Manning visited each conference to meet with the executives of the constituency associations it encompassed. They interviewed all nominees on each constituency association list and, with the advice of its executive, they arrived at a final selection — 51 candidates in single member constituencies, and two six-member constituencies, Edmonton and Calgary, adding 12 to the list.

The Social Credit League opened its election campaign with a picnic rally on July 6 in the Edmonton Exhibition grounds. Over 5,000 people attended. In his address, Aberhart compared the coming election to a horse race, with the dark horse, Social Credit, being the one to watch. He likened Alberta's position to that of a deep sea diver struggling with a money octopus.The diver still had one hand free to strike the menacing octopus by voting for that dark horse in the coming August election.

At the close of the picnic, 1,000 people, accompanied by flags and a band, travelled with Aberhart to Calgary. The train ought to have been called "The Election Special." Whether so named, it must have created an impact on the intervening towns as it carried this boisterous crowd through the province's heartland.

On Sunday afternoon, the election crowd attended Aberhart's broadcast from the Prophetic Bible Institute. They were given special seating arrangements and entertained by Calgary's Welsh choir. Before the program commenced, Aberhart welcomed them warmly. The program opened with announcements to the hundreds of study groups throughout the province, followed by the singing of the hymn "Oh God Our Help in Ages Past."

Aberhart then recognized financial contributions to the movement. After this he turned to the letters, damning and otherwise, he had received during the week, commenting on their contents. Finished with these epistles, he sarcastically belittled the hostile press, ending with a diatribe against the latest broadcast by Norman Priestly. Throughout all these comments, he pilloried his opponents with scorn, contempt, and savage humor. He played on his audience's emotions, both his visible and invisible listeners, with all the skills of a performing artist.

During July, the Social Credit League published the Blue Manual, a 64-page booklet entitled "Social Credit as Applied to the Province of Alberta," with a subheading "Sixty Puzzling Questions and Answers." It was designed to relate the basic principles of Social Credit to the Alberta scene and to answer the criticisms of Aberhart's opponents. It provided a basis for the speeches of Social Credit candidates throughout the province.

The contents of the Blue Manual argued that the introduction of Social Credit would accomplish seven objectives. It would banish fear and worry from the Alberta populace. It would maintain individual enterprise and, at the same time, improve the standard of living. It would solve the problem of high interest rates. It would provide better opportunities for youth and protect honest producers from low prices. A Social Credit government would achieve all this by replacing the present medium of exchange with issues of non-negotiable certificates.

Some businessmen feared the impact of Social Credit on the province's economy. The Drumheller and Medicine Hat boards of trade organized the Economic Safety League, with the Hon. William Egbert, a former lieutenant governor of Alberta, as president. They solicited membership among those who disagreed with Aberhart's proposals. Those members pledged themselves to oppose Aberhart's election for the good of the province. The Economic Safety League hired Henry Angus, head of the Department of Economics at the University of British Columbia, to write and speak against Social Credit doctrines.

The Economic Safety League entered actively into the campaign during the month previous to the election slated for August 22, 1935. The press gave wide and elaborate publicity to the materials published by the League, and the speeches delivered by Professor Angus. Manning questioned the propriety of a former lieutenant governor becoming involved in an election campaign. Others, such as Mrs. Gostick of Calgary, called the League "The Elevated Society of Lunatics."

The most bitter criticism of the League came from the Social Credit candidates, with Aberhart undoubtedly the source. The candidates alleged that financial support for the Economic Safety League, was being generated among business interests on the St. James and Bay streets of Montreal and Toronto. Whether these rumors were true or not, they were nonetheless devastating, making the efforts of the League counterproductive. Whoever those vague eastern interests might have been, they had become objects of scorn to many Albertans long before Social Credit had appeared on the western political scene.

An irrational even ugly mood settled over the province. Incidents occurred displaying behavior that would have been unthinkable during previous elections. Gerry McGeer, a well-known Liberal from British Columbia, flew into Drumheller to assist his party in that constituency. He had difficulty in landing and once on firm ground he was prevented from speaking. He returned home convinced that at least some Albertans had taken leave of their senses. Brownlee attempted to address an audience in the Ponoka constituency, one that he had represented since his entry into politics. A group of men pounded on the outer walls of the school house with clubs, creating such a noise that Brownlee was forced to end the meeting. Although such incidents were not numerous, they did occur.

The victory for Social Credit could only be described as phenomenal. The Social Crediters elected 56 members, the Liberals, five, and the Conservatives, two. Not a single UFA member was elected, bringing to an end the reign of the farmers government in Alberta. This political reversal came at a time when the rural vote in the province still dominated elections. The western revolution had taken a different turn.

Aberhart and his cabinet being sworn in, September 3, 1935.
Photo courtesy of the Provincial Archives of Alberta, KS-828.

Chapter Seven
Aberhart's Premiership

1

During the week following the August election, Aberhart had taken the oath of office as premier of Alberta and had submitted the names of his cabinet ministers to Lieutenant Governor Walsh. These preliminaries over, Aberhart was ready to explore the duties of his new office.

To lead a political party to victory is undoubtedly a rewarding experience. Aberhart's first political campaign had been demanding, requiring a continuous round of speeches delivered over the radio and in public meetings. Now he had to assume a completely different role, that of governing a province.

To move from radio evangelist and school principal to provincial premier in a single step had been a challenge that few undergo. Aberhart had met that challenge and was understandably elated over the outcome. His first reaction was to share his feelings with his Social Credit mentor. He immediately sent a cable to Douglas which read, "Victorious, when can you come?"

This mood was short-lived. Within a brief space of time, perhaps only a few hours, Aberhart learned of the province's financial problems. The provincial treasury was not only bare, the province was actually destitute. The government was unable to pay its own servants. Aberhart's first task was to attend to operational needs. The financial revolution promised his followers had to wait until the pressing chores of governing the province received attention.

Aberhart had only one source from which he could borrow funds — the federal government. Fortunately, he knew the prime minister personally, though probably not well. Whatever Richard Bedford Bennett may have thought of Social Credit, which was undoubtedly not much, Aberhart was a fellow Calgarian. Bennett and Aberhart were unlikely to have moved in the same social circles. The status of a wealthy, politically ambitious corporation lawyer and that of a relatively obscure high school

William Aberhart and R.B. Bennett, circa 1930.
Photo courtesy of the Provincial Archives of Alberta, A-1797.

principal were in no sense equal, even in a city the population of which had not yet reached 75,000. Bennett, however, was quite likely aware of Aberhart's political activities. He was, after all, a former member of the Alberta legislature.

On his first official trip to Ottawa, Aberhart returned home with a two million dollar grant to carry on the affairs of government. One wonders what the reception might have been had the wily Mackenzie King been in power. Actually, Aberhart barely missed meeting Canada's perennial prime minister. King defeated Bennett during that same year, making him a one-term historical artifact.

One action Aberhart had taken in eastern Canada seemed inconsistent with the mandate for monetary reform Albertans had granted him. He was apparently looking for an orthodox financial expert who could assist him in appraising the state of Alberta's fiscal health. He learned of the achievements of J.S. Magor, a Montrealer who had been employed by the Newfoundland government to prescribe a cure for its financial ills. Aberhart hired Magor to carry out a similar study for Alberta.

Magor resigned in June of the following year without having made any apparent contribution to Alberta's financial well-being. Magor's appointment and his subsequent resignation would have gone unnoticed in the province's history, except for one outcome. It later became one of the many factors souring relationships between Aberhart and his mentor, Major C.H. Douglas.

2

In responding to his mandate for the introduction of Social Credit, Aberhart's first preoccupation was to secure Douglas' assistance. His opening message revealed the direction he proposed taking — to persuade the founder of the Social Credit movement to oversee its introduction into the only jurisdiction yet to elect a government controlled by a Social Credit party.

Furthermore, Douglas was already under contract to the former Alberta government to provide a plan for exactly the same objective. This contract had so far not been fulfilled. One might have expected Douglas to complete the contract with even greater enthusiasm, considering the change in government.

This was not to happen. The two men entered into a series of communications by letter and cable that extended over seven months. Douglas terminated the series in a letter dated March 24, 1936, in which he unequivocally refused to have anything further to do with Alberta's premier. He said he had made great sacrifices by keeping himself at the disposal of the Alberta government. Despite Douglas' dedication to the cause he had founded, Aberhart was obviously pursuing a policy that did not require that founder's assistance.

An examination of the various messages that passed between Douglas and Aberhart provides a perception of why this breakdown in communication occurred. As noted earlier, the first source of friction was stimulated by the Magor appointment. Douglas saw this as a serious error for a political leader bent on leading a financial revolution. Magor was obviously a supporter of orthodox finance, someone who accepted the current role of the banks in manipulating credit to their own advantage. In his messages to Aberhart, Douglas returned again and again to this unwarranted departure from acceptable behavior.

Some of the suggestions Douglas offered Aberhart to meet his short-term financial needs readily reveal the difficulties he might have encountered had he chosen to follow them. He suggested, for instance, that

Aberhart should place the moral obligation of support for his policies on the shoulders of the well-to-do. Douglas advocated that for those who refused, he should publicly pillory them by announcing their names. As another approach, Aberhart might arrange an interest-free, non-callable loan of $5 million with a chartered bank.

If Aberhart was prevented from following these recommendations, Douglas offered a final solution. He must take a census of the stocks and shares held by private individuals in Alberta. Aberhart should then ask the owners to exchange these for short-term Alberta bonds bearing a yearly interest rate of one percent. This, however, ought not be out-and-out confiscation. The owners would receive any dividends declared on these stocks, but had to have no lien against them. Presumably these stocks would serve the government as collateral for the negotiation of loans.

From the outset, Douglas warned Aberhart against the perfidy of bankers. He was confident that these wily individuals would, in some way, plot his downfall. Aberhart, however, found them both pleasant and accommodating. He had no desire to antagonize these dispensers of credit during a period when the province was desperately in need of financial support.

In February 1936, Alberta was facing the redemption of a sizeable bond issue with nothing in its treasury to meet this obligation. Douglas suggested that the federal government take over the loan, renewing it at the nominal interest rate of two and one half percent. If Canada refused to do this, Aberhart would have to force any Albertans holding these maturing bonds to accept their true value in exchange for credit issued by the provincial treasury. With this credit an Albertan would be able to purchase any product for sale within the province. Aberhart was apparently not prepared to act on this recommendation.

Douglas' recurring threats to terminate unilaterally his contract with the Alberta government characterized his contribution to this ongoing interchange of messages. Aberhart, on his part, ignored these threats while constantly repeating his invitation for Douglas to visit Alberta. Occasionally, he lectured Douglas on the responsibility of the Alberta government. Although he continued to stress his desire for Douglas' presence in Alberta, he warned him he would have to convince both the government and its people that accepting his proposals would be in their own best interests.

The following cable sent to Douglas on March 13 reflects the pattern in this flow of messages:

"Your refusal to come makes cooperation difficult. We wholeheartedly accept the Social Credit principles underlying your suggestions. Government will cooperate fully when you come."

Douglas replied:

"Since your election, you have taken the view that my function to provide an SC plan is comparable to providing an improved automobile, while I have consistently made it clear that there is a monopoly of gasoline. The problem is to get sufficient gasoline before worrying about the automobile. You are at present pursuing the policy of capitulation to orthodox finance, under the label of a Social Credit government. Until actual steps taken to carry out advice I have given, further advice is useless, even presumptuous."

From Douglas' point of view, communications broke down because of Magor's appointment, and the refusal of Aberhart to accept his advice. Aberhart, in turn, insisted that the break came through Douglas' failure to provide a plan and his demand for the exercise of dictatorial power. Aberhart repeatedly stressed that as an elected official, the responsibility for government resided with him. He could not delegate it.

One can only conjecture as to what might have happened if Douglas had accepted the invitation to spend time in Alberta. The two men would probably have parted company after an argument as bitter as that which occurred in the Calgary Officers' Mess. Douglas' doctrinaire views — such as his obsession for punitive action against bankers and his essentially anti-Semitic world view — would have come directly in conflict with Aberhart's pragmatism. Aberhart's 50 faceless big shots may have been bankers, but they did not belong to any particular religious faith. If a greater degree of anti-Semitism exists in Alberta than in other Canadian provinces, and there is some reason to think that this is the case, it is a legacy of the Douglasites, and not the generality of Social Crediters.

3

The Aberhart-Douglas correspondence occupied the first seven months of the Social Credit regime. While the exchange was between the two men, both the cabinet and the Social Credit caucus were involved on occasion. Aberhart revealed the contents of every communication to the members of his cabinet. On one or two occasions, the cabinet as a whole reinforced the warmth of Aberhart's invitations to Major Douglas.

The entire Social Credit party expressed its loyalty to the principles of Social Credit in at least one message to its founder. Quite obviously, a close rapport existed within the Social Credit political family during its extended flirtation with the coy major.

The break between the two leaders, along with Douglas' criticism of Aberhart, created uneasiness within Social Credit ranks. Although most caucus members remained loyal to Aberhart, the rupture engendered some dissent. The convinced Douglasites, of whom there were several despite Aberhart's careful selection, were predisposed to agree with the major. These early criticisms of the premier were undoubtedly muted but nonetheless prevalent. The seeds of the insurgency were sown as the prophet and his disciple severed their relationship.

The first attempt to establish a form of Social Credit occurred in August 1936. The government issued a medium of exchange known as scrip. This was a certificate of sorts, supposedly equivalent in purchasing power to that of a dollar bill. Its ultimate validity was assured by requiring the current holder to affix a stamp, available in drug stores and post offices, weekly to each piece of scrip in his or her possession. This stamp represented one percent of a scrip's purchasing value.

At the end of 100 weeks, a piece of scrip was fully validated by having acquired 100 stamps from its various possessors. A piece of scrip in passing from hand to hand not only acquired 100 stamps, it also served as a *modus vivendi* for several business transactions. It was obviously advantageous for those holding several pieces of scrip to use them immediately in the purchase of goods and services.

The Alberta government eventually abandoned the experiment, leaving few records of how it affected trade. Nonetheless, the cabinet actually honored $12,000 worth of scrip it had issued. The issuance of scrip obviously contravened section 93 of the *British North* America Act since only the federal government had the authority to establish a national medium of exchange. The Canadian government, however, withheld its disallowance, permitting the venture to flounder by the weight of its own cumbersome validating process.

Though the first session of the eighth legislature had passed serenely for the new government, little had altered in Alberta's economy since the early '30s. The Bennett buggy, so named because it symbolized the prime minister, an old car chassis drawn by a team of horses, provided the decade with its characteristic image.

The government, still in a honeymoon relationship with Alberta voters, had absorbed seven of the 18 months Aberhart had requested to produce a viable Social Credit plan. The summer of 1936 passed with remnants of scrip scattered throughout the province as reminders of a yet-unrealized dream. The Douglasites in the Legislative Assembly still withheld their ire despite Douglas' repudiation of the Alberta movement.

Aberhart's behavior during the first session dismayed his followers, and puzzled Albertans generally. Although he attended every meeting of the session, patiently responding to all questions, he did not once present an address to the Legislative Assembly. Unlike Brownlee, who rose to the premiership because he was the one cabinet minister capable of defending government policy against opposition attacks, Aberhart appeared to ignore the opposition. Considering its limited size, an opposition of only seven members, one can understand how this was possible. Several sessions passed before he delivered a speech of any consequence in the legislature.

One reason advanced in explanation of his reticence was that of the Douglas view on a government's function. Douglas held that an elected government should voice the demands of its people and then appoint experts to fulfill those demands. He had little respect for the concept of government as an institution for reaching decisions through debates between two adversaries, each representing different points of view. Douglas doubtless favored a single-party state not unlike those of Germany and Italy, then in the zenith of their popularity.

The third session of the eighth legislature opened on February 25, 1937, with the Throne Speech being delivered by the chief justice of the Alberta Supreme Court. The mood of the legislature had changed from that of its opening session. Other than some vague references to a new economic order, there was little in the Speech from the Throne to suggest the introduction of Social Credit legislation. Though few anticipated what might happen, a small group of Social Credit members gathered for whispered consultations in the corridors of the Legislative Assembly following the chief justice's delivery. The end of the probation period had almost arrived.

Aberhart may have been aware of the extreme discontent among his followers but if so, he had done little to forestall the coming rebellion.

On February 29, Aberhart consulted with his radio audience. He announced over the air that he could not keep his promise. He would be unable to introduce a Social Credit bill by the end of the session. He suggested that various constituency associations meet throughout the province and consider as to whether or not he should resign. Conceivably, he was asking for a public vote of confidence with which he might quell any insurrection within his caucus.

The broadcast served as a signal to the malcontents in the legislature. Three leaders among the Social Credit backbenchers — Ansley, the former constituency organizer in central Alberta, S.H. Unwin, the third member of the Rogers' troupe, and A.L. Blue — commenced their campaign for support among caucus members. Two members of cabinet — C.C. Cockroft, provincial treasurer, and C.C. Ross, minister of lands and mines — resigned. With the announcement of these two resignations, the public for the first time became aware that all was not well within the Social Credit party.

The insurgents, as they were so recognized during this political rebellion, made their first move on Friday, March 12. It occurred following the presentation of the budget by Solon Low, newly appointed provincial treasurer. Ansley rose to criticize the budget, saying it contained not one single item that even remotely resembled Social Credit.

This highly critical address precipitated the insurgency. The internal conflict festering within party ranks spilled out on the floor of the Legislative Assembly. Albertans were astonished at the display of bitterness that erupted during the debate. Many people were dismayed, others jubilant, and all were fascinated by this battle between those whose sympathies had gone to Douglas during the recent Trans Atlantic duel, and those who remained loyal to Aberhart. Members of the press gallery were obviously delighted by the opportunity to report on an insurgency that threatened to unseat the government.

The insurgents insisted that the acceptance of the budget depended on the introduction of Social Credit legislation. A.L. Blue, one of the trio of backbench leaders, threatened to bring down the government by defeating its interim supply bill. The insurgents had already demonstrated their strength by a motion to adjourn debate before the customary hours of closing. The government was defeated by a majority of 27 to 25. Since it was a procedural motion, Aberhart had chosen to ignore it as a vote of nonconfidence. A defeat on a supply bill, however, could not be ignored for that reason.

The insurgents met nightly in the Corona Hotel throughout the rebellion that unfolded in the Legislative Assembly during the day. They actually plotted the defeat of the government in these nocturnal meetings, going so far as to select a premier and the members of his cabinet to replace those currently exercising power.

On March 29, the insurgents once more demonstrated their strength, and the vulnerability of the government. Aberhart moved a motion of closure to the budget debate that had gone on for several days. The government met its second defeat. The insurgents then announced their intention of defeating the interim supply bill, a defeat that would force the government to resign.

These events were occurring prior to and during the Easter holidays. The Alberta Teachers Alliance, the forerunner to the Alberta Teachers Association, was holding its annual convention in a large downtown church building. As minister of education, Aberhart appeared at the convention to wish his provincial teaching staff well. As he stood in the pulpit, he picked up a copy of the agenda to make the following comment.

"I see by the agenda you are interested in security of tenure."

He paused, then grinning widely he said, "I too am interested in security of tenure." The convention broke into laughter and applause.

Aberhart apparently decided to attempt a reconciliation in a caucus meeting that included the dissidents. He appealed to the insurgents to meet him half way. After some debate, the caucus unanimously agreed to support him if, during the next day, he introduced a Social Credit Measures Act. Following the fulfillment of this promise, Aberhart brought forward the Interim Supply Bill, providing the government with enough money to carry it through the next three months. The Social Credit Measures Act was debated for a week and then withdrawn. It apparently was unacceptable in its present form.

4

On April 12, Solon Low introduced a second attempt entitled the *Alberta Social Credit Act*. It contained provisions, some of which have become permanent structures within the scope of the provincial government. It provided a *modu vivendi*s for introducing and testing the validity of a series of Social Credit measures. At least one of the structures was a marked departure from the traditional practises in cabinet responsibility.

The overall pattern in structures might be described as a "troika." The responsibility for introducing Social Credit measures was divided among three different bodies. The first of the three was the Executive Council, popularly known as the cabinet. The Executive Council ordinarily takes the lead in introducing legislation to the legislature.

The second structure, called the Social Credit Board, was an innovation in parliamentary government. This board, made up of five ordinary members of the Legislative Assembly, had the power to appoint a third body — a commission of experts responsible to it. The commission would be expected to make recommendations to the board on how the machinery of Social Credit should work. This would include the legislation necessary to distribute dividends, the date of their commencement, the amount of each dividend, and who should receive them.

The act provided that social credit should be created, in an amount equivalent to the unused capacity of the industries and people of the province, to produce goods and services. The commission would be expected to determine, from time to time, what that unused capacity might be. It would then calculate the equivalent amount of credit to be deposited in the provincial credit account. This would govern the flow of credit to the individual residents qualified to receive it.

A proposal that has since become a permanent feature of Alberta's business life is that of the credit houses. These were created to release credit to Albertans, and to provide subsidies to industries. The houses were known at first as credit branches, the forerunners of the present treasury branches. Although they have distributed few dividends to individual Albertans, they have since served the province much like ordinary banks.

The most interesting feature of this legislation historically was its provision of a Social Credit Board. In some respects, the powers granted the board superseded those of the Executive Council. The concept of the board derived, not from the cabinet, but from a majority of caucus members. It was, in reality, a device to reconcile the insurgents to Aberhart's retention of the premiership. Aberhart was permitted to carry on with regular government operations. With respect to matters related to Social Credit, however, the board was supreme.

Following the appointment of the board, its chairman, Glen Mac-Lachan, went to England in search of experts to act on the Commission. He succeeded in persuading two members of the Social Credit

Secretariat in London to serve on that body. They were L.D. Byrne, an Anglicized Irishman, and G.F. Powell, a Welshman, but not Scotsman Douglas who refused to come to Alberta. These technical envoys arrived in June of 1937.

To further enhance the power of the board and its commission, each Social Credit MLA was asked to sign an agreement of association. The MLAs had to agree to uphold the board and its technicians while they devised a way of distributing $25 a month to appropriate Albertans. Forty-nine of the 56 MLAs signed, six others assured Powell of their support; one, who refused, was read out of the party.

This established the board as the real government of the province. The majority of the members in the Legislative Assembly, including those in the Executive Council, had sworn subservience to the board and its commission. Responsible government in the traditional sense was placed on hold.

5

This agreement ushered in the period of enactment followed by disallowance. By the end of July, experts had drafted three measures ready to be transformed into legislation. The measures were designed to control the institution that was anathema to Douglas, the commercial banks. The first, called the *Credit of Alberta* Regulation Act, had as its objective the licensing of every bank in the province and its control by local directorates.

A second, entitled the *Bank Employees Ci*vil Rights Act, closed the courts to any employee of a bank that was not licensed under the *Credit Regulation Act*. The third measure, labelled the *Judicature* Amending Act, was designed to prevent further constitutional challenges of Alberta's legislation. It prohibited anyone from taking action against any enactment of the legislature without the consent of the lieutenant-governor-in-council.

These acts were unquestionably revolutionary. They limited the rights not only of organizations, but also of individuals. The *Judicature Amending Act* was a brazen attempt to close the courts to Canadian citizens. The Social Credit Board, guided by its experts, was obviously intent on using the legislature to give the province absolute control over its credit institutions.

To achieve this the board considered it imperative to present a solid front to its opponents. Not content with the pledge it had exacted from the MLAs in June, the board asked them to sign yet another of these binding documents. In a special session called for August 3, it demanded an undertaking to support the government and the board until they had achieved their objective. The wording of the second pledge reflected the strength of the drive the board, guided by its two oversea experts, was creating.

"I also realize the Government of which I am a member is virtually at war and that in war what (sic) may appear unimportant is often vital. I promise I will not reveal to any unauthorized person any information which is imparted to me concerning legislation until it is discussed in the Legislature."

The impact of these somewhat sinister demands was divisive. Six members refused to sign and were ejected from the caucus. The atmosphere was charged with tension and intrigue. Cabinet ministers refused to meet with reporters.

The three bills were introduced in the special session during August and were rapidly enacted. Aberhart and J.W. Hugill, the attorney general, visited Lt. Gov. J.C. Bowen requesting his assent. During the course of the visit, Hugill offered his opinion that the three acts violated the *British North America Act*. Despite this, Bowen gave his assent, perhaps because he recognized the depth of feeling behind this revolutionary legislation. Aberhart immediately asked for Hugill's resignation from cabinet for his gratuitous advice to the lieutenant governor. He then assumed the portfolio himself, presumably to guard against any future repetition of the incident.

The three acts were disallowed by the lieutenant-governor general-in-council on the grounds that the federal government controlled banking, currency and credit.

In the special session held during September, the Alberta government challenged the validity of this disallowance, declaring the acts to be still in force. At this session, the Social Credit Board brought forward three new bills for the province's legislative steam roller. These were summarily introduced and rapidly enacted. They were as follows:

The *Bank Taxation Act* was designed to increase taxes on all banks operating in the province. The *Credit of Alberta Regulation Act* was a reenactment of the disallowed August act.

The third was entitled the *Accurate News and Information Act*. The intent of this particular piece of legislation was to ensure accurate reporting without restricting the freedom of the press. The *Edmonton Journal* challenged the act, establishing it to be unconstitutional. For this action, the *Journal* received an honorable mention by the Pulitzer Prize Committee, the first and only paper outside the United States to be recognized by that distinguished committee.

Lt. Gov. Bowen, taking his cue from previous disallowances by the federal government, refused to give his assent to the September acts. Instead he referred them to Lord Tweedsmuir, Canada's governor general.

The governor-general-in-council disallowed this legislation as it had done with previous enactments. Aberhart asked Prime Minister Mackenzie King if he would refer these acts to the Supreme Court of Canada. In every case, the Supreme Court upheld the disallowances. The acts were then submitted to the British Privy Council, at that time Canada's highest court of appeal. This court rendered the same judgment.

Of the entire group of acts, the most significant was that of the *Credit of Alberta Regulation Act.* The intent of this particular piece of legislation was that the province must gain control of the right to issue currency or credit. Without this right, the central objective of the Social Credit movement could not be achieved. Its disallowance actually terminated any hope of the Aberhart government establishing Social Credit in the province of Alberta.

The Social Credit Board, nonetheless, continued to exist for another 10 years. It brought forth other legislative proposals throughout that period which were also disallowed. It remained as a symbol of the government's origins, a constant reminder of its reason for being. With each legislative failure the board suffered decreasing influence. It eventually became nothing more than a sanctuary for the confirmed Douglasites, a haven for those who clung to his murky anti-Semitic views. Its demise occurred during Manning's first term in the office of premier by his own right.

An incident occurred following the establishment of the Social Credit Board which brought it discredit. Powell, one of the experts secured from the London Secretariat, and Unwin distributed a document in the Legislative Assembly labelling nine prominent businessmen of Edmonton as "Bankers' Toadies." This was accompanied by the following description of such individuals:

"My child, God made Bankers Toadies just as he made snakes, slugs, snails, and other creepy, crawly, treacherous and poisonous things. Never therefore abuse them; just exterminate them."

Both men were charged under the criminal code through a protest by D.M. Duggan in the legislature. Both appeared in court. Powell was given six months and deported to England, thereby ending his career as an expert in Alberta. Unwin served three months in the Fort Saskatchewan jail.

L.D. Byrne, the more discrete of the two experts, became deputy minister of economic affairs, attached to the Social Credit Board. He remained in this post until the board's existence was terminated in 1948. Following his employment with the provincial government, he was appointed British consul in Edmonton, a position he held until his retirement during the early '60s.

6

On September 11, 1939, Canada declared war on Germany. Albertans, not yet fully recovered from the depression, wondered uneasily what this might mean. Few disagreed with the reasons for declaring war. Nazism was an evil that called for extermination. Parents were nonetheless concerned about their sons entering the army. Young men speculated on the effects the war might have on their careers. Young wives stifled fears of their husbands leaving them to join the Armed Forces.

Aberhart sought re-election within a few months following Canada's entry into the war. The final session of the eighth legislature occurred in February 1940, with the writ of election being announced on the 11th of that month. Aberhart actually presented the basis of his election platform through the Throne Speech opening the session. He pointed with pride to the many miles of highways his government had built in an effort to stimulate employment. He stressed that his government had succeeded in reducing the abysmal wastage of gas in the Turner Valley Oil field. This, he had done by reducing the number of flares burnt to secure the oil released by the pressure of escaping gas.

The Throne Speech recognized the war, still in its initial stages, by pledging the Alberta government's wholehearted support to its prosecution. Two regiments from Alberta had gone overseas, and 70 members of the civil service had volunteered for active service.

Aberhart expanded on the government's record in educational reform. Although many at the time may have disputed it, his achievements in school district reorganization has earned him a place in the history of Canadian education. The ideas were not necessarily his, but Aberhart's readiness to introduce essential, but unpopular reforms in rural school administration established his reputation as an outstanding educational reformer.

Aberhart had assumed responsibility for the education ministry following the 1935 election. He and the then current deputy minister, G. Fred McNally, established a good rapport immediately. Dr. McNally was also a dedicated Baptist layman, well-known for his class in biblical studies. Aberhart asked McNally what particular problems existed in Alberta's educational system that required attention. McNally pointed to the desperate conditions of rural teachers, such as salaries well below the poverty line, and their frequent domination by petty rural school boards.

McNally outlined for Aberhart a reform that Perren Baker, the former minister of education in the Brownlee government, had considered introducing. The proposal was to establish school boards with enlarged responsibilities for administering anywhere from 50 to 150 rural school districts.

With a much broader taxation base and with a style of operation not unlike that of a large urban district, not only would the salaries but also the independence of teachers be greatly improved. Brownlee, however, fearing the antagonism of rural school trustees toward any loss of power, decided against any changes in school organization.

Aberhart directed McNally to prepare the legislation, and he would pilot it through the legislature. This legislation resulted in the formation of large school divisions, under the charge of divisional boards, having responsibility for the administration of all rural school districts within divisional boundaries.

The local districts were left intact, each with a local school board as heretofore. These local boards, however, played an advisory role only, exercising little or no authority over their teachers. The Department of Education appointed a professionally trained school administrator, known as a divisional superintendent and inspector, for each school division. This provincial official acted as an adviser for these newly created divisional boards.

By the end of the eighth legislature, the organization of the province into some 50 school divisions was almost complete. This coordination among the province's rural school districts increased school services immeasurably, leading to much better supervisory, library, and building facilities.

Ultimately the reform led to the increased availability of high school services, through school centralization combined with modern transportation procedures. The children of several rural districts, were transported by school buses to a central point, often in some neighboring village or town. The larger enrollments in these centralized schools, made it possible to teach grades nine, ten, eleven and frequently, twelve. Rural education had entered the 20th century.

The 1940 election results were far from the victory Aberhart had achieved in 1935. His following in the Legislative Assembly had been reduced from 56 to 36 members, giving him the greatly reduced majority of nine. Alberta's voters had given surprisingly strong support to a group of independents. These MLAs had campaigned on the need for a strong opposition to examine critically the proposals of a government that had made several attempts to introduce radical reforms.

In retrospect, one finds difficulty in deciding whether Aberhart's loss of support was generated by the public's fear of his proposed monetary reforms, or his failure to have yet achieved any such reforms.

The Liberals had succeeded in electing only one member, and the Conservatives had been wiped out completely. Most former supporters of the old-line parties had obviously united under the politically neutral title of Independent to oppose a common enemy. The election ushered in the years of the ninth legislature.

7

The last three years of Aberhart's political career encompassed most of the ninth legislature's term. During those years, the Alberta government adopted a holding pattern in most activities. These were war years during which the nation's human and physical resources were dedicated to waging a war in Europe that would end in victory. The federal government was the one most involved in orchestrating the war effort. Provincial governments played only minor roles during this period of extreme centralism.

The overriding purpose of a nation at war is to win at all costs. No expenditure is too formidable, no sacrifice too great toward the achievement of that objective. A nation that had failed to deal imaginatively with the problems of the depression, that had been hopelessly adrift throughout a decade of economic malaise, was suddenly galvanized into action. Canada's war effort was total. It encompassed every facet of the national life, its financial, industrial and social institutions. For the period of its duration, the war became the major focus of public attention.

Despite the province's remoteness from the war's active centres, Albertans were conscious of its realities. A major training centre within provincial boundaries enhanced this awareness. The Commonwealth Training Program for airmen — pilots, navigators, gunners, and ground crew — was located in Alberta. The governments of Great Britain, Canada, Australia, and New Zealand conducted this joint training venture, commencing in 1941 and lasting throughout the war's duration.

Young men from every part of the Commonwealth spent several months on the prairies, learning to fly, navigate planes, and bomb ground targets in preparation for active service. During their time in Alberta, they were welcomed into its homes and communities, and they travelled its highways. The province was transformed from a remote, predominantly rural and backwoods colony of eastern Canada into a thriving and widely known aviation centre.

Once deeply involved in the war, most Albertans lost interest in Social Credit. The war's events took precedence over provincial affairs. They listened to different newscasts on their radios, recounting the war's story as it unfolded. The series of actions such as the battle of Britain, Hitler's European victories, the bombing of Germany, and the D day invasion — the landing of Allied troops on the continent — dominated these broadcasts.

Albertans in time came to recognize the voices of the war's political leaders, particularly those of Roosevelt and Churchill. They followed the successes and failures of the war's military commanders, they being the major players in this exciting, fascinating, and awesome succession of events.

For those who had sons or husbands in the war's different theatres — in the Italian campaign, flying with night bombers over Germany, among the invasion forces — it was a time of anxiety and dread. To them it was not a spectacle from afar. They lived with these events constantly, with little hope of release until the final surrender of Hitler's forces.

Although the federal government under MacKenzie King had scorned Social Credit as a western aberration, it, nonetheless, unwittingly followed some of its basic principles in administering the war effort. By the total organization of the nation's human resources, the government solved the problem of unemployment overnight.

The government leaned heavily on the Bank of Canada to issue the currency essential for financing the war effort. Obviously, this placed more money in circulation than was necessary to purchase a diminishing supply of consumer goods. The government sopped up this excess purchasing power by selling victory bonds, using patriotic appeals to stimulate their sale. The ostensible reason for the sale of victory bonds, however, was to pay for war production, with a promise to repay the buyer after the war when the demands for war materials would be substantially reduced.

Furthermore, the government rationed certain goods, including liquor and automobiles, both of which were in exceedingly short supply. It imposed price controls to prevent the inflation of prices on scarce commodities. The prices of farm produce, particularly those of wheat and meat, rose dramatically, with farmers responding by increasing output. The farmers' major problem became that of labor shortages.

8

One incident during Aberhart's second term in office, reflects the deep dislike some Albertans held toward their premier. This was the episode of the honorary degree. The University of Alberta — the only university in the province until 1966 — had established the custom of awarding the honorary degree of Doctor of Laws (LLD) to the premiers of the province.

The decision to award this degree rested with the University Senate, a prestigious body charged with the responsibility of making the university's academic decisions. The senate was made up of a selected group of university staff and members and of well-known Alberta citizens drawn largely from the upper-middle class.

President W.A.R. Kerr consulted with the senate's executive, on awarding this degree to Aberhart during the spring convocation of 1941. Having secured consent from the executive, Dr. Kerr approached the premier to ascertain if he would accept the honorary degree. Mr. Aberhart was delighted to be thus honored, later sharing this pleasant news with his family.

At the senate's next meeting, the executive presented Mr. Aberhart's name for the customary award, assuming that the body would approve the recommendation. A majority of the senate voted against the recommendation. Admittedly, the vote was close — a difference of one — but nonetheless decisive. After a discussion and a strong protest from the president, a second vote rendered the same result.

It now fell on Kerr to inform Aberhart of what had occurred. Aberhart accepted the information gracefully but with obvious disappointment. Kerr expressed his indignation by resigning his position as president. Later the Social Credit government altered the *University Act*, stripping the senate of all its responsibilities, and transferring these to the university's faculty association. A puzzling feature of this revision was that it left the senate with only one real responsibility — that of awarding honorary degrees!

The ninth legislature saw little movement toward the achievement of Social Credit. The Social Credit Board turned its attention toward the national scene in a publication entitled *National Reforms*, published in 1941. It focused on the role of the Bank of Canada in the conscription of wealth, by stressing the need to issue sufficient money for meeting the nation's requirements. This was to be accomplished without borrowing and without creating inflation.

The booklet recommended that the federal government establish a national finance committee as an arm of the finance ministry. This committee would exercise control over both the issue and withdrawal of all money and credit. These decisions would be reached, in terms of the national need, in the interests of true democracy.

This national finance committee would have to wrest control over the issuance of credit from the banks. In effect, the banks would become the agents of the committee. They would be required to hold currency or credit issued by the committee through the Bank of Canada against their total deposits.

The core of the Social Credit faith is expressed in the following obligation of the national finance committee: Through a proper system of accounting, it should ascertain the total price of all goods available for purchase by consumers, and the current purchasing power of the public. If the public had more than enough funds in its possession to purchase these goods, the government would then withdraw some of that purchasing power through taxation. If, on the other hand, there existed a deficiency in purchasing power, this would be corrected by reducing taxes, or by increasing the issue of credit as equitably as possible.

The Social Credit Board was finally convinced that the provision of Social Credit could operate only within the national framework.

The Throne Speech for the third session of the ninth legislature — the last to be read by the lieutenant governor during Aberhart's premiership — touched on many of the problems the province was encountering during the third year of the Second World War. The demand for manpower in the armed services had exhausted the supply of skilled farm labor. This was affecting agricultural production. The government proposed expanding such activities as agricultural education and research in the improvement of field crops as a means of increasing the productivity of Alberta's farms.

The speech dwelt on the serious shortage of teachers, particularly for rural schools. Steps were to be taken to improve teachers' salaries. The government announced its intention to enlarge some rural municipalities in much the same way as it had done with school administrative units. Its purpose was to improve the efficiency of their administration. It also indicated that it would set up a committee on post-war reconstruction.

Such were the concerns of the Aberhart government during the third session of the ninth legislature. During the fourth session in the following year, the legislature recognized the death of William Aberhart on May 23, 1943.

9

William Aberhart had made his contribution to the western political revolution. The anonymous men and women who denied him his much coveted honorary degree have long since been forgotten. No one, however, can deny him his place in Alberta's history.

In describing him, one is tempted to use the time-worn cliche, that he was larger than life. He aroused in people such conflicting emotions as loyalty and hatred, faith and skepticism, devotion and contempt, admiration and scorn. Irrespective of what he undertook, he expended limitless energy and a strong belief in the divinity of his purpose. Although he was strongly egotistical, he was also capable of deep compassion. During the worst depression of this century, he was genuinely concerned for the people who suffered its effects.

His critics scorned the Social Credit faith he had adopted. Unquestionably, the theories he voiced had no rational defense. He was, however, the only political leader during that disastrous decade to pose any sort of solution. Had he been permitted to distribute an amount of

Aberhart escorting Queen Elizabeth, wife of George VI,
during the Royal Visit, 1939.
Photo courtesy of the Provincial Archives of Alberta, A-2046.

currency to each family no greater than the typical family allowance that was to come later, the effect might have been salutary. As it was, the nation was saved by a war, one that placed it on the road to several decades of economic prosperity. One wonders which solution was preferable.

Chapter Eight
An Approach To Power

Aberhart's death on May 23, 1943, left the Social Credit party bereft of its leader. Not unexpectedly, the Social Credit caucus unanimously elected as his replacement Aberhart's young lieutenant, Ernest C. Manning. He had served as acting premier during Aberhart's occasional absences since the 1935 election.

On June 2, Ernest Manning took the oath of office as Alberta's eighth premier at the age of 34. Though Manning was the youngest yet to have achieved that office, he was equal to his peers in governmental experience. He had been a cabinet minister since 1935.

Manning's position was far from enviable. He had assumed the leadership of a bankrupt province without any credit rating, predominantly rural, and entirely dependent on a single product as a source of outside income. Its two major cities were small, with acres of empty land within their overly optimistic boundaries. The total population of the province did not exceed 700,000.

When Manning resigned 25 years later, the province had been transformed into a vital, highly urbanized jurisdiction, with twice the population and with a triple A credit rating. How that transformation occurred constitutes the story of the Manning years.

Ernest Charles Manning was born in Carnduff, Saskatchewan, on September 20, 1908. His parents, recent immigrants from England, had rented a farm in the southeast corner of Saskatchewan. Fugitives from drought, the Mannings moved to the emerging community of Rosetown, Saskatchewan, on the Goose Lake line running between Saskatoon and Calgary. Here Manning Sr. took up a homestead on which he raised his family. Ernest Manning received his early education in the rural schools of the Rosetown area.

Manning's attendance at a one-room rural school was not atypical for the period. Throughout western Canada during the early decades of this century, there were literally thousands of such schools serving pupils in school districts small enough to permit them to attend school by walking, riding horseback, or by driving a horse-drawn buggy.

Those seeking an escape from the drudgery and isolation of rural living frequently pursued the public education route. If they were successful in passing the provincial grade 8 examination, they attended high school in some neighboring town or city. Further success in departmental examinations at the end of grades 11 or 12 provided these rural fugitives with access to one or the other of the province's normal schools, or the provincial university. Many members of western Canada's professional classes, during the first half of this century, boasted of their rural backgrounds.

Manning followed a different route in his escape from the farm. One might describe his freedom as being fulfilled by the Word of God. Manning would doubtless deny that he was being held in bondage by the lifestyle on a prairie farm, even though its strictures at that time were singularly demanding. He might agree, however, on it being an exercise of Divine Providence that led to his meeting with William Aberhart.

During the early '20s, the invention of the radio had begun to alter the quality of rural living. At first the broadcast range of this 20th century miracle was decidedly limited, not exceeding eight kilometres or so. By the mid '20s, however, that range had been extended far beyond a city's boundaries. As noted earlier, a member of Aberhart's conference had persuaded him to broadcast his biblical sermons over the air. On November 23, 1925, Aberhart initiated his first broadcast over CFCN, from the stage of Calgary's Palace Theatre.

In the province of Saskatchewan, a 17-year-old youth, like many others of his age group, had become intrigued with this new invention. Ernest Manning had saved enough money to purchase a radio, one that could pick up a signal broadcast from a station within the range of a few hundred kilometres. He described, in his interview series, how he and his brother had attached the antenna to the roof of their house one cold December day. Whether he immediately tuned in on Aberhart's "Back to the Bible" hour is difficult to say. It seems apparent, however, that he soon became an ardent Aberhart fan.

In 1926, Manning decided to visit Aberhart in Calgary with a view to enquiring about his proposed Bible institute. He spent two weeks there, during which he met and visited with the Aberharts.

Aberhart did not record his first impressions of Ernest Manning. Considering his extensive experience with youth, Aberhart must have been immediately taken with this rather tall, slim young man with his hair combed straight back in the style of the period. His serious manner and obvious intelligence would undoubtedly have appealed to Aberhart, the teacher. His avowed interest in Bible study must have registered with Aberhart, the evangelist. The close rapport that developed between these two men of disparate ages, lasting until Aberhart's death, had its origins in this first meeting.

The next year, Manning returned to enrol in the three-year program of the Prophetic Bible Institute. As observed earlier, the institute's curriculum was built around Bible study, combined with the art of preaching and the skills of public speaking. Aberhart was Manning's major teacher, though he may have had others.

Those three years must have passed rapidly for this Saskatchewan farm boy. During the winter months, he was immersed in Bible studies. With the coming of spring, he returned to Rosetown where he worked as a farm laborer to finance his way through Bible college. He commented in his interview series on nights spent in a bunk house reading the scriptures by the inadequate light of a lantern.

Manning completed the three-year program in 1930, thereby becoming the first graduate. Had the institute been granted the authority to award degrees, Manning would, undoubtedly, have earned a Bachelor of Theology. Considering his effectiveness as a public speaker and his excellent use of the English language, one must conclude that Bible studies may, in certain circumstances, provide a sound basis for a general education.

Following Manning's graduation, Aberhart suggested he remain with the institute as its secretary. Aberhart stressed that he needed someone to help him with his radio broadcasts. Manning must have found this a most attractive opportunity. He had lived with the Aberharts during his final year at the institute, and this arrangement was to continue.

Manning recalled the many conversations he had with Aberhart in his second-floor study. He commented on the assistance Aberhart gave him.

Manning as Premier, 1962.
Photo courtesy of the Provincial Archives of Alberta,
Edmonton Journal Collection, J-107.

"I was a farm boy quite unacquainted with city living, and unaccustomed to dealing with people. Mr. Aberhart helped me make the transfer from rural to urban living. Furthermore he taught me how to deal with people, a skill that I had little opportunity to acquire."

Manning was not only cognizant of, but party to, the birth of the Social Credit movement. As secretary of the institute, he attended the board meeting during which Aberhart secured permission to include Social Credit philosophy in his radio sermons. He travelled with Aberhart in his visits to study group meetings throughout the province. He was at Aberhart's side when they met with constituency associations to make the final selections of Social Credit candidates.

Manning was usually the lead-off speaker in these ostensibly educational, but essentially political meetings. As the demands on Aberhart's time increased during the hectic years immediately prior to the 1935 election, Manning would often fill in for Aberhart as the main performer. He had studied the views of his mentor carefully, and was able to carry the message of Social Credit effectively. He, in fact, adopted Aberhart's mannerisms in addressing a crowd. His radio voice became indistinguishable from that of Aberhart's. Irrespective of whether Manning spoke on biblical interpretations or political philosophy, he assumed an evangelical preaching style. He retained this style throughout his active political life.

Manning competed as a Social Credit candidate in Calgary during the 1935 election. Since Calgary had been the birthplace of the study group movement, Manning, through his involvement in its organization, had become well known to Calgary voters. Still in his mid-20s and looking even younger, Manning led the polls to become one of the youngest, if not the youngest, MLA in the province's history.

2

Manning accompanied Aberhart and Hugill on that historic trip to Edmonton to meet with Lt. Gov. Egbert. During the visit, Premier Aberhart appointed him provincial secretary, not by any means a senior portfolio. Within a few weeks, however, he was awarded a second portfolio as minister of trade and industry, a new government department.

From that time, until his resignation ending his career as a provincial legislator in 1969, Manning continued to hold two portfolios, though not always presiding over the same departments. Manning's administrative and legislative duties combined to provide him with his second set of educational experiences. If his years at the Prophetic Bible Institute might be likened to undergraduate studies, then those which he embarked upon in government could be described as his graduate training. He underwent, during Aberhart's premiership, an intensive and practical program in political science.

Manning had available a well-stocked legislative library containing many sources on political theory. Recognizing his English background, and his high regard for the Mother of Parliaments, in all probability he complemented his biblical studies with generous overlays of British history and political philosophy. He displayed a knowledge of parliamentary procedure that reflects this kind of intellectual experience.

On his entry to the legislature, Manning held certain very firm convictions. He believed in Social Credit, not merely as a set of procedures to achieve monetary reform, but as a philosophy of life. He saw monetary reform as a means of providing the individual with freedom from certain pressures, the demands imposed on him or her by the need to secure food, clothing, and shelter. Relieved of these pressures through monetary reform, the individual could then turn his or her energies toward fulfilling other aspirations, whether intellectual, social, or spiritual. He, in fact, favored a society that fostered the development of free and creative individuals.

Ernest Manning believed that these objectives could be achieved by monetizing the resources of the province. He accepted the thesis that citizens of an industrial society did not possess sufficient monetary instruments to buy all the products coming off its many assembly lines — that our economic system was suffering from an illness endemic to its operation, i.e., a chronic shortage of purchasing power.

Each and every one of the of the 56 members elected to the provincial legislature in 1935 was convinced that he or she had identified the problem. We have seen earlier how their impatience with Aberhart's failure to produce legislation providing a solution to the problem led to the so-called insurgency of 1937, one that threatened the security of the Social Credit government.

As a result of an illness, Manning was absent from the legislature during this fracas. Had he been there, he would not have participated in such a palace revolt. His loyalty to Aberhart was such that he objected to the term "insurgents," preferring to use label "overanxious members" for those involved.

Members of the Aberhart government faced puzzling questions that caused them to move slowly in introducing legislation to implement Social Credit. According to Manning, the Aberhart government during its first 18 months in office faced such questions as these: How does a government monetize the unused productive capacity of a province? How does it distribute credit? How can it assure its people that, if they needed legal tender, they could get it? The introduction of Social Credit was predicated on the voluntary acceptance of credit transfer. The Alberta public, however, was not prepared to accept credit vouchers as a substitute for money.

Manning touched on the highlights of the province's eighth legislature in one of his interview series. He recalled the work of a cabinet minister, Dr. W.W. Cross, MLA for the Hanna constituency. Dr. Cross was a small-town physician who held strong views in the field of public health and was minister of health in the Social Credit government for 25 years. During those years, he introduced legislation on such things as the care

Premier Aberhart and E.C. Manning campaigning, 1940.
Photo courtesy of the Provincial Archives of Alberta, A-2048

of cancer patients, maternity care, and mothers' allowances. The Cross Cancer Institute in Edmonton stands as a monument to the leadership of this dedicated Albertan in the public health field.

Manning also recalled other significant contributions of the Aberhart era. He commented on the debt adjustment legislation designed to protect the debtor from losing his farm, his home, and probably his livelihood. He recalled, as well, the government's many legislative defeats through federal disallowances. The government had been seeking some way of transferring credit represented by figures in a book which would not infringe on federal jurisdiction. It had partially succeeded through the device of the credit houses. The longevity of these quasi-banking organizations attests to their role in the economic life of the province. Needless to say, the Canadian Bankers' Association was highly critical of their establishment. The association accused the Alberta government of going into affairs that it shouldn't, with ideas that were wrong.

The sudden death of a political leader in full control of government shocks the citizens of any jurisdiction. It also creates anxiety and concern within the ranks of the party in power. That party, obviously, has to find a replacement immediately in order to arrange for the transfer of power.

Leadership conventions have their advantages in the interest they arouse during a party's search for a leader. Ordinarily, such conventions require careful planning to gain the greatest advertising benefits possible. The race between competing candidates usually attracts widespread public interest.

The selection of Aberhart's successor was in direct contrast to these political extravaganzas. The decision was reached in a caucus held by the Social Credit members of the Legislative Assembly. E.C. Manning, heir apparent to Premier Aberhart, was elected unanimously as party leader, becoming thereby the premier of Alberta. One might describe this transfer as bearing the aspects of a monarchical succession.

Chapter Nine
Alberta's Youthful Premier

1

Ernest Manning assumed the role of Alberta's premier on June 2, 1943, three months before his 35th birthday. The Alberta newspapers announced the event, treating it as front page news. The probability of it being recognized beyond provincial boundaries was not great. Provincial premiers of the period were not viewed as significant political figures. The attention of all Canadians, including Albertans, was focused on the major players in the military drama that was occupying worldwide attention.

As noted earlier, during the '30s a movement emerged in Germany that was to affect the entire world. The impact of this movement actually influenced Alberta's future, even more than either of those originating in Calgary within that unusual decade. This was the Nazi movement, led by a former corporal in the Austrian army of the First World War who had since become a German citizen.

During the early hours of September 6, 1939, the citizens of Calgary and Edmonton were awakened by newsboys shouting this frightening information. England and France had declared war on Germany.

Within the next five days, Mackenzie King's government also declared war on the Nazis, making Canada a participating member of the Second World War. Australia and New Zealand, as well, joined their mother country, England, in waging the second European war of the 20th century.

During the years 1942-1943, Alberta became the centre for a Commonwealth air training scheme. This was a vast undertaking by the Commonwealth including Britain, Canada, Australia and New Zealand, to prepare pilots, air gunners and bombers for aerial combat. Alberta's skies provided an excellent training space for these emerging Commonwealth forces.

Albertans welcomed these men into their homes and communities. For those two brief years, Australian, New Zealand, British and Canadian airmen travelled Alberta's highways. A hitherto unknown and backwoods province became the focal point of a worldwide training enterprise. This was one unanticipated outcome of a decision generated by the Nazi movement.

2

As noted earlier, Canada's federal government occupied a position of unparalleled power during the years of the Second World War. Entirely responsible for Canada's war effort, the government had preempted from the provinces their right to levy taxes in such fields as personal income, succession duties and the like. It gave the provinces direct payments of support in lieu of these tax preemptions.

The provinces' financial positions, as expressed through their budgets were decidedly circumscribed. Their legislative roles were limited to the maintenance of essential provincial services. No province during the war years embarked on any new program that was not directly related to the war effort, and the federal government was obviously in charge of orchestrating that effort.

Manning's dedication to the enhancement of the war effort was unquestioned. Though he was outspoken in his criticisms of certain aspects of modern democracy, his radical views, nonetheless, did not redound on his reputation as a loyal British subject. That he was the son of English parents was undoubtedly to his advantage. Aberhart, whose name was obviously German in origin, had not been so fortunate. Although his support of the war effort was equally laudatory, he did not escape comments on his Germanic background. The social climate during a war period is not marked for its tolerance.

Manning's leadership qualities were those of a deeply religious man, a dedicated and devoted follower of the Christian faith. Those who accept Christianity completely and without reservation gain from it an inner strength. They know who they are. They need no outward support, no evidence of status, no insignia of office. They achieve security through the strength of their personal convictions.

Manning held firmly to the Christian view that human nature is basically bad. The only way to overcome a sinful nature, to become spiritually regenerated, was to accept Christ. Through this acceptance, man achieves a new outlook on life, one that is expressed through a different concern for his fellows. Presumably Manning's relationships with his close associates, and with those he encountered as he carried out his political duties, were shaped by such an outlook.

A premier's most intimate associates, other than the members of his family, are those who make up his cabinet. Over the 25 years of his premiership, Manning selected and appointed many cabinet ministers. Those who shared his faith respected him for the strength of his beliefs and for the integrity he displayed in their exemplification. The more skeptical, and there were such, respected him for the genuine sincerity of those beliefs.

Manning rarely exercised discipline over the members of the executive council, though he was capable of doing so. The members knew or could anticipate his stance on a variety of matters. They sedulously avoided proposing policies or courses of action of which he might not approve. One suspects, nonetheless, that sharp divisions of opinion within the cabinet sometimes occurred, one or two of which became public.

Though he was doubtlessly unaware of doing so, Manning cast the shadow of his faith over the entire government. Civil servants generally, and those in senior management positions particularly, were fully cognizant of Manning's religious views. The occasions when members of government departments, other than those over which the premier actually presided, might encounter him directly were exceedingly rare. Nonetheless, some departmental issues did reach the premier's attention. Departmental officials involved were sensitive as to what might be the appropriate responses.

Alberta was not necessarily a theocracy during the Manning years, but with a government headed by a lay preacher, it bore certain resemblances to that form of state. One illustration was the slowness with which the province altered its liquor laws to permit cocktail lounges, even though public attitudes had changed markedly on the consumption of alcohol.

Manning displayed attributes that in some degree, counterbalanced the intensity of his religious convictions. He made frequent references to the term "common sense" during his interview series, an approach to political decision making which he apparently held in high regard. One definition of common sense indicates that it is descriptive of a sensitivity to issues or actions commonly held by members of any particular group. A common sense solution is one that the majority of group members would accept as being eminently sensible. Any politician who follows a "common sense" approach to political decision making is likely to build wide support within the jurisdiction he serves.

During 1943, Alberta's youthful premier gave a series of 15-minute radio talks on provincial affairs under the sponsorship of the Alberta Social Credit League. This series gave Manning an opportunity to express his views on post-war reconstruction, and on what must be done to prepare for the post-war period. He stressed the role of Social Credit in shaping a society worthy of those who had sacrificed much to make the world safe for democracy.

Manning argued that Albertans must welcome members of the armed services back to a post-war democracy distinctively different from that which they had left. He insisted that Canadians had not yet known, nor enjoyed a true democracy. In Manning's view, a true democracy would offer the individual the ultimate in security, combined with the highest degree of freedom.

Manning had assumed the leadership of a government that had been in control of the province's affairs since 1935. As a cabinet minister and as Aberhart's closest confidant, he was fully acquainted with the government's record, with its successes and its failures. He was not only aware of the strains within the Social Credit party, he was also sensitive to the problems that party might encounter during the post-war period.

He undoubtedly realized the limitations of a provincial premier seeking to establish monetary reforms in a province within which interest about such matters had been displaced by wartime concerns.

The only avenue open to provincial premiers beyond that of maintaining the status quo, was to focus on post-war planning. The end of the war was not yet in sight. Hitler was still in control of Europe. His armies had not yet met any defeat of consequence. Nonetheless, Canadians generally felt confident that victory would be achieved. Political leaders such as Roosevelt and Churchill, and military commanders in the persons of Eisenhower and Montgomery, inspired confidence in the future.

Not surprisingly, post-war reconstruction became a topic of absorbing interest. People looked forward to a better society, free from the prewar depression, with its dreadful scourge of unemployment and poverty.

Manning did not hesitate in seeking the support of Albertans for his premiership. He called an election during the summer of 1944. He campaigned vigorously on the need for monetary reform following the war's termination. To the surprise of many, he revived the fortunes of the Social Credit Party. He increased Social Credit representation in the legislature from 36 to 51 members.

In commenting on the outcome, Manning suggested that a new and youthful face may have accounted for his success. He had decimated the opposition, reducing it to three independents, two Cooperative Commonwealth Federation (CCF) supporters, and one representative of the War Veterans.

3

When a party in power chooses a new leader, the change in government policy is barely perceptible. The new leader inherits all the unfinished business of the previous administration which he must complete. When Manning assumed the premiership following Aberhart's death in May 1943, he faced three major problems which would absorb his attention throughout most of the '40s. These were the issues of post-war reconstruction, Alberta's debt, and the ultimate fate of the Social Credit Board.

As we saw earlier, Alberta, in common with other Canadian provinces, had established a committee on post-war reconstruction. The purpose of the committee was to plan a program of reconstruction, rehabilitation and re-establishment, ostensibly the three Rs. As the report indicates, reconstruction had to do with things, rehabilitation was directed toward people, and re-establishment focused specifically on members of the armed forces returning from combat.

The Second World War, as with all wars, had its darker side — the loss of life endured by Canada's armed forces. At the same time, it had its altruistic manifestations, with Canadians submerging their immediate and more selfish interests in the pursuit of victory. The war's events were a form of catharsis energizing Canadians not only to assist in winning the war, but also in planning a lasting peace. Considering the nature of the enemy, one could only conclude that this was a war to retain our democratic way of life.

As indicated earlier, the advent of the war had plunged provincial governments into a deep freeze of inactivity. Each of the provinces remained in a holding pattern until the war was won. The federal government dominated the war effort through the recruitment of men and women into the armed services and through the accumulation of war material to be employed by them in the achievement of victory. The federal government spoke for all Canadians, irrespective of where they might live. It became the most powerful government in Canada's history.

Alberta was not unique in focusing its efforts on post-war planning. Every province had its committee on post-war reconstruction. Alberta, however, was the only province boasting a Social Credit government. Considering that the memory of the 1935 election victory was still very much in Albertans' minds, one is not surprised that the report of the post-war reconstruction committee emphasized the Social Credit concept of democracy. The following quotation from the report bears this out:[1]

"The broad objective of Post-war Reconstruction is a properly functioning democracy within which the individual will have the greatest measure of economic security with independence, together with the utmost personal freedom consistent with social life."

The Report of the Committee on Post-War Reconstruction, published in 1945 before the war ended, contained statements stressing such Social Credit principles as the following:

"It is important to distribute purchasing power in the economic sphere, particularly so with Modern Industry eliminating the need for human labor through the use of power driven machinery, and improved processes of production."

The report recommended that old age pensions should be granted to the province's workers at the age of 59 without any means test. It recommended, further, that the federal government provide block grants to each and every province, computed on an equitable basis. These grants, designed to support certain definite programs, were to serve as equalization payments among the provinces.

The subcommittee on finance, more than any other of the several subcommittees, reflected Social Credit views. This subcommittee recommended the establishment of a national monetary authority. The authority would have to work very closely with the Bank of Canada. In fact, it would be the bank's responsibility to carry out the objectives of the proposed monetary authority.

The federal parliament, in voting money to carry out certain national programs, would request funds from the monetary authority. The authority would then direct the central bank to issue money or credit to parliament for the financing of such programs.

The reader may wonder what was to become of the parliamentary power to levy taxes. Parliament would continue employing its right to impose taxes on Canadian citizens. The purpose of such levies, however, would not be to secure income, but to serve as an instrument of control over the economy.

If at any time there existed surplus purchasing power, i.e., more money in circulation than was needed to purchase the products available for sale — this was a method of eliminating that surplus. A highly respected British economist by the name of John Maynard Keynes made a similar proposal, that taxation should be used to control inflation during periods of excessive economic activity.

The document reflected a strong undercurrent of creative, even spiritual feeling. The subcommittee on industry, for instance, recommended the province's entry into fields of endeavor that would provide Albertans with the security, freedom, and happiness as yet unknown to history. Social Crediters saw a rich life as being that of meeting a series of limited objectives which, in the end, would achieve the realization of a better hereafter.

The document is unequivocal in its recognition of the Christian viewpoint. It defined that point of view as a policy of freedom. Those who followed a policy of force were creating the antithesis of a free society. They were, in fact, pagans. Presumably, all those supporting the Nazi and Fascist regimes in Europe had departed from the Christian tradition. One would certainly concur that the rituals of the holocaust were far from Christian.

Alberta's post-war society must emphasize the Christian, and democratic principle of cooperation. This statement identified the origin of the term Christian democracy,[2] one which had become a watchword in Alberta's government, following the Second World War.

The report pointed to three phases in the operation of a Christian democracy. The first, perhaps most significant, was that of policy formulation. The group, in this case all Albertans, decides on policy. Group members then elect administrators whose responsibility it is to administer the policies these members have generated. The administrators then develop sanctions which they may impose on group members in the fulfillment of group policies. If group members find these sanctions objectionable, or if they are dissatisfied with results, they have to secure other administrators to provide more appropriate sanctions and/or better results. Under no circumstance should there be a parliamentary opposition. An opposition does nothing positive other than challenge the administration, an action which, in reality, is counterproductive.

Not all subcommittees dwelt on facets of Social Credit policy. Some made recommendations that bore little resemblance to the government's philosophy. Considering the significance of the rural voter at that time, one is not surprised at the report's emphasis on agriculture. The agricultural subcommittee recommended the establishment of an agricultural service board for every rural municipality. Furthermore, it recommended that each municipality enjoy the services of a district agriculturalist who was to study local needs and make recommendations as to the fulfillment of these needs.

The subcommittee considered ways and means of assisting young farmers to become established on appropriately sized farms. It dwelt on the importance of such matters as soil conservation and weed control. It considered that both these activities were essential if farming was to become a thriving industry. Farmers had to be persuaded to follow methods that would contribute to the achievement of these objectives.

The subcommittee on education made several significant recommendations. It advocated improvements in teachers' salaries, and underscored the importance of teachers' pensions. It insisted that the school leaving age should be raised to 16 years. The subcommittee, as well, turned its attention to the community school movement, stressing its importance toward the achievement of more effective schooling. This movement advocated that the school become not only the educational centre for all age groups, but also the social and recreational centre of the community.

This subcommittee also focused on post-secondary education as an expanding field. It recommended a building program on the University of Alberta campus, an activity that had been static for several decades. It proposed that the provincial normal schools be taken over by the university, thereby placing the preparation of teachers on the same level as the preparatory programs for doctors, lawyers, and engineers.

The subcommittee identified several new departments that should be established by the university: sociology, physical education, and physiotherapy, as well as another foreign language, namely Russian.

Finally, the subcommittee on education introduced the debate on junior colleges, one that was to continue throughout the '50s and '60s. At the termination of this debate, a community college system in Alberta had become a reality.

To guard against the deficiency in purchasing power — a Social Credit shibboleth — the report recommended that old age pensions be made available to all Canadians at the age of 59. It also advocated the payment of family allowances.

The report recommended the establishment of an industrial development board. The purpose of this board was to bring new industries to the province. It was, as well, to encourage and maintain the export of Alberta-made products. Obviously, the board would have to open new markets for these products. Furthermore, it would have to emphasize the development of a tourist industry, a preoccupation of succeeding generations.

Inevitably, the post-war reconstruction committee struck a subcommittee on natural resources. Alberta's oil industry was still in its infancy with, as yet, no discoveries of any consequence. The subcommittee recommended that the government retain the ownership of all undiscovered oil to ensure that exploration, drilling, and production be conducted in the best interests of the province. The government would then have to seek out markets for the products derived from natural gas, popularly known as petrochemicals.

The subcommittee identified the importance of Alberta as potentially one of the world's largest producers of coal resources. It also recognized the extent and potential of the province's forestry reserves, as revealed in the following proposal:

"That in cooperation with the Department of Trade and Industry, and with the assistance of the Alberta Research Council, a study be made to determine the possibility of establishing pulp mills, and investigating the practicability of utilizing birch and poplar in the pulp wood industry."

The public works subcommittee recommended that the government build more highways, increasing the number of kilometres from 6,080 to 9,600, and that district roads be doubled from 3,200 to 6,400 kilometres. It recommended, as well, that 1,100 kilometres of roads for the convenience of tourists be constructed, leading to such provincial attractions as the Waterton, Banff and Jasper national parks. Alberta's roads at that time were far from adequate for either native Albertans or its tourists.

Finally, with the rapid growth in Alberta's urban population, town planning had become an essential activity. The need for waterworks was mounting, with that need particularly prevalent outside the cities. In total, Alberta had only 40 communities with any sort of water and sewage system,

The report maintained that home and family life had to be improved. Few farm homes had been modernized through the provision of electric lights and sewage disposal facilities such as septic tanks. Yet these homes were still homes to most of the province's children. In 1941, the number of rural children was double that of those living in urban settings — 206,681 rural as opposed to 100,129 urban.

The Marsh Report, published during the '40s, made certain observations on life in the Canadian provinces. Insurance plans against the hazards of life were unknown. No protection against unemployment, the frailties of old age, sickness, and the economic results of bereavement were as yet in existence.

The Report of the Subcommittee on Post-War Reconstruction for Alberta is an historic document. It reflected the severe limitations of Alberta's society at that time. It pointed directions for change and improvement that would merit attention for the next several decades. It shaped the subsequent history of the province more than any other single document. Albertans owe a debt to the people that framed it.

2

The Manning government in 1943 faced a serious issue of unfinished business in the size of the provincial debt. By 1945, it had reached the staggering sum of $160 million. At least $30 million had been in default since 1936 when the Aberhart government had arbitrarily cut interest payments in half.

Investors in both Canada and the United States had formed bondholders' protective committees. These committees, each acting for its particular group of bondholders, had kept in constant communication over the years with the appropriate government officials. Together, they had exerted continuous pressure on the Alberta government, through the office of the provincial treasurer for a settlement. They had met with Solon Low who was provincial treasurer in Manning's first cabinet. Low was determined to remove this blight on the province's credit rating. Manning, however, did not agree that the government was yet prepared to deal with this issue.

Following the 1944 election, Solon Low left provincial politics to lead the group of Social Credit representatives in Canada's House of Commons. Manning assumed responsibility for the treasury portfolio as a way of keeping in touch with the activities of all government departments.

He now dealt directly with the two bondholder's protective committees. Whether he was influenced by the same pressures from these committees as Low had received, or had concluded that Alberta was now ready to undertake the refunding of its debt, is difficult to determine. In any event, he set in motion certain actions that would lead to the restoration of the province's credit standing.

In retiring the debt, it was necessary to sell Alberta securities in the financial markets of both Canada and the United States. To do this, Alberta had to seek permission to offer these securities in the U.S. bond market from the American Securities Exchange Commission.

As head of the government, as well as provincial treasurer, Manning had to explain to the commission why the province was eight years in default. To make matters worse, $32 million of that amount was actually unpaid interest. Commission representatives might have conceivably asked why the province had not at least paid the interest on its debts.

The Canadian syndicate involved in the sale of these securities was Wood Gundy Ltd. Its American counterpart was First Boston Inc. Manning and his advisers travelled to New York to complete the refunding arrangements.

The Albertans were eminently successful in this refunding enterprise. The debt totalling $160 million was serialized over 30 years, with the first maturities coming due in three years time. The interest agreed upon was 3.5 percent. The interest rate had been following a downward trend for some time to reach an all-time low. Not long after this agreement had been reached, the rate reversed directions to commence rising again. The deal had been struck at a most favorable time for the province.

One hundred and sixty million dollars changed hands at this meeting. Alberta was now on the its way to becoming a debt-free province. With this achievement, Manning had taken his first step toward political immortality.

3

Manning faced a third significant item of unfinished business in the form of the Social Credit Board. The board, established in 1937, had been in existence for six years. As described earlier, it had been created following the insurgency against Aberhart's leadership, and had been given wide powers to institute a system of social credit.

During the eighth legislature, 1935-1940, the board had been exceedingly productive, devising several legislative enactments all of which met the same fate. They were disallowed by the governor-general-in-council. By the end of the Aberhart regime, however, the board members had settled into a routine of speech making and information processing. Each year they presented a report to the legislature on the board's activities, at the same time proclaiming their dedication to the Social Credit cause.

In presenting its 1944 report to the ninth legislature, the board stressed its role as a source of information, by commenting on the books and pamphlets it had published. This statement revealed the board's perception of its major purpose: "A new social and economic order can be built only on the sound foundation of informed public opinion."

Following his first election as premier in 1944, Manning made two significant changes. He established a department of economic affairs, which, in effect, was an outgrowth of the work accomplished by the Committee on Post-War Reconstruction. He selected Alfred Hooke, a member of the Social Credit Board, to head this new portfolio who, in turn, appointed L.D. Byrne, the Social Credit expert attached to the board, as his deputy minister.

Manning then invited Earl Ansley, currently chairman of the Social Credit Board, to join his cabinet as minister of education, a ministerial post vacated by Solon Low when he became a federal member. In making these appointments, Manning was obviously intent on healing the rupture endemic within the Social Credit party between Aberhart loyalists and the Douglasites.

The several reports of the Social Credit Board to the tenth legislature leads one to wonder what its members were attempting to do. The most kindly interpretation of their purpose would identify the board as the conscience of the Social Credit movement. The material emanating from board members' deliberations may have been designed to remind the government of its original mandate, an appeal to remain true to the revolutionary fervor of its first election. A more realistic interpretation might lead one to conclude that the board members had become intoxicated on the emotional jargon they were producing.

The 1944 report described the interim program in action until that of genuine Social Credit could be introduced. This program was based on a network of treasury branches throughout the province. The device that enabled Albertans to exchange goods and services without legal tender was that of the transfer voucher.

It was possible to transfer claims on goods and services by bookkeeping records maintained in the treasury branches. Granting a 3 percent bonus to the ultimate consumers of goods produced in Alberta persuaded Albertans to make use of credit vouchers. This policy stimulated sales of Alberta-made products.

The experiment, however, had its limitations. The province's wholesalers were uncooperative. They refused to accept vouchers from retailers in payment for goods they had imported from outside the province. This disrupted the cycle of transfer vouchers from consumer to producer and back again.

The problems were also exacerbated by wartime conditions. Canada's wholesalers found it difficult to buy goods of any kind, even with the currency of the realm. Persuading eastern suppliers to accept credit vouchers, rather than legal tender for scarce commodities, would have been virtually impossible.

The central focus of the Social Credit Board existed in this statement:

"It is mathematically impossible, especially in a peace-time economy, for the total aggregate purchasing power to equal the total aggregate prices of the goods and services available, with the present monetary system. What is needed is a national dividend."

This had become a familiar theme for all Social Crediters, whether Aberhart loyalists or Douglasites. Members of the Social Credit Board probed more deeply into the writings of Major Douglas to discover the villains responsible for this deficiency in purchasing power.

Having identified the problem creating economic malaise, the Social Credit Board posed a solution. It insisted that a national dividend issued to every citizen would solve the problem. The economic system, it felt, though identified as capitalist, fell short of a capitalistic reality and was actually a financial dictatorship.

The board saw that reality as power vested in a small group. This group formulates policies and imposes them on others. This is achieved through the establishment of an overriding bureaucracy responsible for applying regulations. The individual is permitted to do only those things ordained by the bureaucrats. The trend is toward the entrenchment of power.

Members of the Social Credit Board were completely opposed to any form of socialism. In their view, it expressed the doctrine of the supreme state, ridiculing all democratic ideals. Statism placed wide powers in the hands of central planning boards, thereby creating the possibility of interference with personal initiative and freedom.

Board members argued that an enormous centralization of power in the federal government had already taken place. A socialist state would advocate even further centralization. Canada now had numerous national boards controlling an ever-widening share of individual enterprise. These were controlled by a government that increasingly depended on formulating legislation through promulgating orders in council. For instance, compulsory contributory insurance schemes were now in actual practise through government decree.

This particular report was presented during the midst of the Second World War. The board's accusations had considerable validity for a nation at war. Whether these would have had equal validity in times of peace is moot. Board members concluded that socialism would destroy our Christian way of life. This is tantamount to saying that Christianity can only exist in a capitalistic society.

Members of the Social Credit Board were exceedingly suspicious of international movements such as the League of Nations. They feared the creation of an international government that would control the money supply, establish a world police force, and impose taxation on a worldwide basis. Such a government would undoubtedly destroy any semblance of a Christian and democratic civilization. The board members were convinced that this world order was being planned, not only by socialists, but by international financiers as well.

Socialists might be amazed at being linked with the world of high finance. Members of the Social Credit Board saw socialists as the enemies of free enterprise, prepared to eliminate private ownership, but doing little about monetary reform. This viewpoint expressed the essential difference between the radicalism of the Cooperative Commonwealth Federation, and that of Social Credit.

The board members' fear of internationalism in any of its manifestations, led them to condemn organizations and activities that had worthy objectives and commendable ideals. The Dumbarton Oaks Conference, for instance, held in Washington during 1944 by the Great Powers, planned an organization for the maintenance of peace following the Second World War. This conference gave birth to the concept of the United Nations, with a security council made up of 11 nations, five of which were to be permanent members. In all probability, members attending this conference were unaware that the Social Credit Board strongly disapproved of this proposed organization.[3]

The Social Credit Board condemned even more vituperatively another historic meeting that occurred during 1944. The Bretton Woods Conference, the membership of which consisted of outstanding monetary experts of the United Nations, had as its objective the establishment of an international monetary fund to control exchange rates. The Social Credit Board, in its annual report of 1945, expressed fears that the fund would become a powerful weapon for disaster in the hands of international bankers.

The board was equally vehement in its denunciation of the United Nations Relief and Rehabilitation Association (UNRRA). This association was expected to provide relief and assistance to those nations liberated from Nazi domination by the victorious forces of the United Nations. UNRRA was designed to stabilize prices, prevent the growth of black markets, and encourage the restoration of self-government. Board members saw opportunities for bankers to exert their nefarious influences toward the establishment of a world dictatorship.

Board members argued that permanent peace could only be achieved through each nation taking control of its own monetary system to provide economic security and democratic freedom for its citizens. Having set its own house in order, each nation would trade its own real surplus of goods on the basis of value for value. At the same time, each would loan its surplus capital to less-developed countries.

These reforms, locally initiated and fulfilled, would eliminate the dangers of war. The board was not opposed to international organizations as long as they were voluntary. Every nation was to respect the sovereignty of other nations. Any nation crossing the boundaries of another would be in conflict with the total association of nations.

The board members' fear of international associations verged on the pathological. They did, nonetheless, appear to favor some form of international action. The root cause of their fears, obviously engendered by the writings of Major Douglas, were the alleged insidious pressures of international financiers, mainly German and Jewish in origin. These were the "bogeymen" of the Douglasites.

Board members were comprehensive in their denunciations. For them, the United Nations Educational, Scientific and Cultural Organization, (UNESCO) illustrated an attempt to place education under the control of an irresponsible group of internationalists. They vented their ire on Julian Huxley, a famous English writer active in UNESCO, whom they accused of being an atheist and a socialist. They denounced Lord Rothschild, the richest man in the world, who currently led the socialist group in the British House of Lords. They poured vitriol on Clement Atlee, a member of the British Labor party who was a lecturer in the London School of Economics, later to become England's prime minister. They expressed alarm that 67 members of the British House of Commons had studied under Harold Laski, an eminent socialist and lecturer in that same subversive school of economics.

The increasingly strident vocabulary of each succeeding report to the Legislative Assembly, dutifully recorded and commented on by the provincial press, became embarrassing to the Manning government. The 1947 report, delivered in 1948, spoke out on two matters, making politically unacceptable proposals. The board, in this its final report, advocated that since land was a heritage to society in general, the government should retain its ownership, leasing it to those best suited to be its guardians.

In its second proposal, board members argued that the secret ballot should be abolished and all should vote openly to reveal how they stood on issues. A secret ballot made it impossible to identify the power that controlled public voting patterns. People hid behind the secret vote.

These two items caused Manning to act. As long as the board attacked international financiers quite remote from the Alberta scene, it was unlikely to arouse local opposition. When the board questioned the private ownership of land, it was striking close to the interests of all rural voters. Furthermore, to attack the secret ballot was to challenge a basic instrument of democracy.

Manning dismissed the members of the Social Credit Board thereby repudiating its report. This created a furor within Social Credit ranks. L.D. Byrne, deputy minister of economic affairs, publicly defended the board, not a politically wise action for a civil servant. Manning immediately terminated Byrne's appointment.

Earl Ansley, a former member of the Social Credit Board, and then minister of education, sprang to Byrne's defence. He defended Byrne's right to speak out about the board's dismissal. As a committed Douglasite, Ansley did not see any problem in implementing the theoretical views expressed in the board's report. Nor did he see any reason to resign from the cabinet because he had publicly defended the former deputy minister. Manning replied in these words, "I can give you a reason right now. I am asking for your resignation." [4]

This request terminated Earl Ansley's career as a cabinet minister. He remained a member of the legislature until the next election.

In dismissing the board, Manning returned the Executive Council to its paramount position in government. The board actually had ceased to have much influence since 1943. It could still, nonetheless, submit legislation on Social Credit to the legislature for its approval, though it was unlikely to have it accepted without the government's blessing.

By 1943, Albertans were actually losing interest in Social Credit. The events of the war, full employment and an expanding population had created other interests. With the demise of the Social Credit Board, Albertans now had a government nominally Social Credit but, in reality, owing its allegiance only to Ernest C. Manning.

Notes

[1] Alberta. "Report of the Post-war Reconstruction Committee" The membership of this committee was as follows:
  A.J. Hooke, Chairman.
  Robert Newton, President, University of Alberta
  C.E. Gerhart, Cabinet Minister
  N.E. Tanner, Cabinet Minister
  Fred Anderson, MLA

Cornelia Wood, MLA
Frank Laut, MLA
E.J. Martin, MLA
H.E. Tanner, Veterans' Representative

[2] During those years the author was employed by the provincial department of education as a school inspector. The provincial director of curriculum, also an employee of the department, was an exponent of Douglas' views. He introduced the term to a social studies curriculum committee established to develop a curriculum guide in that field.

As a committee member, I found it difficult to prepare a curriculum for a Christian democracy. I insisted that a society was hardly democratic that assumed a particular religious label. Admittedly most Albertans at that time probably identified with one or the other of the many Christian sects. Nonetheless, those that did not were seemingly excluded from full participation in such a society.

[3] Mrs. Eleanor Roosevelt, in a speaking tour related to the formulation of the United Nations Organization, was denied an opportunity to address the Alberta legislature on that topic, though she was welcomed in all other provincial legislatures across Canada.

[4] Manning related this exchange to his interviewer during the interview series mentioned in the Sources.

Chapter Ten
The Miraculous Decade

1

Albertans have been singularly blessed by the geological background of their province. The most important occurrence in geological antiquity contributing to this blessing was shaped by a complex of mountains cutting across from what is now the province of Ontario to the present state of Montana. A second complex ran north of Alberta's topmost boundary into the Yellowknife area. These two mountain ranges together created a natural seaway over which the Pacific Ocean flowed in an easterly direction to reach as far as what is currently known as the province of Manitoba.

Two oceanic movements created embayments over the land that was to become Alberta. In the shallow waters along the edges of that inland sea, the forerunners of crabs, shrimps, and lobsters eventually appeared, fulfilling their evolutionary destiny. These early forms of life contributed to Alberta its wealth of oil and gas. That wealth is found in rocks far below the earth's surface, which were formed after the Cambrian era, some 500 million years ago.

The eastward sweep of the Pacific Ocean occurred at least twice unimpeded. During the last repetition of its prehistoric trek, another range of mountains had emerged in the direction of Fort Nelson. This relatively recent obstruction forced the ocean to follow a northerly route. This time the ocean swept over the land that was to become Alberta by pursuing a southeasterly course.

During the course of the Pacific Ocean's end run around this western barrier, it left a trail of coral reefs in the wake of its eastward bound shores. A map of Alberta's oil and gas fields reveals the legacies of those reefs stretching from Rainbow Lake in the province's northwest corner, to Fenn-Big Valley and Drumheller, on its southeastern boundary. Within the range covered by that ancient seaway, some 320 kilometres in width, one may identify the sources of the province's vast supply in energy resources.

The Paleozoic era lasted from 600 million to 225 million years ago, an eternity in time. Much occurred during that geological period of significance to Albertans. The province passed through a succession of dry-land and inland sea periods. Life evolved from the marine existence of simple plant and animal forms to land vegetation and complex vertebrates.

During that era, the source of Alberta's gas and oil industry was stored in rocks thousands of metres below the surface of the earth. The potential wealth provided by that rocky formation has been realized only through discoveries made during the 20th century.

2

The gas and oil — products of early marine life — stored in porous rocks during the Devonian period, some 400 million years ago, were to remain untouched for countless eons in time. During succeeding geological eras, these deposits were covered by layers of rock and other substances.

Primitive man was indifferent to what was stored deeply beneath the earth's surface. Had the Indians who inhabited the land that was to become Alberta discovered oil, they would not have regarded it as liquid gold. A 19th-century fur trader would also have dismissed such a discovery as insignificant, compared to that of the beaver pelt which he sought so zealously.

The oil stored in the Devonian rocks would have remained encapsulated forever had it not been for the demand created for it by the internal combustion engine. The unending search for oil is a 20th-century phenomenon. Those nations blessed with this subterranean wealth have indeed reaped a fortuitous harvest.

There were early signs that Alberta might be one of those fortunate jurisdictions. The first indications of this existed in drilling wells that produced natural gas. In 1909, Bow Island # One, located on the banks of the South Saskatchewan River, stimulated an initial flurry of excitement over Alberta's hidden treasure. The supply of gas was such that a pipeline was laid to Calgary, taking no longer than 80 days to complete.

Further exploration was rewarded by discoveries in Chin Coulee, north of Foremost and around Barnwell. Albertans living in the villages, towns, and cities of the Lethbridge-Medicine Hat region enjoyed the comforts of natural gas heating prior to the First World War.

A further discovery of natural gas, occurred in the Viking district southeast of Edmonton. This strike was sufficiently productive to serve the Edmonton market, a city at that time of 65,000. Edmontonians were forced to wait, however, until after the First World War before discarding their coal bins and ash cans. During the early '20s, they joined Calgarians as beneficiaries of Alberta's geological past.

The Turner Valley field soon became the focal point of Alberta's interest in oil exploration. The first oil strike occurred in 1914. That discovery, unfortunately, turned out to be naptha oil, which meant that it was actually a by-product of naptha gas. To secure the oil, owners of the well found it necessary to burn off the naptha gas. Since naptha itself is useful, this meant sacrificing it to secure a more valuable product — a process which proved to be exceedingly wasteful.

The First World War terminated Alberta's initial oil boom. Its second boom was generated by further discoveries in the valley following the end of the century's first great war. During 1924, Royalite Oil brought in a well, renewing a keen interest in the Turner Valley field. Successes along its western flank in 1936 accelerated the boom. All of the valley's wells, however, produced naptha oil. For a period of 10 years or more, the flares in Turner Valley lit up the surrounding environment, becoming visible as far away as Calgary. These beacons, combined with the odor of escaping hydrogen sulfide gas, identified Turner Valley by both sight and smell.

Many complained about this wasteful method of refining oil. The provincial government was, however, loath to order an end to the practise, though it eventually was forced to do so. While the major companies might have agreed to follow other, less profligate ways of securing oil, their smaller compatriots would have been much more hesitant. They found it necessary to sacrifice the less valuable naptha gas quickly for the treasured oil it produced.

Turner Valley remained the focus of oil seekers' attention throughout the decades of the '30s and well into the '40s. Much of the action took place in North Turner Valley. Although the large integrated companies such as Imperial Oil were the major players, smaller independents concerned mainly with such upstream activities as accumulating land, and exploring and drilling for oil also participated.

A well-known independent — a completely Canadian company — called Home Oil, was quite successful in these endeavors. The company was founded by John Lowery, an Ontario teacher who had been attracted to the West. The board of directors included many prominent Albertans of the period. Ray Milner and Marshal Porter of Edmonton, and Reuben Ward of Calgary, all Alberta businessmen, as well as Herbert Greenfield, premier of the province from 1921 to 1924, were board members.

Consistent with most jurisdictions desirous of stimulating oil exploration, the Alberta government offered very good terms to companies intent on discovering this liquid gold. As a result, the province, throughout the '30s and '40s, was covered by seismographic crews boring deeply beneath Alberta's surface to secure rock samples that might indicate possible oil caches. These crews obviously followed a course marked out by the coral reefs along the eastward-bound shores of those ancient inland seas.

3

On November 20, 1946, Imperial Oil spudded in an exploratory well, southwest of Edmonton not far from the village of Leduc. During the early months of the succeeding year, the head driller, bearing the nickname of Dry Hole Hunter, was convinced that, despite his ominous sobriquet, this time he would not leave a dry hole behind him. So confident was he of success, he invited several government officials and other prominent citizens to take part in the "bringing in" ceremony on February 13, 1947.

The Hon. N.E. Tanner, minister of mines and minerals in the Manning government, was invited to turn on the well. This would occur when the drill finally penetrated the rocks that had encapsulated the oil. These rocks were now buried some 1,500 metres below the earth's surface.

After several hours of steady and monotonous pounding there came a moment of silence. The driller signalled the minister, who stepped to a wheel on the pipe, giving it a few swift turns. With a powerful "whoosh" the well blew in. The oil commenced flowing into huge metal tanks. Cheers from that hardy crowd ushered in Leduc # 1.

A single winner, no matter how productive, does not guarantee the presence of an oil field. Imperial Oil now had to ascertain that presence

"Bringing in" Imperial Leduc #1, February 13, 1947.
Photo courtesy of the Provincial Archives of Alberta, P-2725.

by boring other strategically located wells around its initial discovery. Throughout the next two years, Imperial completed several successful wells, confirming that the Leduc field was indeed a major find.

One incident occurred during the early years of the field's development that caught the attention of the major oil companies in America. This involved a well called Atlantic # III owned by Pacific Petroleum, a firm established by a well-known Calgarian, Frank McMahon. The well went out of control during the course of its "bringing in," spewing oil in great quantities over its immediate surroundings.

For the short period of time necessary to regain control of this "wild well," it became front page news. All other activities in the field came to a halt during the struggle to subjugate this fiery outlaw. Following this display of uncontrolled power, the oil was retrieved and sold. This sale of oil is said to have placed McMahon en route to becoming a millionaire.

A most significant outcome of the worldwide interest created by the spectacular behavior of this unruly outlaw was the recognition accorded the field by certain major oil companies. Such firms as British Petroleum, Belgium Petrofina, and Mobil Oil began to display an interest in Alberta as a potential source of oil.

The discovery of the Leduc-Woodbend field was significant for a number of reasons: it was located on the doorstep of a market, a city with a population approaching 100,000, whose citizens had adopted the automobile as an indispensable mode of transportation. Within a few short months, a refinery that had proven to be something of a "white elephant" at Norman Wells in the Northwest Territories was dismantled and moved to Edmonton. A pipeline was soon constructed to feed it with crude oil from the Leduc-Woodbend field. The oil was intended to be refined in that city, and its products to be consumed locally.

The discovery of Leduc #1 confirmed what some geologists had suspected, the presence of oil in the Devonian strata of rocks 1,500 metres below the earth's surface. This formation, stretching from Rainbow Valley in the northeast corner of the province to its boundary with southern Saskatchewan, along a subterranean course 320 kilometres in width, provided exploratory challenges to oil seekers for several decades.

On this broad subterranean fairway they played their exploratory games in the never-ending search for oil. They did this, not only during the years of Alberta's miraculous decade, but for many years thereafter. In fact, the search for oil has become one of Alberta's major industries.

No one knows precisely at the outset of an oil field's development how extensive it might be, or its ultimate potential. The amount of oil in any field is, however, finite. The Leduc-Woodbend field, now fully explored, will render up some hundred million barrels of oil, through production coming from 1,300 wells. Unlike the oil produced by Turner Valley wells, that which poured out of Leduc #1 was identified as pure crude, ready to be distilled into gasoline and other products. There was no need to dispose of naptha gas during the process of its refinement.

4

If the interest of the major oil companies had been titillated by the discovery of Leduc #1, it must have been fully aroused by that which occurred in 1948. Imperial Oil had confirmed the presence of a new field by bringing in Imperial #1 in the vicinity of Redwater, a way station on the Edmonton-St. Paul Railway. This new field, some 80 kilometres north of Leduc-Woodbend, was well within the confines of the Devonian fairway.

The Redwater field extended from Egremont, in a southeasterly direction, to cross the Saskatchewan River near the town of Fort Saskatchewan. This new field was equally as large, if not larger than its precursor, Leduc-Woodbend. Edmonton was now surrounded by two major oil fields and Alberta had entered the major leagues among oil producers, with recoverable reserves exceeding one billion barrels.

The Redwater field had its impact on the region over which it extended. The town of Redwater grew from its original nucleus, a way station and railway water tank that had been built during the construction of the Edmonton-St. Paul railway some 30 years earlier. Similar to the Leduc-Woodbend field, the farms within that of Redwater became dotted with pumps raising crude oil from its Devonian sources to be piped to Edmonton's refineries.

The discovery of the Redwater field led to a review of provincial government policy. A major distinction between the two fields existed in the ownership of mineral rights. Within Leduc-Woodbend, a large number of settlers owned not only the surface of their land, but also the wealth that lay beneath it. They had settled on the land prior to 1887, the year during which the federal government had decided to retain the ownership of any minerals that might lie below the earth's surface. In Redwater, this was not the case. The Manning government found itself in the enviable position of having inherited a windfall.

The government issued regulations which set patterns for the development of all Alberta's oil fields. Oil companies could reserve a large area of land within which they must agree to undertake a search for oil. If an oil firm decided to drill a well, it had to inform the government of its intent. The government would then grant the company a lease, comprising 9 sections in one total block and would also award the company 9 more sections scattered throughout the township. However, the oil company had to return the rest of the original reservation to the government. The government then proceeded to place the remaining unleased land on auction to be bid on by other competing oil companies.

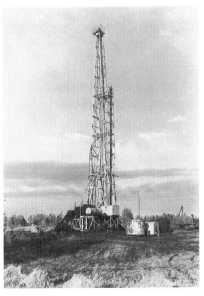

Redwater oil well, Redwater oil field.
Photo courtesy of the Provincial Archives of Alberta, H. Pollard Collection, P-2121.

The Alberta government, during the years following the Redwater discovery, had two sources of income from Alberta's oil fields. Since the government owned the subsurface rights, not only on crown lands, but on all lands acquired by private owners after 1887, it obviously owned the oil brought to the surface by the oilseekers. This, however, did not include oil discovered on lands granted to the Canadian Pacific Railway, nor on those lands held by the Hudson Bay Company.

The government consequently could charge a royalty on each barrel of oil from a producing well. Recognizing, however, that the finder was entitled to recompense for his discovery, the government prorated the royalty according to the productivity of a well.

To illustrate: if a well produced up to 660 barrels monthly, the government claimed up to 5 percent of its total output. For a well producing from 1,500 to 1,800 barrels, the claim increased to 12 ½ percent of the total production. A high-producing well with an output in excess of 4,050 barrels rewarded the government with 16 ⅔ percent of that which it ultimately rendered up from the earth's Devonian substructure.

The second source of income came from the sale of crown reserves. These included leases, blocks of land on which oil companies purchased the right to search for oil by sinking wells, not more than one on every 16 hectares. The government also sold reservations, large areas on which companies might search for oil through seismographic exploration. On some of these reservations the companies also purchased drilling rights. The government, as well, collected rental income on certain leases, which was frequently as remunerative as the actual sales.

For the years from 1947 to 1956, those of the Dynamic Decade, the revenue earned by government from these various sources, was $589,427,954. The income for 1957 was $134,359,861. For each succeeding year, until 1971, the revenue increased gradually to reach $260,486,956 in the final year.[1]

Each year during this decade brought new finds. Although these discoveries did not always identify a major field, the announcements of these discoveries, irrespective of their size, enhanced the interest of Albertans. Even though few of them were directly involved in the oil industry, they were interested observers of the events that occurred during this intensely exciting decade — events which could only be described as extraordinary.

Between 1950 and 1952, several fields were located, though none equaled that of either Leduc or Redwater. In 1950, the government sold 1,800 hectares for exploration in the Fenn-Big Valley field, at $5,360 per hectare. During the next two years, discoveries in the Wizard Lake and Bonnie Glen region led to the sale of leases comprising of 400 hectares for $11,500 a hectare. The Sturgeon Lake find was equally remunerative, leading to a sale of leases containing 2,350 hectares at $6,500 a hectare. Minor discoveries also occurred in the Rimbey and Erskine districts.

One of the largest discoveries during this remarkable decade was that of Pembina Valley. The field was located near Drayton Valley, a settlement on the north side of the Saskatchewan River, about 120 kilometres southwest of Edmonton. One immediate result of this discovery was to bring into existence Drayton Valley, first as a village, then as a new town, and finally as an incorporated town with a population of 5,000.

The Drayton Valley field was estimated to have a potential production of a billion barrels of oil. The estimated size of the field, was 17,850 hectares, over three times the size of Redwater. The average depth of producing wells was 1,590 metres, indicating that oil was located in the earth's Devonian substructure. This field was, unquestionably, the most impressive discovery up until that time.

These projections obviously influenced the sale of leases. The first auction was held in 1954. Although the price per hectare was quoted as $43,450, certain sections were sold at $500,000.

Swan Hills, the last major find, one of the three most important fields in the province, was discovered in 1957. It lies in the boreal forest region, between Lesser Slave Lake and the town of Whitecourt. The estimated potential of the field was two billion barrels; as one writer described it, a triumph in the wilderness. The discovery was the achievement of Home Oil of Calgary, an Alberta company, the owner of which, R.A. Brown Jr., has had a career of interest to Albertans.

Notes

[1] Informative materials provided by a senior government official, Hubert Sommerville, during the Manning era.

Chapter Eleven
An Alberta Wildcatter

Bobby Brown registered in an accountancy course at the University of Alberta in 1931. This story, probably apocryphal, reflects his unlimited confidence. He was alleged to have told the professor that he was not interested in the details of the course. He merely wished to learn how to read a balance sheet. He could, as he said, hire bookkeepers to look after the details of accounting.

Bobby Brown, when he first appeared at the University of Alberta to register in the Faculty of Arts, was 18 years of age, of medium height, with a shock of brown curly hair. He could be best described as having a baby face, startlingly white, open and remarkably innocent. His manner was friendly, even warm. One would not, however, have considered him effeminate, though he was far from rugged. None of his friends expected him to try out for the university football team.

The Calgary students who introduced Bobby to one of the men's fraternities knew his family background. His father, R.A. Brown Sr., had been head of the Calgary Street Railway System. He had recently resigned from that post to become involved in the search for oil in Turner Valley. Brown Sr. had already initiated Bobby into the oil business. His brash statement to the professor of accountancy had not been without foundation.

R.A. Brown Sr., who had established Turner Valley Royalties, brought in his first well during June 1936. As with most Turner Valley wells, it produced not only oil but naptha gas. Nonetheless, the flow of oil reached a 1,000 barrels a day, making it an outstanding producer. During October of the previous year, the Brown family had organized a firm known as Brown, Moyer and Brown Ltd., an operating company to look after all of the Brown interests.

By 1950, Bobby Brown, 36, had become the major player in this family firm. Still a small operator in the activities of the miraculous decade, Bobby was ready to expand. He and his lieutenants conceived the idea of buying Home Oil, a firm that was located in the same building as the Brown enterprises — the Lougheed Building. Home Oil, a Canadian company, though not to be compared with Imperial Oil or Texaco, was, nonetheless, earning a yearly revenue of $5 million and was debt free.

As noted earlier, Home Oil had been developed by Jim Lowery, an Ontario school teacher who had come to Alberta in 1905. He had been responsible for the incorporation of the company by the Dominion secretary of state in 1925. Since that time, Home Oil had been controlled by a board consisting of some well-known Albertans and several Vancouver businessmen.[1] The company had been reasonably successful in Turner Valley and had been active, as well, in the Leduc and Redwater fields.

Bobby Brown's capacity for friendship, apparent in his university years, had provided him with useful connections. To assume control of Home Oil, Brown would need to purchase a large number of shares, approaching a figure in the hundreds of thousands. A friendly banker, Neil McKinnon, offered to loan Brown the millions of dollars he would need to secure a controlling interest. Having obtained financial support, Brown then commissioned another friend, Jim Weir, to purchase the shares on the Montreal Stock Exchange.

Weir bought some 481,571 shares at $16 a share over a period of 12 months. By April of 1951, Brown possessed 400,000 shares, which gave him control of Home Oil.

The takeover of Home Oil was a dramatic event in the career of this unusual Albertan. Brown's representatives walked into the annual meeting of Home Oil in 1951 to stun its assembled shareholders and their board of directors with the announcement of a takeover. Brown's henchmen included Jim Weir, his stock broker, Ronnie Brown, a younger brother, and Douglas McDermid, a long-time friend dating back to university days who was also his lawyer.[2]

With the appointment of Weir and Moyer to the board of directors governing Home Oil, it became an Alberta company completely controlled by Albertans. By uniting Federated Oil, his original company, with Home Oil, Brown now controlled the fourth-largest oil producing firm in Canada.

As more oil fields came into production during the miraculous decade, 1946-1956, Home Oil expanded its holdings. The company followed a policy, described by one writer in these words:

"The development of exploratory plays based on regional geological studies, followed by the acquisition of land, geophysical exploration, and, if desirable, exploratory drilling."[3]

Geological opinion was actually nothing more than an informed guess. It had to be verified by seismic crews who bore deeply into the earth's surface to secure samples of rock for examination and study. Having gained some hard evidence, an oil firm engaged in exploration would finally decide to sink a wildcat well, one which might or might not be successful. Home Oil made such a discovery in a wildcat well at Westward Ho, immediately north of Calgary.

R.A. Brown, Jr.
Photo courtesy of Home Oil.

The oil industry, in common with all natural resource industries, is dependent on access to markets for its various products, the most important being gasoline. The production of gasoline involves moving crude oil from the well head to a refinery which then transforms this liquid gold into a form more acceptable to its final consumers — the owners of trucks and cars.

Closely related to the industry of oil and gas production is that of pipelines. The production of piping, and the burial of these long cylindrical objects in trenches a few metres below the earth's surface, is as essential to the oil industry as the wells that bring crude (i.e., unrefined) oil to the surface of the earth.

In 1955, Home Oil spent $2.2 million on exploration largely in the Pembina field. Bobby Brown's appetite for funds was insatiable. The lending agencies were apparently prepared to satisfy that appetite.

Farmers of the period approached in trepidation the managers of their local banks for a loan of a few hundred dollars to tide them over the harvest. They would have been shocked to learn of the ease with which Bobby secured a loan of $2 million. Perhaps Alberta's bankers were also infected by the oil mania that pervaded the province throughout this decade of miracles.

Brown secured the right to construct a pipeline for gathering oil from the various wells in the Cremona field. The destination of this oil was to those refineries located in the city of Calgary.

The most important find of Home Oil was that of Swan Hills, the last discovery of a major Alberta oil field. Bobby Brown first drilled exploratory wells at Virginia Hills, some distance from the Swan Hills location. He then turned his attention to Swan Hills, deciding to explore four townships, a huge block of land approaching 41,000 hectares in area. The results were decidedly rewarding.

Bobby immediately applied for authority to build a pipeline. The Manning government granted him this authority readily. The completed line to Edmonton refineries carried oil from several fields in the Swan Hill region such as Swan Hills, South Swan Hills, Judy Creek, Carson Creek, and Virginia Hills.

As the end of the miraculous decade approached, the issue of marketing grew in significance. Bobby Brown showed a keen interest in pipelines early in his career. This interest was shared in varying degrees, not only by Albertans, but by Canadians generally. It was aroused particularly by the issue of the Trans Canada Pipeline.

The House of Commons' debate on this issue during 1957 riveted national attention on its substance. The debate focused on whether the pipeline should follow an all-Canadian route across the bleak, uninhabited regions of northern Ontario, or pursue a southern route with a detour through the United States.

The opposition parties raised two objections to the Trans Canada Pipeline. The NDP insisted that the pipeline should be publicly, rather than privately, owned. The Conservatives criticized the American influence in the company that was to undertake the construction. The Liberal government, under the leadership of Louis St. Laurent, imposed closure to end the debate, an action which infuriated both opposition parties.[4] C.D. Howe, the minister in charge, wanted to terminate the debate in order to get on with the construction of the line.

Brown was very much in favor of the project. He invested heavily in it by purchasing some 700,000 common shares. Home Oil actually became the largest single shareholder, holding around 12 percent of the issued shares.

By the end of 1958, Home Oil owned 4,044,073 shares, costing $30.4 million. Most of that money had been advanced by the Canadian Bank of Commerce.

These purchases placed a heavy load of debt on Home Oil. Brown had traded such assets as 40 percent of Home's gas reserves in the Nevis field, as well as its interests in nine Harmatton and eight Pembina wells. Together these represented a total daily production of 677 barrels of oil. Unfortunately, the Trans Canada shares did not pay dividends for five years after completion.

Brown's luck held. During 1958, Home Oil discovered the Carstairs gas field. This was located south of Westward Ho and the Harmatton oil discoveries. It turned out to be one of the richest gas fields in the province. By 1970, that field was producing much of the revenue Home was earning from natural gas and its by-products.

By 1960, three years after the last major oil discovery in Alberta, two organizations represented companies involved in the production and

Pipeline suspended over coulee west of Leduc.
Photo courtesy of the Provincial Archives of Alberta, H. Pollard Collection, P-2758

distribution of oil and its products. The Canadian Petroleum Association was dominated by the big foreign companies such as Imperial Oil and Texaco. These companies controlled around 80 percent of the oil and gas reserves in Canada. The independent Canadian Petroleum Producers was made up of smaller local firms such as Home Oil. They held the remaining share of Canada's oil and gas reserves.

These independent producers were convinced that Canada should have a national oil policy. They wanted a share of the Montreal market. This meant extending the Interprovincial Pipeline from Sarnia through to Montreal.

By 1959, Home Oil's bank debt had reached $31.4 million. Its assets were estimated at $82 million. Brown was encouraged by his advisers to reduce Home's outstanding debt. Since the company's gross income was only $7.7 million, it would have been difficult to pay off this debt from production income.

Chase Manhattan, a New York bank, gave Brown a short-term loan of $15 million, which in Canadian funds amounted to $15.8 million. Brown was actually "robbing Peter to pay Paul."

As an example, Brown sold $20 million, 6 percent Home Oil debentures convertible into Trans Canada shares at $27. At conversion, Home was relieved of a $20 million debt by giving up 740,741 Trans Canada shares. He also sold $10 million worth of secured bonds to a group of U.S. insurance companies headed by Mutual and New York Life.

He disposed of all Home's interests in the Redwater field to Triad Oil for $7 million. A few months later, he managed to pay Home's debt fully by repeating the sale of $4 million worth of 6½ percent secured bonds to two American insurance companies. This time the firms were Mutual of New York and the Prudential Insurance Company of America.

With its financial problems solved for a time, and with the advantages created by the National Oil Policy of 1961, Home's income capabilities began to improve.[5] Other events also contributed to its success. Home's production of crude oil and natural gas doubled during the '60s from 7,849 to 16,666 barrels per day. Its gross revenue increased from $9.2 million in 1960 to $27.7 million in 1969.

While Home's position improved, Brown personally remained heavily in debt. The Bank of Commerce had given him a large personal loan to acquire United Oil in 1954. He was forced to increase this substantially in 1958. United Oil, which he had purchased in 1954, owed the bank $11.3 million. The only assets which that company possessed were Home shares. At this point, Brown might easily have lost Home Oil.

Brown's final solution was the formation of a company called Cygnus. Cygnus actually controlled Home Oil since it held 43 percent of its shares. If he could have sold those shares at a good price, he might have maneuvered his way out of debt completely.

This however was not to occur. Canada was undergoing one of its periodic bouts of extreme nationalism. Sensitive to the prevailing mood of most Canadians, the federal government would not permit this sale to a foreign buyer. It objected to yet another Canadian company coming under foreign control.

Bobby Brown was finally forced to accept an offer from Consumers Gas. This was an Ontario firm controlled by Oaka Jones, an American who had become a Canadian citizen. Though the antithesis of Brown, the two men got along well together.

Brown died in 1973 at the age of 60. He had lived life in the fast lane for most of those years. Wildcatter that he was, Bobby continued his search for oil until the end. His last big failure was in Alaska's Prudoe Bay, one that may have led to his ultimate financial disaster.

Bobby Brown's career is illustrative of events during a brief, but fascinating period in Alberta's history. These were the province's most dynamic years, those which transformed its society from its widely dispersed rural settings to its two modern urban concentrations.

The dominating share of provincial oil development was undertaken by large companies such as Texaco and Mobil Oil of New York, Chevron from San Francisco and Amoco of Chicago. These companies made little pretence of being other than international organizations that gave little recognition to the countries whose oil they exploited. Imperial Oil, Shell and Gulf did, apparently, provide their Canadian subsidiaries with a degree of independence that permitted them to, at least, recognize the country in which they operated.

The firms most closely associated with Alberta were the independents, that small group of firms that shared about a fifth of the oil development with the multinationals. Bobby Brown, and the firm with which he was closely identified, was an independent.

Historically, Bobby Brown belongs to the Manning era. He was among the first group whose members established themselves as

Calgary's upper class in a city unaccustomed to such social distinctions. Peter Newman, in his book *The Canadian Establishment*, presents the view that Calgary is a business town, and that it is the only place in Canada within which the commercial and the social elites are indistinguishable.

One commentator in this book identified the group of which Bobby was a prototype as the "nouveau riche." Unquestionably, Bobby may have given that impression during much of his lifetime. He certainly moved in circles not open to the vast majority of middle-class Calgarians living in a predominantly middle-class city. Albertans have always prided themselves as being members of a society free from class distinction. If pressed, they may admit that they are members of the middle class and that they live in a middle-class neighborhood. They generally refuse to accept any other designation.

The records show how frequently Bobby Brown skirted disaster. His career, including his lifestyle, might well have been portrayed in the popular television show of the '80s, "Dallas." The backgrounds of his career are somewhat comparable to those employed in this well-known TV "soap opera." Certainly Alberta and Texas have much in common.

Bobby Brown obviously used his attractive personality to further his own selfish interests. He could be, and was, ruthless in the pursuit of those interests. Those who worked most closely with him rarely, if ever, commented about him. Whether this reticence reflected indifference, fear or condemnation, one can only conjecture. Dying at the age of 60, which Bobby did, suggests that life in the fast lane, no matter how exciting, has its disadvantages.

In retrospect, perhaps one can only say of Bobby Brown that he was an Albertan who should be recognized.

Notes

[1] See Chapter Ten, p. 164, the formation of Home Oil.

[2] Douglas McDermid was later appointed to the Alberta Supreme Court.

[3] Philip Smith, *The Treasure Seekers* (Toronto: Macmillan of Canada, 1978).

[4] The St. Laurent government was defeated later that year by the Conservatives, under the leadership of John Diefenbaker.

[5] The federal government created the National Energy Board to oversee and regulate the import and export of oil.

Chapter Twelve
Shifting Emphases

1

American oil companies played a major role in the development of Alberta's oil fields. Manning at first tried to involve eastern Canadian capital in the exploitation of the province's natural resources. No one in the east, however, showed any interest in undertaking western investments. Eastern capitalists preferred to sink their wealth in either the pulp and paper mills of Quebec, or in the mines of Ontario.

Alberta benefitted from the experience American oil firms acquired during the opening of the Oklahoma and Texas oil fields. Their assistance proved to be most helpful to Alberta's government in the drafting of legislation providing guidelines for both the production and marketing of oil and natural gas.

Although American companies dominated in the development of Canada's oil fields, a major difference existed in the oil industry between the two countries. The Alberta government was the sole owner of the oil rights in all major fields, with the exception of Leduc-Woodbend. Here many of the farms had been settled prior to 1887, the date after which Canada retained the subsurface rights on all lands, with the exception of those already granted to the Canadian Pacific Railway and the Hudson Bay Company.

As a result, the Alberta government had the authority to impose procedures for the production and marketing of oil and gas from those fields brought into existence subsequent to the discovery of Leduc-Woodbend.

The government, for instance, insisted that no export of either of these products to other parts of Canada, or abroad, should occur until there was assurance of sufficient production to provide a 30-year supply for all Albertans.

Manning, himself, assumed direct responsibility for the Department of Mines and Minerals in 1952. Up until that time, the portfolio had been occupied by N.E. Tanner, MLA for the Cardston constituency who retired prior to the election of that year.

During the following election three years later, Lucien Maynard, the province's attorney general, was defeated in the St. Paul constituency. Manning then chose to carry responsibility for that portfolio as well. In effect, he was not only provincial premier, but he also directed the affairs of the government's two major departments.

In response to criticism for these two decisions, Manning argued that with good deputy ministers aided by effective staffs a minister had little difficulty in keeping in touch with departmental affairs. Convinced that government could get oversized, he believed in a small cabinet membership with a limited number of deputies.

During the Manning era, Alberta's civil service entered into a period of growing professional competence. Civil servants were selected and promoted on the basis of their ability to perform the tasks of the department to which they were attached. The issue of political affiliation was seemingly irrelevant. One did not need to be a Social Crediter to succeed in provincial government service.

Throughout Manning's career as Alberta's premier from 1943 to 1968, he led his party during seven elections. Within that lengthy period, he maintained an overwhelming majority in the Legislative Assembly with but one exception. This was in the thirteenth legislature shaped by the election results of 1955. Manning's party held 37 seats, facing an opposition of 15 Liberals, three Conservatives, two CCF and four others, each of whom claimed some form of independent status.

There appears to have been two reasons for this aberration within his quarter century long premiership. Two Social Credit MLAs, John Landeryou and Roy Lee, both from southern Alberta constituencies, had, despite their legislative commitments, entered into contracts with government. When this became known, Manning immediately read them out of the party.

The Liberals under Harper Prouse argued that the Manning government had grown old and tired in office and was obviously ineffective. Manning attributed Liberal Leader Prouse's success not only to his exploitation of the "Lee-Landeryou affair," but also to his vigorous campaigning.

Manning was not long in securing political revenge. During the next election in 1959, Social Credit regained its political dominance by securing 61 seats in the Legislative Assembly. The opposition was reduced to four members — a Liberal, a Progressive Conservative, an Independent Social Crediter and a Coalition candidate.

Manning, perhaps facetiously, recommended that the four get together to decide on which of the four should serve as leader of the opposition.

2

During 1957, the year following the discovery of Alberta's last major oil field, the Manning government reached a decision that aroused memories of Social Credit. It decided to issue citizen's participation dividends. These were, as Manning said, to be paid to shareholders in Alberta Incorporated. The amount of the monthly payment was set at $20.00 and $17.50. In order to secure the dividend, an Albertan had to make application on a form entitled Citizen's Royalty Dividend.

To receive this payment, an Albertan was required to certify that he or she was a Canadian citizen, 21 years of age, and a resident of Alberta for more than 10 years. This statement was to be signed by a commissioner of oaths.

The amount paid out to Albertans during 1957 and 1958 amounted to 20 million dollars. The reaction of the public to these payments was perhaps unexpected. Albertans agreed, almost unanimously, that the government should put the money to better use. In effect, Albertans decided that they didn't want government handouts.

On August 14, 1958, Manning went on television to make an important announcement. That the announcement came by way of television evidenced the change in the means of communication that had occurred during Manning's premiership. During the '40s, this announcement would have been delivered over the radio.

Manning announced that government members of the legislature had reached decisions on several projects to be undertaken over the next five years. This, in its entirety, was to be a gigantic anti-recession program unlike any that had ever been attempted heretofore by any provincial government.

Although Manning made no reference to Maynard Keynes, the British economist who recommended vast public expenditures during periods of depression, it was undoubtedly a Keynesian, rather than a Douglasite or Social Credit, series of proposals that he set forth.

During 1959, the Manning government proposed building 50 homes for senior citizens. These homes, though built by the provincial government, would be turned over to the local municipalities for their operation in the zones within which these residences were to serve.

In the following year, 1960, the provincial government would spend $10 million on local community improvements. These were to include such things as street paving and the construction of local recreation centres. Facilities such as swimming pools and campsites would contribute to the quality of life in the province's various communities.

The year 1961 was to see the completion of a provincial hospital in Calgary patterned after the Mayo Clinic in Rochester, New York. This new medical centre, combined with the province's University Hospital in Edmonton, would give Alberta the most advanced health facilities in Canada.

"During 1962, the province intends," said Premier Manning, "to establish an institution for the care of emotionally disturbed children. It will also provide a school for the training of those with cerebral palsy and other physical handicaps."

Finally, in the fifth year, the government proposed erecting a provincial archives in Edmonton.

Each of the government's major departments would undertake programs of interest to all Albertans. They were such as these: a $350 million scholarship fund for students seeking to enter university; a technical and apprenticeship training centre comparable to that which then existed in Calgary, and a program of guaranteed farm home improvement loans.

In addition, a projected highway and bridge program would be geared to the anticipated needs of the province's various communities. These public work projects would be designed to provide employment during seasonal fluctuations in the demand for labor.

And finally, the government would abolish the gas tax on all gasoline used in farm trucks.

The significance of this speech delivered on August 14, 1958, was not only revealed by its substance, but also by its timing. It obviously had been carefully prepared and discussed at length in the Social Credit caucus. It came at the close of a decade during which the people of the province and its government had been deeply involved in the excitement created by a series of oil discoveries and an accompanying oil boom.

Although the search for oil continued, its pace had slackened. Albertans were ready, both physically and psychologically, for a shift in the tempo of living.

The speech presented a five-year plan of action. The various proposals were far from novel, although some may have titillated the imagination. Certainly most Albertans were aware of and many had experienced the need for more hospitals. Almost everyone of that era knew about and approved of the contribution rendered by the Mayo Clinical Hospital. Many Canadians, including Albertans, had made a pilgrimage to that hospital in search of better health.

Not many, however, were aware of the purposes served by a provincial archives. This proposal reflected a sensitivity to historical interests and needs that was unexpected in this Social Credit province.

In fact, the comprehensive character of these proposals broadened the scope of their appeal. There was something for every social group, for those who lived in the two major cities, for the town and village dwellers, and for the province's yet rather populous rural regions. The Manning government had touched base with every significant provincial group.

That Manning and his government had introduced this awe-inspiring set of proposals at this juncture had certain political implications. As noted earlier, the previous election in 1955 resulted in the Manning government facing the largest opposition in its political career. During the thirteenth legislature, the government's majority was respectable enough, 37 to 24, but markedly below those of previous legislatures. Manning may have been concerned that this diminished support might have introduced a trend. That he was sensitive to this is reflected in the followings:

"I am aware of the current crop of political speculations, by those whose minds are centred in their political party fortunes, rather than on the progress of this province and the welfare of its people. Let me set their speculations at rest by saying emphatically that I have no intention of plunging this province into a premature election ahead of the normal time when the electors properly expect an opportunity to give a mandate to the government of their choice."[1]

It is significant to note that this speech was delivered on August 14, 1958. The next election occurred during the summer of 1959, less than a year later. As noted earlier, the Manning government was returned with an overwhelming majority of 61 members. The opposition was reduced to four members, each drawn from different parties. As Manning implied, it was difficult to determine who should lead the opposition.

3

The year during which Manning introduced his five-year plan marked his fifteenth year as premier of Alberta. He ended his premiership 10 years later in 1968, having spent a quarter of a century serving Albertans. He may well have established a record within the British Commonwealth.

During those years, the province's population was transformed from being predominantly rural to overwhelmingly urban. By 1966, according to census figures recorded in that year, Alberta's population had reached 1,007,437, with percentage ratios of 69 percent urban and 31 percent rural. This was a complete reversal of such ratios over two decades in time.

Most of the growth had occurred in the province's two major cities, Edmonton and Calgary, and in the smaller cities and towns. Calgary and Edmonton, in 1943, had populations well below 100,000. Within their boundaries, there were still large areas of undeveloped land attesting to the fact that their early designers had been overly optimistic as to their immediate future growth.

By the end of Manning's premiership, 25 years later, those empty spaces had been completely occupied. The two cities had commenced their outward growth by absorbing land around their original boundaries. Together, they were on the way toward becoming two of Canada's major metropolitan centres.

Alberta's rural landscape was also transformed during Manning's premiership .At the outset of the Manning years, the early '40s, the countryside looked much as it appeared following the First World War. Farm homes, particularly in the central and northern regions, were located on every half section of land (130 hectares). The country roads leading to a neighboring hamlet or village were busy thoroughfares bearing locally generated traffic.

Children pursued well-marked routes to local schools, predominantly one-room buildings providing education from grades one to eight. A typical rural school district encompassed an area of some 51 square kilometres, within which there might be located between 20 and 30 farm families.

Conceivably two, and sometimes three generations of these families, had passed through the local school. If the district encompassed a hamlet or village, a two- or three-room school might offer instruction from grades one to eleven. The village school, frequently served as a high school centre for several of the surrounding rural school districts.

Futurists are social scientists who develop scenarios descriptive of what might possibly exist two or more decades ahead. By identifying emerging trends, they project their future impact on the current social and economic scene.

If futurists are astute in the identification of a trend, and imaginative as to its ultimate consequence, their futuristic perceptions may be quite accurate. Obviously such knowledge has great importance to industries, in preparing for change. A good futurist is invaluable; a poor one may well prove disastrous.

4

Trends evidencing the directions of future change were emerging throughout certain parts of the province at the outset of the Manning years. Not surprisingly, the evidence of shifting directions became apparent in a provincial region immediately north of the American boundary. This vast prairie region was pierced by a railway that ran from Stirling, south of Lethbridge, through such hamlets and villages as Foremost, Etzikom, Orion and Manyberries, to end in Shaunavon, Saskatchewan.

At the bottom of the province, stretching along the American border, there were ranches reminiscent of the West's 19th-century ranching era. The Gilchrist brothers, three sons of an English family that had settled in a place called White Mud, south of Maple Creek, Saskatchewan, in the late 19th century, had created a vast ranching empire.

The story of this family is not widely known. One wonders what motivated these first generation Canadians of English immigrant parents to re-enact the experiences of others derived during an earlier century.

By the early '20s, the Gilchrist holdings stretched from the Alberta border in One Four, (Township One, Range One, East of the Fourth Meridien) west to Milk River. Reuban "Reub" Gilchrist owned the Wild Horse Ranch, named after the border crossing into the United States, located in the southeastern corner of the province. Chester "Chay"

Gilchrist's ranch called the BAR Z — the brand used to identify his cattle — came next. Joe Gilchrist's Lost River Ranch completed the Gilchrist holdings, on its western boundary.

The estimated size of the three ranches, covering hilly land unattractive to homesteaders, was 1,000,000 hectares. The vegetation on which their cattle fed was called short grass, a well-rooted succulent plant that had long ago adapted to the vagaries of prairie weather. During earlier centuries, the buffalo probably fed on those grass-covered hills.

Further west toward Aden, a settlement located midway between two American entry points — Wild Horse and Coutts — ranches equally as large occupied land shunned by earlier homesteaders. The Mac Higdon and the George Ross ranches were both well-known spreads in southern Alberta.

Immediately north of these ranching regions, during Alberta's earlier years, homesteaders had settled south and north of railway stations and their accompanying hamlets and villages. As noted earlier, these were such as Foremost, Nemiscam, Etzikom, Orion and Manyberries. Typical of other parts of the province, one-room schools dotted the prairie landscape, providing schooling for the children of these early settlers. By the beginning of the Manning Years, the enrollments in these white-frame school houses had begun to diminish.

The Foremost School Division was one of the earliest, large administrative units deriving from Aberhart's educational reforms.[2] The division included all the rural school districts in a territory stretching from Coutts and Milk River on its western boundaries, to the Cypress Hills and the Alberta-Saskatchewan border on the east. The division stretched northward from the Foremost coulee to include rural school districts surrounding villages such as Burdet, Bow Island and Whitla. These were located on the railway connecting the cities of Lethbridge and Medicine Hat.

Had this area existed in Europe, it might conceivably have contained a small country. Within the Foremost School Division's boundaries, there were a hundred or more rural school districts, all with diminishing enrollments.

The Divisional School Board, made up of five members, met once a month in the divisional office, located in Foremost, for a one- or two-day meeting. They established policy governing the maintenance of these rural schools, the employment of their teachers, and the delivery of school services. They travelled distances of 80 kilometres or more to attend these monthly board meetings. Each spoke for a particular subdivision of the division, reporting on problems that emerged from time to time during the school year.

The membership of the board during the '40s reflected the essentially rural character of the province's new school divisions. The chairman of the Foremost Divisional Board, Olaf Solberg, was a well-educated, dignified, elderly Norwegian farmer whose farm of 130 hectares was located between Foremost and Bow Island. Foster Gow, a farmer living near Whitla, represented the schools in the northeast subdivision. James Underdahl, a retired mounted policeman and local magistrate, came from Mannyberries. His responsibility was for the schools in the eastern subdivision, up to and including three school districts on the top of the Cypress Hills. He later became an MLA in support of the Manning government. Jack Griffiths, a small rancher from Aden, looked after the schools in the subdivision between Foremost and the American border. Leonard Halmrast, a sheep rancher from Masinasin (Writing on Stone), exercised responsibility for the schools in the southwestern subdivision. He finished his political career as minister of agriculture in the Manning government.

The Foremost School Division employed a full-time secretary-treasurer, David Terriff, whose responsibility it was to keep minutes of board proceedings, look after board finances, and pay the teachers and other board employees. The Provincial Department of Education designated a departmental employee as superintendent of schools within the division, and inspector of schools for the town and village districts not part of the Foremost School Division. This departmental official served as educational adviser to the board.[3]

No one would have considered this group advanced or revolutionary thinkers in rural education, but essentially, they were. They had adopted as an overriding policy, wherever feasible, the centralization of school services. This concept added a new dimension to school management, that of transportation. Their major objective, was to remove the one-room school as a basic organizational unit and they derived much pleasure in performing their public service as divisional school trustees, through planning school centralizations.

Mill Creek school district 355, 1921.
Photo courtesy of the Provincial Archives of Alberta, E. Brown Collection, B-3958.

A school centralization, in its simplest and least expensive form, consisted of four one-room school buildings moved to a central location. This, in effect, made possible a grouping of grades up to and including grade 11.

The divisional board members found the planning for transporting pupils to these centralizations especially challenging. It involved not only securing van drivers and specifying the type of vehicle they should supply, but designing bus routes, and persuading the municipal council to grade the roads designated as bus routes.

Most of the roads so designated had hitherto been nothing more than prairie trails. To assure year-round transportation, it was necessary to build highways of a certain height and contour. During a winter snowstorm, the winds would more readily blow the snow off these improved roads, making winter traffic possible.

The centralization of schooling at first met with local opposition. Rural people had become attached to their one-room white school houses. In many cases, they had served not only as schools, but as community centres. Why was this "big board" from Foremost daring to alter long established patterns in living? Interestingly, the opposition disappeared rapidly after the centralization began operation. It was not so much the improved educational facilities that won approval as the quality of the roads that centralization had generated.

By the end of the '40s, the Foremost School Divisional Board had transformed its school system into a group of centralizations of varying sizes. These were of two types. A rural centralization stood alone on the prairies, remote from any hamlet, village, or town. The teachers generally resided in teacherages on the school grounds. Often they rode in the buses from some distant point along with their pupils. A farmer's wife, for instance, with a teaching certificate secured through normal school attendance, irrespective of its date, might augment the farm income by returning to the practise of her profession. This was particularly true during times of severe teacher shortages, a condition that existed throughout the '40s.

The other type of centralization was established in the hamlets and villages located on the two railway lines that traversed the division. A network of bus routes stretched out in all directions from these centres, along which school buses gathered up their loads of young Canadians each morning, and returned them to their homes in the late afternoon.

Class in session, Horse Hills School.
Photo courtesy of the Provincial Archives of Alberta, E. Brown Collection, B-3955.

These centralizations provided schooling for their pupils in graded classrooms, through grades 1 to 12. Again, one-room schools were moved in from the surrounding rural districts to augment the limited classroom space that existed in buildings built in these village districts prior to the centralization movement.

That movement, emerging first in the province's extremities, became a growing trend that would envelope the entire province during the Manning years. Even an inadequate futurist might have forecast that this would occur. Within the next two decades, those white outposts of learning disappeared from the Alberta landscape to be sold to private owners for a variety of purposes. Many were converted into residences; at least one served as a studio for an Alberta artist for several years.

Interestingly, the last school division to succumb to the centralizing movement was located in the centre of the province — the Red Deer School Division. That division had modernized its rural schools in an attempt to retain this last symbol of an early 20th-century idyllic society.

Evidences of another trend emerged in southern Alberta during the first decade of the Manning years. This trend had both social and economic implications for Albertans far greater than those posed by the disappearing one-room school house. Nonetheless, the two trends in a sense were closely related.

In the Foremost School Inspectorate, which included the hamlets, villages, and towns, as well as the rural areas, the bulk of the student population came from the surrounding farms. Alberta remained a predominantly rural province.

An astute observer, however, might have pointed to evidences of trends that would engender change, unthinkable as that might be. School centralization was actually a response to lower enrollments in rural schools. There was, however, another trend emerging, much more substantial than that of diminishing rural school enrollments. After all, the family farm of 130 hectares was still the norm.

In retrospect, the two following examples in southern Alberta provided evidence of this emerging trend. Art Frankish, a farmer who operated a machine agency in Foremost, had developed a farm containing some five sections of land. His farm was completely mechanized, including even a small aeroplane. Another farm located between Foremost and Stirling, the Wesley holdings, was reputed to embrace more than 30 sections.

These were both single crop operations devoted exclusively to the production of wheat. While the smaller ½ and ¾ section farms were still the norm, the number of full-section farms was on the increase. This trend to large-scale farming was still confined to dry land areas. Farms under the ditch, that is irrigated, still adhered to traditional acreages.

By the end of the Manning years, the farm consolidation movement had enveloped the province. Alberta's agriculture was well on the way toward becoming entirely mechanized. The farmer with holdings of several sections, who produces wheat exclusively and who buys his vegetables at a modern supermarket, was becoming the norm.

Notes

[1] Alf Hooke, *"30 + 5" I know I Was There* (Edmonton: Institute of Applied Art, 1971), Chapter Eighteen.

[2] The enlarged school divisions were later to become part of the modern counties, within which both rural municipalities and school divisions are included. The Foremost School Division became part of the County of Forty Mile, to be governed by the school committee of the county council.

[3] The author of this book was superintendent of the Foremost School Division, and inspector of schools for the Foremost Inspectorate from 1942 to 1947.

Chapter Thirteen
The Turbulent Sixties

1

The '60s was a decade of growth and expansion in Canada generally, including Alberta. It was also a period of protest and change. Because Alberta's history is part of the larger Canadian story, certain historical events within Canada and abroad have tended to influence those in Alberta.

Three leaders emerged during the '60s to affect the course of Canada's history. The first of these, John G. Diefenbaker, a Saskatchewan criminal lawyer and leader of the Progressive Conservative party, became prime minister of Canada following the defeat of the St. Laurent government on the floor of the Canadian House of Commons in 1957.

Diefenbaker, during a federal election called the following year, swept into power with a parliamentary majority established by securing 205 seats in the Commons. With such a phenomenal victory, this western Canadian lawyer had wiped out the Social Credit representation from Alberta, thus ending the hope of that movement ever becoming a force in Canadian politics.

Lester B. Pearson was the second Canadian leader to emerge during the '60s. He was Canada's prime minister from 1963 to 1968. During those years, he introduced certain policies that have become integral facets of Canadian society. One such policy — that of bilingualism and biculturalism (B and B) — recognized Canada as a country of two languages and two cultures, English and French.

Pearson also introduced the *Canada Pe*nsion Act, a program now familiar to all who are members of Canada's work force. Canada's present flag was designed and approved by its parliament during the Pearson administration. Pearson is recognized historically as having contributed to his fellow countrymen the fruits of universal medicare. In effect, Pearson provided 20th-century Canadians with the benefits and shortcomings of the welfare state.

The third leader to appear on the Canadian political scene during the '60s was Pierre Elliot Trudeau. In April of 1968, he became Canada's fifteenth prime minister. Trudeau's prime ministership extended throughout the '70s and, except for a brief interlude at the end of that decade, continued until 1984.

His first contributions to Canadian law were rendered during the '60s when he served as minister of justice in the Pearson cabinet. He gained national attention for his introduction of legislation providing reform in Canadian divorce proceedings. Trudeau also introduced amendments to the Criminal Code, liberalizing laws on abortion, homosexuality, and public lotteries. He became a proponent of a strong federal government, opposing the nationalist ambitions of provinces such as Quebec.

The Cold War had emerged during the '50s to create international tensions that were to continue throughout the next several decades. The Cold War had been exacerbated by the Cuban missile crisis in 1962. Reports were circulated that Nikita Kruschev had decided to install ballistic missiles in Cuba, a small island state off the coast of the United States, with a communist government. These missiles were designed to strike at the United States and Canada in the event of war.

John F. Kennedy immediately announced a blockade of Cuba to prevent this from happening. He also asked Canada to move its military forces to an alert status, a request with which Douglas Harkness, minister of defence in the Diefenbaker cabinet, was prepared to comply.

Prime Minister Diefenbaker, however, was hesitant to agree with this request. He was intent on demonstrating his independence of American influence, irrespective of its purpose. Furthermore, he had met Kennedy and the meeting had been far from successful. This elderly Saskatchewan lawyer, steeped in prairie conservatism, found little to admire in the youthful, vigorous Kennedy with his liberal ideas. Apparently, this lack of regard was mutual. Nonetheless, Diefenbaker grudgingly agreed with the recommendation of his defence minister.

In any event, the forceful opposition of both North American nations convinced Kruschev to withdraw his missiles from Cuban soil. Fidel Castro, Cuba's lifelong dictator, was left without his menacing play things.

The concern aroused by the Cold War led the federal government to plan for national emergencies that might include not only invasions but other forms of national disasters. One tangible step was to create a headquarters in each province to deal with such events. The government directed a company called Fenco to construct a safe retreat at Penhold, south of Red Deer. From this carefully hidden headquarters, certain key people could organize and direct what might be termed disaster services.

The Alberta headquarters, completed in 1964, was built underground. One descends by elevator into a suite of rooms which include a work room, some bedrooms, a kitchen, and storage space, containing sufficient food to last for a long period of time. In the event of a disaster, the provincial premier would direct activities from this centre, aided by a staff selected from senior officials. These would be chosen from such government departments as those of the attorney general, health, highways, provincial treasurer, and agriculture.

For most Albertans during the '60s, this fear of communism meant very little. They saw it, largely, as being generated for political ends. They might have agreed, tacitly, that those who espoused communism were, if not fanatics, at least being misled by false prophets. Few had ever heard of Karl Marx, and those that may have known about him were unlikely to have read his book, *Das Kapital*. The word communism probably aroused, in most people, an uneasy feeling that could be readily dispelled by changing the subject.

There were other matters during that interesting decade that caught public attention. For instance, Canada's 100th birthday in 1967 dominated the attention of all Canadians throughout that year. A feeling of optimism for Canada's future pervaded the country. Canada, during its first century as a nation, had achieved a great deal. Canadians looked forward to even greater achievements in the century ahead.

One of the intriguing events during the '60s might be described as the youth movement. This movement was one of protest, of refusal to accept the views, practises or even values of the older generation. Many young people, bent on discovering themselves, disregarded the expectations of their parents. They preferred, rather, to explore the world with pack sacks on their backs. This movement, in some respects, dominated the spirit of the '60s, a decade during which the unconventional often met with approval.

2

This general description of the '60s decade is a backdrop against which one may view the final events of the Manning era. Although the Social Credit League was still in existence, there was little about those events that bore any relationship to its aims and objectives. As Manning said, eventually one gives up trying to batter a wall down with one's head.

During the '60s, Manning gained another source of information and another perception of a major provincial institution. Preston Manning graduated in 1965 from the University of Alberta with an honors degree in economics. Whatever Manning Sr., with his Bible school background, may have thought about university programs, his views were now being influenced by those of his brilliant young son.

During his undergraduate years, Preston met several students not unlike himself. They were serious-minded, highly intelligent, and likely to find public service roles attractive. None was pursuing a degree from the professional faculties such as medicine, law, or engineering. They were, in the main, students of disciplines in the social sciences or the humanities. It is highly improbable that any one of those youthful Albertans ever considered joining a university fraternity.

For students of this type, the university provides a special type of environment, particularly for those who do not enter the professional faculties. This environment tends to stimulate discussion about contemporary society, its inadequacies and how to solve them. While the intellectual climate of the modern university, may not reach that of Ancient Athens, there are many professors who strive to create such an atmosphere. Those who have pursued a baccalaureate in arts without experiencing this climate have missed its actual essence. One could not hope to have such an experience in a Bible college.

This may well have been that which attracted Ernest Manning to the proposal that certain members of this group of students be appointed to serve the government. He may have seen this as a way of dealing with a problem which he had identified during the final years of his premiership. He concluded that governments long in power find it difficult to foster new ideas. They tend, rather, to re-emphasize their original contributions by cloaking them in new verbal garments.

He developed this concept in the field of political science through an insight deriving from practical experience. As a politician, if not as a preacher, Manning was the supreme pragmatist.

Members of this group entered the pages of Alberta's history as so-called advisers to government. Their presence was not announced by cabinet ministers nor by the long-established and aging leaders of the

Social Credit League. They were well-known, however, and often resented by those within government circles. Members of this young coterie of political experts found it difficult to understand the antagonism they engendered.

The presence of what appeared to be a significantly powerful group not customarily found in government could not long be kept from public knowledge. An ever-watchful press, an essential instrument of any democracy, sooner or later discovers the unusual. How the press became aware of their presence is, in retrospect, difficult to ascertain. Conceivably, someone within government brought it to the attention of the *Edmonton Journal*.

A reporter immediately sought an interview with one or two members of this young elite group. They talked freely, even boastfully, of the access they had been given to cabinet meetings and its proceedings.

The next day the story was headlined in the *Edmonton Journal*. The group was labelled as the "whiz kids," a sobriquet which gave these young elitists their place in Alberta's history. The article identified the group's members, detailing, as well, their responsibilities in government.

The most important member of the group was, of course, Preston Manning. He did not enter government service, but he obviously had a special relationship with the premier. Actually, Preston ran in the 1965 federal election on the Social Credit ticket, but was roundly defeated.

Erick Schmidt was, perhaps, the most influential of those who played a role within government. That he was at one time a candidate for the Baptist ministry may have cemented his very close relationship with Premier Manning. A highly imaginative and far-sighted thinker and practising sociologist, Schmidt was responsible for the establishment of an information magazine called *Land for the Living*, which focused on the impact of urbanization on the future.

Don Hamilton, an ordained minister of the United Church with a strong bent for business affairs, was appointed the first director of the Alberta Service Corps. This organization was a volunteer action group made up of university students. The corps was designed to serve those lacking in opportunities to make a gainful living.[1] Hamilton later became executive assistant to Premier Strom.

Owen Anderson, a graduate in political science from the University of Alberta, had been born and raised in Medicine Hat, a city very close to the county of Forty Mile. Premier Strom, who appears later in this story, commenced his political career in Forty Mile by serving there as a municipal councillor. Anderson was in his late 20s when he received an appointment as executive assistant to Premier Strom during the final years of the Manning era. He shared this responsibility with Don Hamilton.[2]

These were perhaps the most significant of those who were dubbed the "Whiz Kids." Others, such as John Barr, served as advisers to members of the Executive Council. Barr was attached to the Ministry of Education.

3

Many people write books. Writing a book is, nonetheless, not a particularly easy task. It requires a modicum of ideas, some capacity to express those ideas in written prose, and a considerable degree of persistent application to the business of writing. The problem lies not in the writing, but in the publishing. For most people, it is infinitely easier to write a book than find a publisher to preserve one's golden prose in print. This is especially true if the would-be author is relatively unknown and is seeking to establish a literary reputation.

When a public figure decides to write a book, this becomes a different matter. Even if that figure is not too proficient at writing, he or she can readily find a scribe who will provide such a skill. The public figure contributes the ideas and experiences gained in some other field, and behold! A new book appears in the marketplace.

The premier of a province is undoubtedly a public figure. Ernest Manning was not only a provincial premier, but an eminently successful one. By the early '60s, he had won six elections, most of them with sweeping majorities. Any book written by such a political leader might conceivably catch the fancy of a customarily obdurate reading public.

Manning's book was undoubtedly written by the young men he had turned toward during the final years of his premiership. Those responsible for the writing were his son Preston and Erick Schmidt, a youthful sociologist who had exercised considerable influence on both Mannings. Nonetheless, the ideas contained in the book were those of Premier Manning. They expressed his views on political affairs at the federal level.

The book, entitled *Political Realignment, A Challenge to Thoughtful Canadians*, was published by McClelland and Stewart of Toronto in 1967. During this year, Manning fought his final election to win a resounding victory. There was, however, a small opposition of six Progressive Conservatives elected as MLAs, a portent of what was yet to come.

A particular organization assisted Manning in the publication of this book that was highly unlikely to recover its production costs. This organization was known as The National Affairs Research Foundation. A rather obscure body, the foundation was apparently intent on fostering private enterprise. It has been labelled by one writer as being "right wing." R.A. Brown Jr. was currently head of the organization.[3]

Manning had concluded in *Political Realignment* that Social Credit had no future at the federal level. The party had been almost completely decimated by the Diefenbaker sweep during 1958. He called upon all members of the Social Credit League to support what he termed a social conservative party.

He insisted that there were basic defects in the organizations and structures beneath and behind Canada's national leaders. These political organizations overlapped in their policies. They were too much alike.

Social conservatism would combine the best elements of two traditions in Western thought. Its purpose would be that of creating an internally consistent ideology, one specifically oriented to the character and requirements of the Canadian nation.

In effect, a social conservative party would harness the free enterprise economic sector to the task of attaining those humanitarian goals for which socialists had been clamoring.

The following are some of the ideals toward which this realigned party would strive:

1. The attainment and conservation of liberty for each individual.
2. Conservation of a national community of diversity.
3. Prosperity for each Canadian.
4. Attainment of liberty, community and prosperity.

Manning concluded that the Progressive Conservative party possessed the greatest potential as a vehicle for this realignment. He dismissed members of the New Democratic party (NDP) as reactionary socialists. As for the Liberals, they were too much inclined toward collectivism. Needless to say, the Progressive Conservatives ignored the invitation to participate in realignment.

Many dedicated adherents to the Social Credit movement consider Manning's book to have rung its final death knell. This is probably true. Although Manning's book is important in that it reveals the evolution in his political thought, by the time the book was published, for most Albertans, Social Credit had become nothing more than a dim memory of a decade that few wished to recall.

4

During March 1967, immediately prior to the final election under his leadership, Premier Manning presented to the provincial legislature the *White Paper on Human Resource Development*. A white paper, traditionally, is a thought-provoking statement designed to generate debate on proposals for political action.

This particular paper set government policy for the remaining years of the Manning administration. This long, repetitive, and somewhat tedious document contains many ideas of merit. To understand Manning's views during the final years of his premiership, one must endure at least some of its turgid prose. A companion piece to Manning's book, the paper was similarly prepared, in part, by Manning's executive assistant, Erick Schmidt.[4]

The basic theses of the White Paper was that people in young communities, such as Alberta, turn their attention first to the exploitation of physical resources — an activity labelled in the paper, as Physical Resource Development, (PRD). As wealth is accumulated through PRD, people then direct their efforts toward the development of human resources. This activity is recognized in the White Paper as Human Resource Development (HRD). The relationship between PRD and HRD is set out in the White Paper through both language and diagrams.

The paper stressed certain principles which doubtless reflected Manning's political philosophy toward the end of his premiership. They were:

1. Human resources will be treated as intrinsically more important than physical resources.
2. Prior consideration will be given to human beings individually, rather than to human beings collectively, i.e., society.
3. Changes, and adjustment to changes will be proposed, but these must always be related to fundamental principles.

4. A free enterprise economy, one in which all individuals will be regarded as more desirable than in a state regimented economy.
5. A supporting function, rather than a domineering function, will be ascribed to the state relative to resource development.

In addition to stating Manning's philosophy, the White Paper contained the philosophical orientation of the Social Credit government. One finds difficulty in distinguishing between Manning's views and those of his government. Doubtless, some members of the Executive Council differed with Manning on occasion. Nonetheless, the quiet strength of this man was such that his views usually predominated. Their respect for their chief was so great, they had little desire to challenge him.

Manning was convinced that a government should express, through its policies and actions, certain basic principles and values. Presumably this is its ideology, the driving force that dominates a party in its quest for power. This view had been expressed, as well, in his recently published book.

Not content with the first outline of principles and values, the authors of the White Paper expanded on these further in the following series of numbered statements:

1. Individual human beings are more important than nonhuman things.
2. No two individuals are exactly alike. Variety in human life, associations, and culture should be recognized, appreciated and encouraged.
3. Society exists to enhance the development of free and creative human beings, and should aspire to the full and free development of the human resources of that nation.
4. The supreme objective in developing the physical resources of a nation should be to make possible the full and free development of the nation's human resources.
5. The institution of government is both a product and an instrument of human development and good government is responsible to the people it serves.
6. The primary rights and responsibilities for the development of the human resources of a nation should reside with individual citizens and associations of citizens with responsible government performing a supporting function.

7. The primary rights and responsibilities for the development of the physical resources of a nation, (i.e., the national economy), should reside with private citizens, with responsible government performing a supporting function.

This new emphasis, deriving from the above statement of guiding principles, was set out in the following paragraphs:

"The time has come for government to declare its emphasis on human resource development. This new emphasis will be directed toward the individual, rather than society. We must avoid the error of collectivist or socialistic reforms, coercive measures to force individuals into a mold. This emphasis is oriented toward encouraging the individual to achieve his or her full potential. We need a society, the characteristics of which will be determined, not by state planners, but by free and creative individuals.

"The acquisition of physical resources is not an end in itself. That wealth must be used to facilitate that which is infinitely more important — the development of human resources — of free and creative people.

"To achieve this, Alberta needs a free enterprise economy. The exploitation of the province's physical resources should be the responsibility of the private sector. Harnessing an economy, based on the principles of economic freedom, to the task of achieving objectives stemming from humanitarian values — that is the major challenge. In meeting this challenge, the individual human being is the supremely important unit of consideration."

Although the White Paper continues beyond this outline for several pages, this provides the reader with its essence. Quite obviously, provincial resources accumulated during the Dynamic Decade were now to be devoted to the production of free and creative individuals.

Notes

[1] John Barr, *The Dynasty. The Rise and Fall of Social Credit in Alberta* (Toronto: McClelland and Stewart Ltd., 1974).

[2] Don Hamilton ran for the political post of mayor of Edmonton in 1989.

[3] Brown's career in the Alberta oil industry was described in Chapter Eleven.

[4] Erick Schmidt first made his mark in Alberta's history as director of human resource development.

Chapter Fourteen
Institutions for Human
Resource Development

1

According to views expressed by Premier Manning in his White Paper presented to the Alberta legislature in 1967, he thought his government should turn its attention to the development of human resources. These resources were the free and creative people that would build a Christian democracy.

How were they to be developed? One can only assume that they were the products of post-secondary institutions, the universities, colleges, and technical institutes that evolved during the '60s — the most creative decade of the 20th Century.

Many movements converged during the '60s, all of which contributed to the transformation of Alberta. The most significant, as noted earlier, was the urbanization of Alberta. Other movements, not caused by this but closely related to it, altered the nature of Alberta and its people.

One of these had to do with people. Following the Second World War, a boom in babies emerged in Canada, as it did throughout all countries that had been involved in the conflict. This phenomenon is not unusual after a war, particularly one as devastating as that which occurred in Europe during the early '40s.

By the mid '60s, these Baby Boomers had finished grade school, and many were intent on pursuing some form of post-secondary or vocational studies. The demands of this greatly enlarged group of young men and women stimulated growth and change in the province's educational organizations.

The University of Alberta had commenced its institutional existence in 1908, shortly after the province was born. It had grown, not only in student enrollment but in the breadth of its curriculum under the skillful administration of its first president, Henry Marshall Tory, from 1908 to

Panoramic view of the University of Alberta, 1929.
Photo courtesy of the University of Alberta Archives.

1928. By the end of the '20s, the university was offering degree programs in the arts and sciences, law, medicine, dentistry, commerce, and household economics. Starting with an initial enrollment of 45, by 1929 overall student attendance had reached 1,560.

In 1945, the university had assumed responsibility for the preparation of all teachers, including those both elementary and secondary. This ended existence for the provincial normal schools of Edmonton and Calgary, teacher training institutions which, along with Camrose Normal, had supplied staff for provincial schools throughout the century's earlier decades. The Calgary Normal School, as with that of Edmonton, became part of the university's Faculty of Education, thereby providing the University of Alberta with its Calgary campus.

Immediately following the Second World War, in Alberta and elsewhere, university enrollments began to mount. In the University of Alberta, full-time enrollment, that had hovered around the 2,000 mark for almost half a century, accelerated. By 1958, it had reached 4,280. This increase led to a vigorous building program on both campuses during the '40s and '50s.

The Baby Boom generation exerted pressure on a number of university places at the beginning of the '60s. The full-time enrollment on the Edmonton campus tripled between 1957 to 1966 to arrive at a figure of nearly 16,000. Likewise, enrollment on the Calgary campus increased ten times throughout those years to reach 1,400, a spectacular growth within a nine-year time frame.

During 1960, the Calgary campus had moved from its original location on the grounds of the Institute of Technology to the first buildings on its

permanent site. These new buildings, and the increasing student enrollment, tended to focus the attention of Calgarians on this relatively recent
addition to the city's cultural and educational life.

By the mid '60s, the University of Alberta faced such questions as
these: Could it meet the rising demands for university places through its
southern campus? Could the University of Alberta administer its
southern campus effectively by remaining as a single administrative
unit? The University of Alberta had established separate faculties in
Calgary for the arts and the sciences, for education, and for engineering
between 1963 and 1965. Was this adequate?

Calgarians, in general, began to exert pressure on government and on
university authorities. Calgary students, specifically, took up the cause
of autonomy for their campus with vigor and enthusiasm. Autonomy for
Calgary became their favorite watchword. Whether their views were
shared by staff members of the southern campus has never been
recorded; the probability of this having been the case is reasonably high.

Ultimately, the Manning government responded to these pressures
from the southern city. Perhaps the most telling influence toward this
response was exerted by a recommendation from the University of
Alberta Board of Governors. The board had sought and received advice
from a committee headed by Justice Hugh John MacDonald. The committee had recommended that Calgary become an independent university. This led the board to suggest a departure from the policy of a unified
university, one that had been in vogue for some 60 years.

The Manning government in 1966, made the most sweeping revision
in university legislation since the original 60-year-old act had been
formulated giving birth to the University of Alberta. This new legislative
version created the University of Calgary and at the same time extended
to it control over the Banff School of Fine Arts.

Furthermore, the revised act made provision for the creation of future
universities. Rather than by acts of the legislature, the government could
now establish a university through an executive order-in-council.

This act not only created Alberta's second university, it also set up a
universities' commission. The purpose of the commission was to coordinate the province's emerging university system by serving as an
intermediary between it and government.

The commission performed this coordinating role by advising government on the system's financial needs; by aiding the universities in

preparing and implementing developmental plans; and by regulating their expansion in programs. The commission did this regulating to avoid unnecessary duplication in services.

During 1967, the government used its new powers to found, through an order-in-council, Alberta's third university, the University of Lethbridge. At the same time, it directed the commission to examine the need for a fourth university.

The Manning government, during the course of the fifteenth legislature, had altered the pattern of provincial university organization. It had abandoned the principle of a unified, or centralized, provincial university such as the State University of California. It had chosen, instead, to substitute a university system composed of two or more institutions, each fully autonomous and depending on two sources of income — student fees and government support.

2

A second group of human resource institutions deeply rooted in Alberta's past was that of the colleges. Within this group there existed greater institutional variety than among those falling under the rubric of university. The term "college" actually encompassed a wide diversity in types. These various types had emerged at different periods throughout the province's history.

By 1916, 11 years following the province's birth, Alberta boasted no fewer than 14 institutions of higher, or post-secondary education. These encompassed a university, a technical institute, two normal schools, three agricultural schools, and seven privately supported colleges.

The colleges were, with one exception, church related. The exception, a Calgary institution, lasted from 1912 to 1915. While it had only a brief period of duration, Calgary College caught the attention of Albertans for a much longer period. Its story involved at least one very prominent and newsworthy Calgarian.

The action that first aroused Calgarians was of political origin. Since Calgarians had failed to have their city designated as the province's capital, they expected that, at least, the provincial university should be theirs.

This was not to happen. A political decision intervened. Dr. Alexander Rutherford, Alberta's first premier, appointed by the Laurier government at the time the province was created, remained in that office until 1910. He was not only leader of the government, but also minister of education.

Rutherford decided to locate Alberta's first university in his own riding, which happened to be Strathcona. He very conscientiously did not select Edmonton as the site, thereby avoiding the criticism that he was favoring the northern city over its southern competitor. That the site he selected was directly across the North Saskatchewan river from the capital city was sheer coincidence.

A number of Calgarians including R.B. Bennett, a future Canadian prime minister, immediately began a campaign to secure a university for Calgary. Calgary at that time had a population of 40,000, large enough to justify becoming a university town. It was also an important rail centre, with railway lines branching out from it in all directions. While the West of an earlier ranching period gave Calgary much of its local color, the flood of immigration during the century's first decade had increased the importance of the city's surrounding farming areas.

Bennett was elected as a member of the Alberta legislature in 1910.[1] One of the first actions Bennett undertook in the provincial legislature was to introduce a bill proposing the establishment of a university in Calgary. The provincial government, however, took the position that a second university would lead to inter-institutional competition, while a single university would tend to unify the province. The government amended the bill to grant Calgary a non-degree granting college.

The privately financed Calgary College opened in 1912. Those who were financing the college continued their campaign in the legislature to secure degree-granting status for their venture into higher education.

This legislative issue did not disappear during the years of the college's operation from 1912 to 1915. Finally, the Alberta government in 1914 set up a commission of three university presidents from other provinces to study the matter and make recommendations.

The Falconer Commission, as it was then called, agreed that a second university, in competition for both students and funds, would not be in the best interests of higher education within the province. However, the commission did agree that the Calgary College's proposal for an institution emphasizing science and technology had merit.

Accordingly, the commission in its report recommended that the government should create an institute of technology and art in Calgary rather than a second university.

The government did not act immediately on this proposal. The decision as to which government, provincial or local, should support this new institution had to first be settled. The Canadian government showed increased interest in an institution for the training of disabled veterans from the First World War. With federal assistance, Alberta agreed to pay for the operation of this new institution and the Calgary Public School Board provided space in its Colonel Walker School.

In October of 1916, the first publicly supported technical institute on the continent, the Provincial Institute of Technology and Art, opened its doors.[2]

Alberta College, the province's first institution in higher education was established in Edmonton by the Methodist church during 1903. It extended the college's services, further, by creating Alberta College South for the preparation of ministers. The church located this extension on the University of Alberta campus in Strathcona during 1911.[3]

Robertson College provided a Presbyterian presence on the campus during the same year. These two church-related colleges merged to become St. Stephen's College, following church union in 1925.

Camrose Lutheran College came into existence in 1910, reflecting the religious identification of the surrounding settlers. College St. Jean, a Roman Catholic school, first began operation in Pincher Creek, Alberta, to settle permanently in Edmonton during 1910.

Affiliation of these colleges with the University of Alberta came gradually. Through an affiliated relationship, the University of Alberta recognized instruction within a college as valid standing toward the granting of its baccalaureate degree. St. Stephen's College had such a relationship on the date of its creation. Concordia College in Edmonton had entered into this relationship during 1921. St. Joseph's College, a Roman Catholic institution, was built on the University of Alberta campus in 1926 to become affiliated immediately with the university.

The University of Alberta, during 1930, set up a committee on college affiliation. The purpose of the committee was to establish criteria for such a relationship. These criteria included the qualifications of staff members, the availability of a well-stocked library, and the extent of laboratory facilities. The committee was also responsible for the application of these criteria and for monitoring affiliation arrangements.

Mount Royal College in Calgary, during 1931, commenced offering first year courses in the arts and the sciences leading to a baccalaureate degree. It was, in fact, the first junior college with university affiliation in the province.

The demand for post-secondary education following the Second World War grew from both industrial and demographic pressures. Accompanying industrial growth in Canada came the need for people with knowledge and skills beyond those required for farming. Furthermore, the service industries, which had become an integral part of an information society emerging during the '50s and '60s, also required people with higher education. Combine these demands with the presence of a Baby Boom generation seeking ways of entering the labor force and the pressures for advanced education became irresistible.

The forerunner of the modern college first emerged in one of Alberta's smaller cities. Lethbridge was the first city to plan and evolve a new type of public college. There were many reasons for this, the major being that Lethbridge was without any post-secondary institution in the '50s, whereas the two larger cities had access to a university and a technical institute.

Furthermore, Lethbridge had excellent leadership in its city school board. Gilbert Patterson and C.M. (Kate) Andrews, trustees of Lethbridge public schools, became active in promoting some form of post-secondary education.

The Lethbridge School Board, in 1950, commissioned a Dr. S.V. Martorana from the United States to make a survey of the post-secondary needs of Lethbridge. He submitted his report in 1951. He concluded that there was insufficient population in Lethbridge to support a college. He recommended that the board add a thirteenth year to the high school program that would include some university transfer courses.

A committee composed of representatives from the various school boards and education committees in the Lethbridge area considered the report. Martorana's main proposal was not accepted. The committee decided to press forward with the creation of a community college.

In 1955, the Lethbridge School District sent an application to the University of Alberta's Board of Governors and to the province's Department of Education. The request was for a college that would provide a university transfer program and other forms of general and vocational education.

Dr. Walter Johns, dean of arts and sciences and president of the University of Alberta from 1959 to 1969, favored the establishment of junior colleges as feeders to the university's degree programs in the arts and the sciences. Anders O. Aalborg, minister of education, 1952-1964, speaking for the government, insisted that as a condition of support these colleges should offer, as well, non-university courses of a vocational or general nature.

The *Junior College Act* of 1958 authorized the establishment of junior colleges by school boards. The purpose of these colleges was to provide university transfer courses of the first year leading to a university degree, and non-university courses of a general or vocational nature.

Under this act, the Lethbridge College came into existence, during 1957. By 1962 it had moved to its own campus. The college, right from its inception, attracted an increasing number of students, not only into the university transfer courses, but into those not leading to university.

Throughout the '60s, junior colleges were established in Red Deer in 1964, Medicine Hat in 1965, and Grande Prairie in 1966. Of the five colleges during that period, only Lethbridge and Mount Royal offered non-university courses. The other three devoted their resources to providing university transfer courses.

The debate on the role of junior colleges continued. Which were they to be? Local service stations for those en route to a university degree, or community colleges serving a broad range of students intent on achieving a variety of purposes?

During the '60s, the debate on the role of the colleges intensified while the population of college students rapidly expanded. Starting with 31 students, the first-year enrollment in Lethbridge, the numbers had grown in the five public colleges to 2,000.

The years 1967 to 1971 saw a transition to a coordinated college system. During 1967, the minister of education, Ray Reierson, appointed a board of post-secondary education, with Gordon Mowat from the University of Alberta as chairman. While this board was short-lived, not more than three years in duration, it was during that time an influential body.

The board was directed to coordinate the work of the several junior colleges. By studying provincial needs, it was to make recommendations to the minister on the future directions of these post-secondary institutions. The board also assumed the role played by the University of Alberta for several years. It was to determine who should be admitted to the colleges, the qualifications of their instructors, and their affiliations with universities. This, the board would do in consultation with the Universities' Coordinating Council.[4]

The Post-Secondary Board recommended a consolidation of the institutes of technology, the agricultural and vocational schools, and the publicly supported colleges into a college system to be supervised by a colleges commission.

Each member of the system would have its own board of governors. Each would be quite distinct and separate from the public school system. These various institutions would no longer depend on local financial support. They would, in fact, be financed much like the universities — by provincial grants and student fees.

The outcome of these recommendations was the *College Act* of 1969. The act revamped the administrative and financing mechanisms for public colleges and shaped the nature of public colleges for the remaining decades of this century. Furthermore, it reiterated and re-emphasized the Manning government's policy, one that favored comprehensive education.

The act established, in line with the recommendations of the Post-Secondary Board, the Colleges Commission, an autonomous corporation analogous to the Universities Commission.[5] This new commission was to advise the government regarding financial support for the college system. It would review for approval the colleges' operating and capital budget. It would act as an intermediary between the universities and the colleges, and between the colleges and the government.

The act was to apply only to public junior colleges. However, if the government so decided, the terms of the act could be extended to include the two technical institutes, the agricultural schools, and the vocational centres. In effect, it might encompass the total non-university sector of post-secondary education.

The act, in fact, eliminated completely the universities' statutory power over university affiliation. Affiliation of the colleges with any of the three provincial universities was still possible. It was, however, no longer necessary. It was now permissible to operate a public college without any university transfer program.

As noted earlier, the various junior colleges had begun to expand their range of general and vocational courses under the short-lived board of post-secondary education. Lethbridge, during 1966, had offered a broad range of programs in the fields of business, technical and vocational studies.

The University of Lethbridge became a reality in 1967, located on a site at some distance from the college. With the removal of all university instruction from its curriculum, Lethbridge College commenced its evolution into a true community college. It focused on the needs of the community rather than the expectations of a senior institution.

The Red Deer, Medicine Hat and Grand Prairie colleges, hitherto way-stations for the university bound, began to follow in the footsteps of the renewed Lethbridge Community College. They not only offered courses in general and vocational studies, but also undertook the delivery of diploma courses in nursing education.

The crowning achievement in community college development occurred in 1970. Grant McEwan College in Edmonton became the first public college to offer exclusively, from the date of its inception, vocational and other non-university courses.

In review, the three final years of the Social Credit government under Manning and Strom, 1967-1971, saw the traditions and practises of the junior college give way to those of a comprehensive, community college. In effect, a network of junior colleges had developed into a distinct system of community colleges.

3

Alberta's government has been interested in agricultural education from its earliest years. The University of Alberta established a faculty of agriculture, providing for a degree in agricultural science in 1915. This degree program did not, however, meet the needs of all farm youth in this predominantly agricultural province.

In 1912, the provincial Department of Agriculture purchased seven farms located strategically throughout the province. These were intended as demonstration centres for the development of the province's agricultural industry.

By 1916, the Alberta government had opened three schools of agriculture, each located on one of these seven farms. These schools were located in or near the towns of Olds, north of Calgary, Claresholm south of that city, and Vermillion east of Edmonton. At the same time, the government created a board of agricultural education to supervise these schools. Dr. H. M. Tory, president of the University of Alberta, became the first chairman of this board.

The purpose of these schools was to provide training in the fields of agriculture and home economics for the sons and daughters of farm families. In so doing, the government hoped not only to retain these young people in the farming industry, but also to increase that industry's productivity.

Encouraged by the success of these first three schools, the government, in 1920, added three more to the system. These were located at Gleichen, Raymond, and Youngstown.

The future of these schools was in no sense secure. The difficulties they encountered were two-fold. The government found that maintaining these six schools was exceedingly costly. Furthermore, despite the predominance of the farming population at that time, the schools did not always attract sufficient students to operate economically.

Gleichen and Youngstown closed in 1922. Vermillion and Raymond lasted until 1923.

The government then built housing accommodation for students at Olds and Vermillion. This, in the long run, brought stability and success to these two agricultural schools. The others became mere memories of a time when the farm family dominated Alberta's social and economic life.

A revival of interest in agricultural education occurred during the '50s. The Board of Agricultural Education, chaired by the minister of agriculture, was revived after three decades of inactivity to become a permanent fixture.

A third agricultural school was built at Fairview, to join Olds and Vermillion. The changing nature of the farming industry, however, had its impact on attendance at these schools. High costs combined with diminishing enrollments, caused the government to reconsider their future. A disastrous fire at the Fairview Agricultural School also contributed to this concern. By the late '50s the permanence of these schools was uncertain.

The Cameron Commission on Education had been established during this period to examine all publicly supported education in the province. The commission, through its report in 1959, made certain recommendations on the schools of agriculture and home economics. It recommended a complete reorganization and modernization of their instructional programs. The report also proposed the introduction of vocational programs, in addition to those of agriculture and home economics. Finally, the report recommended that these schools become part of the provincial college system.[6]

By and large, these recommendations fell on deaf ears in the provincial Department of Agriculture. However, during 1963, as a result of a brief to the minister of agriculture, Harry Strom, the Board of Agricultural Education indicated directions for change.

The redevelopment of the schools following these studies included a change of name for the three schools. They were to be known as agricultural and vocational colleges. A number of new programs were introduced, including business education, clothing design and trade apprenticeships. The role of the schools was clarified further in 1967 through the *Agricultural and Vocational Colleges Act.*

4

During 1960, the federal government introduced the *Technical and Vocational Training Assistance Act*. The legislation was designed to meet the manpower needs of an industrial society. The purpose of the act was to consolidate the federal-provincial cost-sharing arrangements regarding technical and vocational training in high schools and in post-secondary institutions.

The implementation of the act was achieved through the *Technical and Vocational Training Agreement* (TVTA). The federal government paid 75 percent of approved capital expenditures for the first two years of the program and 50 percent thereafter.

The impact of the program was not unlike that which occurred in the provincial university system during the same period. Technical and vocational education was decentralized throughout the province. Alberta received over $70 million through this agreement between 1961 and 1967.

The most notable illustration of its effect resided in the construction of the Northern Alberta Institute of Technology. This institution, a counterpart of the Southern Alberta Institute mentioned earlier, commenced operation in 1962. Within two years, its enrollment exceeded that of its sister institution. By 1966, that enrollment had reached 6,000, making it the largest technical institute in Canada.

These two institutes were concerned with apprenticeship training programs. They placed a high priority on the preparation of engineering technologists and other paraprofessionals in the applied arts and technologies. This distinguished the role of these two institutions from that of the vocational schools. A vocational school concentrates on shorter term, skill-oriented training.

Vocational training also expanded during the '60s with the introduction of the Alberta Vocational Training Program. This was carried out through various Alberta vocational centres located in Calgary, Edmonton, and Fort McMurray. These centres concentrated on academic upgrading and short-term, employment-oriented training. These programs were administered through the Division of Vocational Education in the provincial Department of Education.

As one outcome of Manning's White Paper, the Alberta government created a Human Resources Development Authority. This authority was actually composed of members drawn from the Provincial Executive Council, with a deputy minister directly involved in its day to day operation. This authority had been directed to initiate and to coordinate developmental programs, particularly in the province's underdeveloped areas.

Illustrations of the efforts undertaken by the authority were numerous: AVC Grouard opened in 1970. This centre offered academic upgrading, and prepared Native teacher aides to staff other community vocational centres. Such a centre was also established at Lac La Biche.

Another effort toward solving unemployment in these Native centres was carried out by New Start Inc. This was a Canada-wide research project aimed at solving problems of unemployment in depressed areas. New Start programs were instituted in the smaller Native communities, throughout northeastern Alberta.

One of the final actions of the Strom government in 1969 was to establish a commission on education planning under the direction of Dr. Walter Worth, a member of the University of Alberta's Faculty of Education. His task was to study the province's total educational system, and to recommend such changes in services, administration, and coordination that might adapt the system toward changing social and economic conditions.

Appointed by Strom's Social Credit government, Worth reported to its successor, the Lougheed government, in 1972. The Worth Commission transcended two periods in Alberta's history.[7] The report of that commission not only described in detail the achievements of the '60s in the area of human resource development; it influenced, as well, the course of that development throughout the following decade.

Notes

1 John English, *The Canadian Encyclopedia* (Edmonton: Hurtig Publishers, 1988) Vol. One, pp 203, ff.

2 B.E. Berghofer and A.S. Vladicka, *Access to Opportunity* (Edmonton: Government of Alberta, Dept. of Advanced Education, 1980) p. 5.

3 The union between Edmonton and Strathcona took place in 1912, extending Edmonton's boundaries beyond the Saskatchewan River.

4 The Universities' Coordinating Council was made up of members drawn from the three, subsequently four, provincial universities. The president of each university was invariably a member of the Coordinating Council.

5 The Lougheed government in 1972 eliminated these two commissions, consolidating their powers in the provincial government's Department of Advanced Education. The new department was set up following the defeat of the Social Credit government by Lougheed, leader of a revived Progressive Conservative party, in 1971.

6 This recommendation was not accepted by either the schools of agriculture or the provincial Department of Agriculture. It was quite unlikely that the department would pay any attention to a commission appointed by the minister of education and his department.

7 Commission on Educational Planning, *A Choice of Futures* (Edmonton: The Queens Printer, Province of Alberta).

Chapter Fifteen
Church and Sects in Alberta:
A Protestant Province

1

Comparing Albertans with Quebecois, one immediately focuses on language and religion. The typical Quebecois speaks French, and if he or she attends church, it is likely to be a Roman Catholic one. The typical Albertan of the Manning Era was an Anglophone and if a church member, probably supported one or the other of the several Protestant denominations or sects.

This is not to suggest that Catholics have not played any role in Alberta's development. French fur traders and Catholic missionaries placed their stamp on the Northwest Territories. Furthermore, the flood of immigrants into the Last Best West contained a proportion of Catholic families.

Roman Catholics have built their churches in the villages, towns and cities of the province, stretching from Coutts in the south to Fort Vermilion in the north. Within the province's two major cities, they have constructed two stately cathedrals, each reminiscent of those found in European cities.

Within the towns and villages, despite the stern discipline exercised by the Roman church over its people during the first several decades of this century, Catholics fraternized with their Protestant neighbors. They entered into community activities, working with members of other Christian denominations toward community improvement. The religious animosities of earlier years and distant places seemed to have had little meaning in this Last Best West.

In the province's two major cities, the division between these two Christian groups was less obvious. Catholics entered freely into the various occupational fields. They could be found among the professional and business classes of the two major cities, in numbers proportionate to their respective populations which was about five to one. They operated street cars, clerked in department stores, served as policemen and postmen, drove milk wagons, and owned corner groceries. There were no limits imposed on their vocational ambitions.

Their private lives were, nonetheless, circumscribed by their parishes and separate schools. Theirs might be described as a socio-religious community. Successful men joined the Knights of Columbus. Women became members of the Catholic Women's League. While they read the *Edmonton Journal* or the *Calgary Herald,* depending on the city, the *Western Catholic Reporter*, a paper devoted to church affairs, bonded this minority tightly together with the printed word. Catholics of that period in Alberta's history were fully aware that they lived in a predominantly Protestant society.

Catholic parents were concerned that their children might commit that most fatal of errors, a mixed marriage. The church refused to sanction such a marital union except under two conditions: the Protestant member of the couple proposing matrimony would agree to "turn," that is to become a Catholic. Failing this, that party in the marriage contract must consent to the children, the issue of the marriage, being brought up in the Catholic faith.

The modern transformation of the Catholic church occurred by decisions reached in 1959. Pope John XXIII convened an ecumenical council in Rome. That meeting, one that has become known as Vatican II, introduced the refreshing winds of change in an institution that had clung to its rigid views of Protestantism for many centuries.

The council recognized the primacy of conscience and the real Christian faith of many non-Catholics. As a result, Protestants were promoted from the rank of heretics to that of separated brethren. The church's views on marriage underwent dramatic reversals. Not only did it allow mixed marriages, it now held that the children should be raised in the religious denomination of the most committed Christian partner.[1]

These views, when fully understood and widely recognized, should have gone far to remove the religious animosities of earlier times. The Catholic church, through Vatican II, became a partner with other Christian denominations in the shaping of Christian democracies. Vatican II may well have ended the socio-religious enclaves that characterized the Catholic populations in Alberta's two major cities throughout the early decades of this century.

2

The fact remains, however, that during the Social Credit era, Alberta's population was predominantly Protestant. That term is inclusive of a wide range of groupings. Within its scope, there are many manifestations reflecting the essence of Protestantism.

In its original meaning, the term was applied to those who protested against the teachings promulgated by the Church of Rome. As various divisions within this protest movement emerged, each defined its own perception of how to achieve salvation. This had led to an almost bewildering variety of expressions in faith that fall under the rubric of Protestantism.

The following table provides the reader with a perception of the various Protestant denominations and their numbers in 1946.[2] This is representative of Alberta's religious groupings during the early years of the Manning Administration.

Religious Denominations	Numbers
Church of England	41,600
Baptist	10,000
Lutheran	21,000
Moravian	2,400
Presbyterian	11,000
United Church of Canada	130,000
Fundamentalist Sects	53,790
Others	
Greek Orthodox and Mormon	60,000
Roman Catholic	130,000

While these are estimates, it seems apparent that there were 250,000, out of a contemporary population of 700,000, that had no religious affiliation. One might define this group as secular, a group that would increase proportionately as Alberta's population expanded.

A church is a religious structure that has become well accommodated to the secular world. It is, for the most part, aligned with the middle- and upper-middle classes. To belong to a church is a token of respectability.[3]

Within Canada, there has not been, since its formation in 1867, an official state church. The separation of church and state was fundamental in Canada's original constitution, the *British North America Act.* This was the constitution that prevailed in Canada until 1982. *The Charter of Rights and Freedoms,* an integral part of the Canadian Constitution, patriated by the Canadian parliament in 1982, guarantees Canadian citizens freedom of religion.4

While there is no state church in Canada, there is one that encompasses the largest number of Protestant adherents. The United church fulfills that role in Canada, and, as the figures in the previous table indicate, particularly in Alberta.

The United Church of Canada was established in 1925 through a union between the Presbyterian and Methodist churches of Canada, Newfoundland,and Bermuda. The union also included the Congregational churches of Canada as well. A few Congregational churches, and about a third of the Presbyterians, remained outside the union.

Through this union with the Presbyterians, the United church lost many of the evangelical features of 19th century Methodism. It might actually be described as modern. In fact, the United church had indicated in 1969 that it sought to express a Christian faith in terms both ecumenically acceptable, and readily understandable to new generations.

Perhaps the most significant decision in determining the nature of United church clergy was the requirement that theological students should have a university education. The bachelor degree in the arts or sciences became compulsory for admission to a divinity degree program.

This educationally broad approach to theological training led almost inevitably to modernist views on the part of the clergy. As a result, United church preachers were reputed to have delivered intellectual sermons that went over the heads of their congregation members.[5] This shift toward modernism on the part of the clergy had other outcomes. Emphasis on personal salvation gave way to an examination of social problems. Rather than stressing eternal security, the church focused on issues of social improvement, on problems of poverty and other discriminatory societal features.

Modernism tended to ignore Protestant asceticism as a way of life. Both the Methodists and the Baptists traditionally had frowned on such activities as dancing, card playing, and theatre going as frivolous and unworthy behavior for Christians. Obviously, a church that now catered to the middle classes was unlikely to proscribe their main modes of entertainment.

The professionalization of the United church clergy had its impact on clerical employment. The tendency of ministers to seek appointments in city churches was marked. City congregations were much larger than those in the villages and towns of the province. They usually varied in their membership of from 400-600. One of the most prestigious of charges was that of Central United in Calgary. This church boasted a membership of 3,000.

3

Protestant sects during the Manning era were religious organizations quite unlike those of the conventional and historic Christian church denominations. Mann lists 35 Protestant sects of varying sizes that existed in Alberta at the time of his study.[6]

As discussed earlier, the Protestant denominations such as the Anglican and the United church have long since accommodated to the contemporary world. These historic institutions have not only shaped society; they have also been influenced, over time, by various social forces. Unlike the early Methodists of England, they are, in Canada, closely associated with the middle and upper classes. As with membership in the Rotary Club, an identification with either of these religious organizations carries with it a badge of respectability.

Membership in one or the other of the 35 Protestant sects does not carry a similar status to that accorded by the Protestant denominations. Sects and denominations are, nonetheless, alike in some respects. They are both socio-religious institutions. Here the similarity ends.

A sect is an institution of social and religious protest. Sects have provided at various times support for the poor and the downtrodden in society. In the Manning era, they tended to be fundamentalist in their beliefs, insisting on a literal interpretation of the Bible. The Holy Book was to be accepted as written. It was the source of all truths, the Word of God.

Having taken this position, the sects were opposed to much that had been accepted by modern churches. They might be described as creationists. They rejected completely the theory of evolution, that man had evolved from lower forms of life. Such a theory would have been quite inconsistent with the story of Adam and Eve.

The adherents of these 35 sects, in the main, subscribed to premillenial views. They anticipated the second coming of Christ. They looked forward to the 1,000 years when the ills of the world would be corrected and mankind would live in peace.

The sects tended to accept the concept of asceticism. The Protestant ascetic renounced worldly values, pursuing a lifestyle of self-denial. He or she exercised self-discipline with respect to such pleasures as dancing, attending movies, and other frivolous pastimes. Some, but not all the sects, pictured hell as being filled with fire and brimstone.

Their emphasis on evangelism led to certain forms of religious expression distinctly different from those of the denominations. These forms might be broadly described as revivalist. Revivalist services are noted for their informality and the enthusiastic participation on the part of the congregation. The preaching is emotional, even fervent in tone. Hymn singing is very much a part of the service but it is quite unlike the controlled participation of church congregations. Extemporaneous prayers are voiced, not only by the preacher, but also by members of the congregation. Frequently worshippers shout out such words as Hallelujah!

During these services conversions may occur. These are described as "a dramatic experience of inner melting and of self-surrender to the Almighty." Conversion gives the assurance of salvation.[7] Obviously, these meetings provided an emotional release to their participants. They, in a sense, compensated for the drabness and dreary existence of those who practised ascetic Protestantism.

Another characteristic shared by most sect members was their liking for charismatic leaders. They responded to dominant individuals capable of arousing their emotions. This, too, might explain the fundamentalist's desire for evangelistic preaching.

The Bible school movement, occurring in Alberta after the First World War, emerged as a means of meeting the religious and educational needs of the Protestant sects. The basic and perhaps overriding objective of these Bible schools was to produce pastors for the growing population of fundamentalists in the province. The schools were of two types, those unaffiliated with any particular Protestant sect, and those operated by a sect.

The first and best known of these schools was the Prairie Bible Institute located at Three Hills, Alberta. This particular school was established in 1921. By 1947, it had a student enrollment of 450. Although fundamentalist in its teaching, it operated independently of any particular sect. By 1947, the school had achieved a national reputation.[8]

During the 25 years following 1921, the Bible school movement spread throughout Alberta. The Calgary Prophetic Bible Institute commenced operation in 1929 under the aegis of the Prophetic Baptist sect. Other schools were located in Red Deer, Medicine Hat, Edmonton, Camrose, Grande Prairie, and Sexmith. In all, there were 15 of these biblical study centres within provincial boundaries.

The curriculum followed by these schools was similar, irrespective of the management. Biblical knowledge was basic. Christian apologetics, a course interpreting and defending Christianity, was also part of the curriculum. An emphasis was placed, as well, on the techniques of serving as home missionaries.

There was little or no relationship between these private, sect-related schools, and the province's publicly supported grade schools, colleges and universities. Nevertheless, some of the Bible schools taught the Alberta high school curriculum. They were accredited to recommend students for provincial high school standing provided they met certain conditions. They were to employ qualified teachers with provincial certification, follow the prescribed program of studies, and use the authorized text books. They were visited each year by a provincial high school inspector to ascertain whether or not these requirements were being met.

The Prairie Bible Institute stubbornly refused to meet these conditions. It did, nonetheless, teach the high school grades, using unapproved texts that, for instance, made no reference to evolution. Institute students, consequently, did not receive provincial high school standing. Considering their vocational objectives as fundamentalist preachers, this probably made little difference in their lives.

Of the 35 sects listed in the Mann study, some originated in Europe, others in the United States, and some were locally produced in Alberta. Those sects, imported from Europe, were protest groups of long standing such as the Mennonites, the Seven Day Adventists, and the Jehovah Witnesses.

The Disciples of Christ, an American-derived sect, arrived in the province in 1913. The Apostolic Church of the Pentecost was a small

E.C. Manning speaking at the Prophetic Bible Institute,
Calgary, in the early '40s.
Photo courtesy of the Glenbow Archives, Calgary, Alberta.

Alberta-born sect. A very large sect, the German Baptist of North America, depending on itinerant evangelism and practising bilingualism, was particularly successful in the province.

The Prophetic Baptist Church and Institute also had a wide following. Then, of course, the Salvation Army, a well-known fundamentalist sect, had become very much part of the Alberta scene.

The sects in Alberta did not work among the poor. They did, however, cultivate those with less than average incomes. They were particularly helpful to the less successful farmers of the Manning era. These were the people who, unable to cope with the changes occurring in Alberta's agricultural industry, found their way into the cities to become part of an unskilled labor force. Many adherents to the various Protestant sects were low-paid office workers and artisans.

One cannot terminate a discussion on Alberta's fundamentalist groups without reference to the radio. As Aberhart demonstrated, this was a very effective medium for evangelistic preaching. It was a medium through which evangelistic preachers could reach out to audiences numbering in the thousands. Aberhart, in his prime as an evangelist, is said to have inspired radio audiences of 350,000. Furthermore, the radio provided a significant source of income for those who could use it successfully.

Dr. Lowry, an American Moody Institute evangelist, arrived in Calgary during 1938. He rented time for a half-hour early-morning period from a local radio station to give a six-week series of religious broadcasts. His response by letter provided him with $10,000, a considerable amount for that time. It paid for all his expenses, including radio time, the salaries of five stenographers, and a suite in the Palliser Hotel.

His programs consisted of stirring evangelistic preaching, hymns, prayers, and frequent references to sexual problems.[9] He is reputed to have made more than a hundred converts. He returned to California with the message that Albertans were generous supporters of evangelistic broadcasts.

Others followed his example. A Baptist preacher, Reverend Sawtell, came to Calgary in 1939. He, with the aid of the pianist who came with him, started the Sunrise Gospel Hour at the Calgary station, CFCN. He later introduced the Home and Heaven Hour, through the services of an Edmonton station, CFRN.

His ways of milking fundamentalist audiences in the rural areas and small towns of Alberta were perfectly legal and quite ingenious.[1] To illustrate: Sawtell organized a "Fifty Club Plan," whereby 50 people pledged to give 25 cents a week toward the support of a missionary. Each member was supplied with a picture of the particular missionary which he or she supported. Contributors usually sent Sawtell a donation with the gift for the "Fifty Plan," all of which suggests that the Bible schools and their graduates had created a ready and responsive audience for such performances.

4

Alberta's four revolutionary leaders might now be reviewed in light of the differences between fundamentalists and modernists, between Protestant churches and Protestant sects.

All four of these men — Henry Wise Wood, John E. Brownlee, William Aberhart and Ernest Manning — were Protestants responding to the political needs and pressures of a predominantly Protestant province.

Henry Wise Wood was a dedicated student of the Bible. He was particularly interested in those parts of the Holy Book that stressed the importance of change. Wood was deeply absorbed in social and economic reform, particularly if it contributed to improvement in the lives of his beloved farmers.

Wood belonged to a Protestant sect known as the Campbellites. One conjectures that his faith may have led him to his concept of group government.[11]

The career of J.E. Brownlee indicates that he too was a religious man. He had taught Sunday School in the Methodist church during his younger years. He was undoubtedly an adherent of the United church following church union in 1925. He was, in fact, a modernist, in tune with the objectives and views of his church.

William Aberhart and Ernest Manning were both fundamentalists. Their activities in the Prophetic Bible Institute attest to that. That the affairs of the Alberta government were directed by these two men from 1935 to 1971 underscores the political importance of fundamentalism in this province.[12] Conceivably many United church members, though ostensibly modernist, were actually sympathetic to fundamentalist interpretations of the Bible.

An intriguing comparison that might be drawn between two western political leaders would be to consider the views of Ernest Manning and those of Tommy Douglas. Tommy Douglas was premier of Saskatchewan until 1961. Manning in his series of interviews commented on many contemporary political leaders. He was strangely silent about Douglas, though they must have met during the earlier years of his premiership.

Both men were Baptists; Douglas was actually an ordained minister of the Baptist church. Here the similarity ends. Douglas adhered to modernism as opposed to Manning's fundamentalism.

Their views on the role of the state stand in stark contrast. Douglas, a socialist, favored state ownership of industry in the interest of serving all people. Manning saw capitalism as an opportunity for man to achieve salvation. Their social and economic perceptions were diametrically opposed. Nonetheless, both served their provinces well.

Notes

[1] John English, The Canadian Encyclopedia (Edmonton: Hurtig Publishers, 1988), Vol. 1, pp 81 ff.

[2] W.E. Mann, *Sect, Cult, and Church in Alberta* (Toronto: University of Toronto Press, 1955), p. 30. A study sponsored by the Canadian Social Science Council.

[3] This definition is one given by Mann. It is a sociological definition.

[4] The term "patriate" is distinctively Canadian. It cannot be found in either the Oxford or Collins dictionaries.

[5] Mann, p. 53.

[6] The tables on pages 30-31 in Mann are dated 1946. The list of sects are given here.

Name of Sect	Membership
Apostolic Church of Pentecost	1,000
Apostolic Faith Mission.	100
British Israel	200
Canadian Sunday School Mission	350
Christadelphians	150
Christian and Missionary Alliance	1,700
Church of Christ	50
Church of God, Anderson, Ind.	900
Church of God. Clevland, Tenn.	150
Church of the First Century	20
Church of the Nazarene	2,900
Cooneyites	1,500
Disciples of Christ	1,600
Evangelical Church of Pentecost	350
Evangelical Free Church of America	400
Evangelical Mission Covenant	750
Foursquare Gospel	200

Free Methodists	350
Fundamental Baptists	350
German Baptists of North America	5,500
Gospel Missions	300
Holiness Movement	250
Jehovah's Witnesses	3,000
Mennonites	8,500
Pentecostal Assemblies of Canada	5,000
Pentecostal Holiness Church	200
Plymouth Brethren, open	500
Prairie Bible Institute Missions	700
Prophetic Baptist Church and Institute	3,000
Regular Baptists	900
Salvation Army	2,100
Seven Day Adventist	4,900
Standard Church of America	350
United Evangelical Brethren	4,800
World Alliance Evangelical and Missionary churches	650
Total	**53,790**

[7] Mann, p. 52.

[8] Mann, p. 83.

[9] Mann, p. 123.

[10] Mann, p. 123ff.

[11] See Chapter Two.

[12] Harry Strom was also a fundamentalist.

Chapter Sixteen
End of an Era

1

E.C. Manning retired as premier of the province on December 12, 1968. He had apparently been thinking of retiring for three years or so before he actually took the final step. It is unusual for a premier to leave office part way through the legislative term. The election of 1967 had given the Manning government a comfortable majority. Furthermore, Manning had just turned 60, hardly the age of retirement for a politician.

Manning had dominated the political life of the province for a quarter of a century. Albertans knew him as a capable and honest premier. They were fully aware that he was a religious man. His radio broadcasts provided evidence of that virtue.

Manning at that time was a confirmed monarchist. He saw the relationship between a monarch and his or her people as highly personal. He described the present reigning monarch, Queen Elizabeth, as a down-to-earth person, possessing both common sense and excellent judgment. He, in fact, attended her coronation in 1953.

He considered the monarchy of extreme importance to the British Commonwealth of Nations as a unifying force. However, he had doubts about its permanency in Canada. He thought, however, that the Canadian government should encourage its preservation.

He expressed regret, during his interview series, that Pierre Trudeau, then prime minister of Canada, had no respect for the monarchy and didn't hesitate to show it. He thought that Trudeau and his "gang" were doing all they could to separate Canada from the British monarchy. For instance, the mail was no longer the Royal Mail, but had become Canada Post.

In fact, there was little about Trudeau that Manning admired. He granted that he had a bright mind and was courageous. On the other hand, his stubborn fight to bring the Canadian constitution home to Canada

Queen Elizabeth and Premier Manning, 1951.
Photo courtesy of the Provincial Archives of Alberta, A-1635.

was not only divisive, but also unnecessary. Furthermore, Trudeau's move to adopt the metric system was out of step with both Britain and the United States. Manning considered the Trudeau government to be the worst in Canada's history.

In speaking of J.F. Kennedy, Manning approved of his approach to government as expressed in the words — " Ask not what your country can do for you, but what you can do for your country." However, he was not confident that Kennedy could have delivered. He saw him as the type of wealthy person who depends on the poor to capitalize on their virtues. He referred, in his series of interviews, somewhat disparagingly to the Kennedy clan.

On the other hand, he approved of Ronald Reagan, the American president during the '80s. He admired his leadership and the new attitudes he had brought to the American people with respect to their country.

He spoke approvingly of Reagan's handling of the air controllers' strike. They had conducted an illegal strike and had broken the law, for which they were dismissed. On the other hand, he criticized Trudeau's behavior during a postal strike. Trudeau had said, "No use legislating them back to work. They wouldn't obey anyway."

Manning spoke about his experiences with W.A.C. Bennett, premier of British Columbia and a contemporary of Premier Manning. Bennett had successfully introduced Social Credit into that province by forming a government under that name. In Manning's view, Bennett was not a genuine Social Crediter. For the B.C. premier, Social Credit did not mean monetary reform. It represented right wing, free enterprise.

The two men were quite dissimilar. Bennett's liking for argument and conflict was in direct contrast to Manning's quiet and friendly manner.

Premiers E.C. Manning and W.A.C. Bennett, 1952.
Photo courtesy of the Provincial Archives of Alberta, PA 2315/9

Manning recounted a story of a Grey Cup play-off which he attended in Vancouver. Manning was keenly interested in professional football. Bennett met him in a car driven by a chauffeur. This flamboyant display bothered Manning; such royal treatment made him uncomfortable. He was certain that there were many other Albertans, at that game, who were chauffeurless.

Dennis Groh, during 1970, completed a study on Manning's political thought as a thesis for a master's degree granted by the University of Calgary. His conclusions are not only interesting, but also useful in understanding this unusual political leader.

Groh maintained that Manning's political philosophy could be interpreted through his religious identification, that of a Fundamental Baptist. The Baptists were the inheritors of Calvinistic traditions. John Calvin was a Swiss religious leader of the early 16th century (1509 to 1564). Calvin believed in predestination, that certain people were predestined by God to become the elect, those who would be granted salvation and everlasting life in Heaven. These electors, God's chosen people, would fullfil their destinies on earth filled with grace, that is free from sin, and consequently ready to receive Christ.

The Baptists did not accept predestination, nor did they agree that financial failure was evidence that one was not a member of the elect. They held that any individual could achieve grace through his or her own efforts. The route to this achievement must, however, be selected voluntarily. One could not, nor should not, be forced to pursue a course in life leading to a close identification with Christ. It was a matter of one's own free will.

Such a view cloaks a capitalistic society with a divine purpose. It is a society within which one may achieve grace by working purposefully as an individual. That individual may become wealthy by so doing. This, however, is not the outcome for which he or she strives. Through the all-consuming struggle to acquire wealth, one achieves grace. Hence the old adage, "The devil finds mischief for idle hands to do."

This, according to Groh, explains Manning's religious zeal in his support of individualism and private enterprise. Manning believed that the world's problems, irrespective of what they might be, would be solved not by organizations, but by individuals.

It explains, as well, Manning's abhorrence of socialism and other forms of statism. A socialistic society directs people toward the achievement of certain social ends. It does not permit them to elect voluntarily that which they might wish to do toward achieving grace. Furthermore, it prevents, or at least discourages, individuals from working to their full capacity. In so doing, that society denies its citizens the opportunity to achieve a close identity with Jesus Christ.

This explains, further, the use of such terms in the White Paper as "human resource development." The purpose of HRD was the development of free and creative individuals. These persons, presumably, would have achieved a state of grace.

The term Christian Democracy was frequently used during the Manning era. This is a type of society within which individuals are free to fulfill their destinies as Christians. These terms are, in fact, interdependent. Only Christians can establish a free and democratic society.

Whether one accepts this view or not, it is somewhat formidable to refute. It is difficult to identify a democratic nation whose people are not, at least nominally, members of one or the other of the many Christian sects.

Whatever the basis for Manning's political thought, he had given Albertans for a quarter of a century a government which they had appreciated. They had expressed this appreciation by supporting him throughout seven elections.

Albertans were fortunate to have had his leadership throughout the dynamic decade until the end of the '60s. Albertans, in general, benefitted from the income generated through the discovery of oil. Unlike Texas, there were few oil millionaires created through the exploitation of Alberta's oil wealth. The income produced from the province's nonrenewable resources was spent wisely toward the improvement of its highways, its towns and cities, its universities, colleges, and schools.

2

Manning announced his retirement on September 27, 1968, two months prior to the date on which he would turn over the premiership to his successor. During the intervening time, the Social Credit party was faced with the task of choosing a new leader.

The Social Credit party had, at that time, several contenders for party leadership. At least three cabinet ministers were intent on replacing Manning. Ray Rierson, who had held the two portfolios of labor and education, immediately announced his intention of seeking the top position in government. Gordon Taylor, minister of highways, had established a reputation as an effective road builder. As a result of his efforts, the province was now served by a network of hard-surfaced highways. He, too, declared his candidacy for the party leadership.[1]

Members of the "whiz kids" group had attempted to persuade Manning that his son, Preston, should enter the leadership race. Premier Manning, however, was adamantly opposed to this proposal. He agreed that Preston had personal attributes favoring his candidacy. Preston's extreme youth, however, would have made it difficult for him to control a cabinet composed of men very much his senior in years. Preston at that time was only 21.

The attention of this young group of advisers then turned to other possible candidates for party leadership. Manning was not prepared to lend his unqualified support to any particular candidate. In fact, Manning had been criticized for not having identified and cultivated a possible successor during his long tenure as leader of the Social Credit party. He did, however, show some approval of Harry Strom, MLA for the Cypress constituency located in southern Alberta, part way between the cities of Lethbridge and Medicine Hat.

Harry Strom, a tall blond man of Scandinavian origin, had entered the legislature in 1955. His early experience in local government was typical of that undergone by many Social Credit MLAs. He had been a member of the municipal council of Forty Mile, and chairman presiding over the board of the Foremost School Division, a position he had inherited from a close neighbor, Olaf Solberg, on his retirement.[2]

Manning had appointed Strom to the Executive Council in 1962. Since that time, he had served as minister of municipal affairs, and also agriculture. He had fulfilled the roles of those two portfolios quite successfully.

In the leadership convention, held by the Social Credit party during early December 1968, Strom was elected as leader of the party. This position carried with it the responsibility of serving as provincial premier. He assumed the premiership role on the day of Manning's resignation, December 27, 1968. He held the post of premier until the defeat of the Social Credit party on August 30, 1971, a period of 33 months.

Strom's place in Alberta's history is a minor one, not unlike that held by J. Reid who completed Brownlee's term following his resignation in 1934. A kindly and considerate man, Strom was open and democratic in his leadership style. He was a member of the Evangelical Free Church, devoutly religious, and a dedicated Christian. He had become a follower of Manning through the attraction of his religious broadcasts.

Premier Harry Strom.
Photo courtesy of the Provincial Archives of Alberta, *Edmonton Journal* Collection, J-8841.

Strom, on his access to power, faced an immediate challenge. He had to, in some fashion, bring a new face to the Social Credit party. It had been a Manning party for so long that its original purpose had been completely obscured. What exactly did the party stand for in a province that had been transformed from rural to urban during the previous 25 years?

This challenge was far beyond the capabilities of Harry Strom. Despite his success in provincial politics and his rise to the premiership, Strom was not a professional politician. To him, there was much about politics that seemed inconsistent with his Christian principles. Developing a new image for the Social Credit party and making it meaningful to urban Albertans would have been, for him, an impossible task.

3

Peter Lougheed had won the leadership of the Provincial Conservative party in 1965. The leadership convention had been held during a time when that party was without a single representative in the Legislative Assembly. In fact, the last Conservative to win a seat in Alberta's legislature occurred during the 1959 election. Furthermore, the Conservatives had never formed a government in the province during its entire existence. So far as Alberta's governmental administration was concerned, conservatism had been an unknown political manifestation.

Lougheed's name was not, however, unfamiliar to Alberta's political history. His grandfather had been leader of the Canadian senate under Robert Borden's administration during the early part of the 20th century.

Peter Lougheed, during 1949-1950, played professional football with the Edmonton Eskimos, thereby establishing himself in the world of sport. At the same time, he was pursuing a combined arts and law degree program at the University of Alberta. He graduated in arts in 1952, and secured his baccalaureate degree in law one year later.

Not content with these academic achievements, Peter Lougheed entered the University of Harvard in the United States. In 1954, he was granted a masters in business administration from that prestigious institution.

Having completed his formal schooling, Lougheed practiced law in Calgary for a brief period before joining the Mannix Corporation. This company was an international giant with diverse interests in oil, coal, pipelines, earth moving, and industrial plants. Lougheed, serving first as secretary, became a vice-president in 1959, and the following year, a director.

During the 1967 election, this fledgling Conservative party, led by Lougheed, succeeded in electing six members to Alberta's Legislative Assembly. This small contingent of MLAs formed the nucleus of a renewed Conservative thrust into the province's politics.

Lougheed had chosen his candidates carefully. They were young, well-educated and presentable MLAs. They included Don Getty, a well-known member of the Edmonton Eskimo's professional football club; Lou Hyndman, an Edmonton lawyer whose grandfather had been Chief Justice of Canada's Supreme Court; and Dr. Hugh Horner, a former Conservative MP.

During the duration of the sixteenth legislature (1967-1971), this small group of six was augmented by the defection of a Liberal, the conversion of an independent, and by victories in two byelections. This made a Conservative opposition of 10 members. Such an opposition did not pose a serious threat to an incumbent government that had been reelected by securing 55 of the 65 seats in the legislature.

Opposition leader Peter Lougheed in the Legislature, 1968.
Photo courtesy of the Provincial Archives of Alberta,
Edmonton Journal Collection, J-172.

Lougheed played the role of opposition leader skillfully. He dwelt on the concept that his party, in reality, was not so much an opposition as an alternative government. He introduced private member bills into the legislature, even though the introduction of legislation was traditionally undertaken by government members. Needless to say, his proposed legislation never reached its final reading.

Lougheed and his cohorts were well aware that there was little to criticize in the many Social Credit programs. Manning's government had built solidly in the fields of education and public health. The government's record was devoid of any obvious scandal.

Lougheed's team capitalized on their comparative youth. Their pictures frequently showed them arm in arm on the run, with Lougheed leading in front. This emphasis on movement created an image of vigor, all of which contrasted with an ostensibly aging government.

Lougheed had mastered the art of television. He was fully aware that this was the political medium of the future. He cultivated the image of a concerned and thoughtful political leader who would be capable of performing as a statesman. The Conservatives used this medium to good effect during the campaign leading to the August election of 1971.

Peter Lougheed and Premier Strom in a hay pitching contest.
Photo courtesy of the Provincial Archives of Alberta,
Edmonton Journal Collection, J-346.

Strom, on the other hand, dismissed television as being unimportant. The Social Credit party made little use of it during the election campaign. Strom was convinced that few people watched television during the summer months.

The contrast between these two political leaders was marked. Lougheed was highly educated and articulate. Strom's formal education beyond high school consisted of a term at the Calgary Institute of Technology. While Strom spoke well and communicated effectively on a one to one basis, he was not a good public speaker. He had no means of creating a public image, nor was he interested in doing so.

In fact, only those who knew Strom personally were aware of the man's true self, his honesty and integrity, and his devotion to Christian principles.

The Strom team took heart from one incident during the summer campaign of 1971. Harry Strom agreed to ride in a parade signifying the opening of Klondyke Days, which is Edmonton's annual exhibition. Strom was entirely at ease on a horse and warmed to the boisterous response of the crowd. This was the genuine Strom, a reigning monarch at one with his people on a joyous occasion.

Though some Social Credit members may have been uneasy about the outcome of the 1971 election, the general feeling was one of optimism. After 46 years of continuous power, with nine electoral victories, it was difficult to imagine a political reverse. A child born in 1935 had now reached the age of 46, well into his or her middle years. Men and women, young at the commencement of the Social Credit era, were now considering retirement. Few, if any, of the MLAs elected in 1935 still remained active in political affairs. The Social Credit government had spanned two generations.

Even to Social Credit party members an electoral defeat was unthinkable. To Albertans generally, the idea that a new government might assume power in Edmonton was equally difficult to imagine. No one would deny the possibility; few would accept the probability.

Nonetheless, governments are not immortal. They can be defeated. Lougheed and his cohorts must have often assured each other of this event's inevitability. The question remained, would it occur August 30, 1971? Perhaps Lougheed quoted from Shakespeare, "There is a time in the affairs of men which taken at the flood, leads on to fortune."

The election day arrived. The campaign was over. The competing candidates waited to learn whether or not they could affix the letters MLA after their names throughout the period of Alberta's seventeenth legislature.

That night they met the truth, either from the radio or television. With the Conservative vote running at 46 percent of those who had marked their ballots, Lougheed was assured of a victory. As usual in Alberta's elections, Edmonton was the bellwether city. Lougheed's forces had taken every seat within that city's boundaries. In northern Alberta, the NDP had shown strength, perhaps due to the vigorous campaign conducted by Grant Notley who had won in the constituency of Spirit River and Fairview.

Not surprisingly, Lougheed's Conservative party had done well in Calgary, though not equal to their achievement in Edmonton. The constituencies south of Calgary remained faithful to Social Credit.

The Progressive Conservatives won 49 seats, Social Credit, 25, NDP, 1. The miracle had happened, proving once more that governments are not immortal. The Manning era was over, that of Lougheed had just begun.

Premier-elect Lougheed and defeated Premier Strom.
Photo courtesy of the Provincial Archives of Alberta,
Edmonton Journal Collection, J-7061.

Notes

[1] Four MLAs sought the leadership in this convention, three of which have been mentioned in the substance of this chapter.

2 Chapter Thirteen describes the Foremost School Division as an illustration of an enlarged school administration unit. There were eventually some 50 of these school divisions formed throughout the province. They were later incorporated in the counties when these came into existence during the '60s.

Sources

Publications:

Barr, John. *The Dynasty: The Rise and Fall of Social Credit*. Toronto: McClelland and Stewart Ltd, 1974.

Berghofer D.E. and A.G. Vladicka. *Access to Opportunity*. Government of Alberta, 1980.

Durant, William. *The Story of Civilization*. New York: Simon and Schuster, 1939, 1969.

Gould, Edward. *The History of Canada's Oil and Gas Industry*. Victoria: Hancock House Publishers, 1976.

Hanson, Erik. *The Dynamic Decade*. Toronto: McClelland and Stewart, 1958.

Hardy, W.G. Ed. in Chief. *Alberta, A Natural History*. Edmonton: Hurtig Publishers, 1967.

Hooke, Alfred. *30 + 5, I Know, I Was There*. Edmonton: Institute of Applied Art, 1951.

Irving, J.A. *The Social Credit Movement in Alberta*. Toronto: University of Toronto Press, 1959.

Johnson, L.P.V. and O.J. MacNutt. *Aberhart of Alberta*. Edmonton: Cooperative Press, 1970.

Lingard, Cecil. *Territorial Government in Canada*. Toronto: University of Toronto Press, 1946.

Mann, W.E. *Sect, Cult and Church in Alberta*. Toronto: University of Toronto Press, 1960.

Manning, E.C. *Political Realignment, A Challenge to Thoughtful Canadians*. Toronto: McClelland and Stewart, 1967.

McHenry, Dean E. *The Third Force in Canada, The Cooperative Commonwealth Federation, 1932-1948*. University of California Press, 1950.

McNaught, K. *A Prophet in Politics*. Toronto: University of Toronto Press, 1959.

McPherson, C.B. *Democracy in Alberta*. Toronto: University of Toronto Press, 1953.

Morton, W.L. *Social Credit in Alberta*. Toronto: University of Toronto Press, 1950.

Palmer, Howard and Tamara. *People of Alberta, Portraits of Cultural Diversity*. Saskatoon, Sask.: Western Producer Prairie Books, 1985.

Province of Alberta. *The Douglas System of Social Credit*. King's Printer, 1934.

Rolf, W.R. *Henry Wise Wood of Alberta*. Toronto: University of Toronto Press, 1950.

Rothrock, George. *Europe, A Brief History*. Chicago: Rand McNally Co., 1971.

Sharp, P.F. *The Agrarian Revolt in Western Canada*. Minneapolis: University of Minnesota Press, 1948.

Shiver, William. *The Rise and Fall of the Third Reich*. Greenwich, Conn.: Fawcett Publications Inc., 1959, 1960.

Schafer, Edward. "Class and Oil in Alberta" cited in Nore and Turner, *Oil and the Class Struggle*. London: Zed Press, pp. 252-271.

Smith, Phillip. *The Treasure Seekers*. Toronto: McMillan of Canada, 1978.

Thomas, L.H. *Alberta, William Aberhart and Social Social Credit*. Toronto: Copp Clark, 1977.

Truman, Margaret. *Harry S. Truman*. New York: William Morrow and Co. Inc., 1973.

Young, W.D. *The Anatomy of a Party. The National CCF 1932-61*. Toronto: University of Toronto Press, 1969.

Zakuto, Leo. *A Protest Movement Becalmed, A Study of Change*. Toronto: University of Toronto Press, 1964.

Documents, Essays, and Other Sources:

Alberta, "Annual Reports of the Social Credit Board, 1936-1947." Edmonton: Provincial Archives.

Alberta, Throne Speeches, 1945 - 1964. *Journals of the Legislative Assembly*. Vol. XLVI.

Alberta, "Committee on Post war Reconstruction, A Report." A.J. Hooke, Chairman.

Brenda, William J. "Building the Cooperative Commonwealth." *Essays on the Democratic Socialist Tradition in Alberta*. Canadian Plains Research Centre, University of Regina, Saskatchewan.

Lyons, William E. "The New Democratic in the Canadian Political System" University Micro Films. Ann Arbor, Michigan, 1965.

Manning, Ernest C. Series of Taped Interviews, with Lydia Semotuik, 1978 - 1983. University of Alberta Archives.

Ibid. "A White Paper on Human Resource Development." Provincial Library, Alberta Legislative Assembly.

Marsh, James, Ed. in Chief. "Canadian Encyclopedia." Four Volumes. Edmonton: Hurtig Publishers, 1988.

Morton, W.L. "The Social Philosophy of Henry Wise Wood." *Agricultural History*, Vol. 22, 1948. Provincial Library.

Ibid. "Western Progressive Movement." *Agricultural History*. Vol 22. 1948. Provincial Library.

Alberta, "Premiers' Papers 1921-1934." Edmonton: Provincial Library.

University Theses:

Berke, Carl. "The United Farmers of Alberta: The Relationship between Agricultural Organization and The Government of Alberta." Masters Thesis, University of Alberta, 1971.

Byrne, T.C. "The Ukrainian Community in North Central Alberta." Masters Thesis, University of Alberta, 1937.

Cullen, L.A. "Petroleum Concession in Iran and Alberta." Masters Thesis, University of Alberta, 1981.

Embree, G.D. "The Rise of the United Farmers of Alberta." Masters Thesis, University of Alberta, 1981.

Foster, Franklin Lloyd. "J.E. Brownlee, A Biography." Doctoral Thesis, Queens University, 1981. (Alberta Provincial Library, Microfiche)

Groh, Dennis. "Political Thought of E.C. Manning." Masters Thesis, University of Calgary. 1971.

Index

Printed in Canada